CONSCIOUSNESS AND CREATIVITY:

transcending science, humanities, and the arts

BILL ROMEY

DRAWINGS BY LUCRETIA ROMEY

Ash Lad Press
P.O. Box 396
Canton, N.Y. 13617

To Cricket, Gretchen, and William: watching you grow gets me going.

Other Books by Bill Romey

Risk, Trust, Love: learning in a humane environment (Charles Merrill Publishing Company, 1600 Alum Creek Drive, Columbus, Ohio, 1972)
Inquiry Techniques for Teaching Science (Prentice-Hall, Englewood Cliffs, N.J., 1968)
Investigations in Geology (with E. Muller, J. Kramer, and J. Lewis; William C. Brown Publishing Company, Dubuque, Iowa, 1967)

Library of Congress Catalog Card Number 75-5095
International Standard Book Number 0-915492-00-8
First Printing. Type by Northern New York Publishing Company, Ogdensburg, N.Y.
Printing by Salina Press, Syracuse, N.Y.

PREFACE

Fat snow flakes tumble about outside my window. The elms reach up as dark arms against a pale-gray sky. Beads of water form on the window and hang there, ready to roll when their weight becomes too great for them to hang there any longer.

> These are my two drops of rain
> Waiting on the window-pane
>
> I am waiting here to see
> Which the winning one will be.
>
> —A.A. Milne

A rounded pebble of coral sits on my window sill. I pick it up and am surprised by its lightness. Where did I get it? Must have stuffed it into my pocket somewhere or the other. I try to enter into it mentally to find more meaning in it. Then I realize that trying won't really help. Perhaps if I can let myself just flow into it I can find more meaning and delight there. Thoughts of beaches near Mombasa last summer flood into my mind. The lightness of the coral suggests to me that it is recent stuff, not long dead, not a fossil. What does "dead" mean, anyway? As I replace the pebble on my window sill I am aware of the gritty sand still on my fingers. I rub my fingers together to experience the grit more fully.

Just at my right elbow lies the completed typescript of **Consciousness and Creativity.** No, it won't be complete until it's printed, for I'll undoubtedly move things around and change them again. Several hundred "discarded" pages lie in another pile. I like many of the "discards" too, and I may put them together in some other combination or context.

As I have developed this final draft I have sought to give the whole at least some minimal sense of flow from what I think a reader's perspective might be. I have rearranged and reshuffled more-or-less separate essays many times. Finally, I am ready to send this out as a communication to others. I do not expect this to be any kind of comprehensive and orderly "treatise". The essays comprise some thoughts on consciousness, knowing, creating, learning, and being. Many of them depart from experiences I have had as a practicing scientist and science teacher. I wrote most of them during the summer of 1973 while nestled in a cottage on the edge of Sykkylvsfjord in west-central Norway. My awareness of the Norwegian scenes forms a thread that extends through much of the text. Other essays I have written more recently, even within the last few days. In the year and a half since I prepared the bulk of this material I have written many other things that could form parts of this book, too. But I have decided to cut the essays included here apart from the web in which they have been enmeshed. These are personal views, and this is very much a "first-person" book. Yet other people have certainly affected many of my views, as you will see in the reading. At the beginning of **Walden**, Thoreau writes something I want to quote:

> In most books, the **I**, or first person, is omitted; in this it will be retained; that, in respect to egotism, is the main difference. We commonly do not remember that it is, after all, always the first person that is speaking. I should not talk so much about myself if there were anybody else I knew as well.

I view creativity as a process in which all of us are engaged throughout our lives. We are aware of this process and give ourselves to it to varying degrees. The creative potential in each of us may be virtually unlimited, but our awareness limits its expression. Our state of consciousness determines the degree to which we can use and enjoy our creative potential.

Because creativity is a process, I want to do more in these pages than write **about** creative activity and consciousness. I want to provide glimpses into how my own processes are involved in the writing of these essays and how my own consciousness and awareness are developing. To some extent I have followed the flow or stream of my consciousness, or at least a small part of it that I have been able to capture on paper. This produces a text that you may see as jumping back and forth from theme to theme, from point of awareness to point of new consciousness.

But enough of the preface. Perhaps you will find things in the reading that will enhance your awareness, just as the writing of it has done for me. Perhaps you will fill in the blanks where I have failed to put into words many elements of my own process. If we can vibrate together on a common frequency, even for a moment, then the interaction between us will have been worthwhile.

Bill Romey
Canton, New York
January 1, 1975

CONTENTS

A FLOW OF CONSCIOUSNESS

CONSCIOUSNESS

Within the flow of our consciousness we transcend many of the divisions and disciplines we have created in attempts to organize our world. **Conscious, unconscious, subconscious, preconscious:** all of these words classify parts of what must be a vast ocean of consciousness where every part is somehow in contact with every other part. Yet in an ocean, too, conditions change with depth; one finds abrupt changes in temperature, salinity, and other physical properties; gradational boundaries separate some zones from others; movement and change are everywhere. Theodore Roszak feels that the things hidden within this sea of our consciousness shape our powers of perceiving and analysing. Unbeknownst to us, they filter, screen, censor. Until we develop at least some dim feeling for these parts of our personalities that lie submerged within us, we have little chance of moving toward higher consciousness, and the reality we perceive will remain limited.

In western cultures we grow up learning to behave rationally, to view reality as fixed, to mistrust our intuition and dreams.

> *"Billy! Stop daydreaming! Pay attention!"*
> *They started telling me this as soon as I*
> *was old enough to understand them.*

Yet a common factor in so-called creative people, be they in science, music, literature, art, is the access they apparently have to states of consciousness beyond the area called rational.

Eastern cultures recognize the value of dreams, passive acceptance, and meditation. Rediscovery of the mystical and the "extra-sensory" seems to be taking place on a large scale in many parts of the western world. Scientists, not satisfied to let themselves flow, continue to analyse these deeper levels of consciousness. Psychologists interested in the neurological bases of human consciousness believe that (in right-handed people) the right hemisphere of the brain, which controls the left side of the body, is involved in aspects of consciousness such as music, intuition, fantasy, orientation in space, art, spirituality. The left, "dominant" hemisphere controls logical and analytical functions—science, language, and reason. The two hemispheres are, of course, connected. Jerome Bruner began to explore this relationship several years ago in his book **Essays for the Left Hand.** Recently, Robert Ornstein devotes much of his **The Psychology of Consciousness** to this topic.

Although I am interested in the process of creativity, I do not wish to get caught in this book in a morass of analytical details.

> *I just looked up "morass" in my dictionary. It means "swamp," "bog." I transport myself mentally into a swamp. Sticky mud holds my feet down as I try to walk. I feel cold water trickling into my boots. It's slimy, and I slide and slip. Swamp plants grow all about me, and I try to push my way through them. Here and there a solid tussock of grass provides temporary support so that I can stop and breathe for a moment. In one place I find a smooth patch of delicate, fine grass, lush green. I want to lie down on it and touch it, experience its softness and even its wetness. A snake slithers away as I disturb him. This makes me start and catch my breath. Perhaps experiencing the feeling of this swamp on several levels will help me understand more about problems I have in the morass of scientific analysis and rationalism.*

I am interested in understanding, meaning, interaction, relationship. I will undoubtedly commit myself to "serious" analysis. Both sides of my brain must work together if I wish to develop an increasingly holistic view of my world. The trouble is that, in today's schools and work-a-day world there is so much emphasis on rational consciousness that many of us have let our intuitive powers get dusty and disused. Much of "hard science" and respectable scholarship has gotten such a narrowed field of vision that I want to spend a great deal of my energy in freeing my underused intuitive powers. There is little danger of losing our analytical capabilities. All of us have had years of training in the use of these, in how to reduce things, how to generalize, how to process conventional information in conventional ways. The question is, how do we transcend rational consciousness, adding to its powers rather than abandoning it?

I am aware that I am "lecturing" <u>about</u> consciousness. So be it. I guess I want to do that now, but I may stop now and then to comment on what I am experiencing at other levels.

Many people are experimenting with attempts to enter into "altered" or "expanded" states of consciousness. Some have chosen routes involving drugs. Not that this is a new approach. Coleridge and Baudelaire were among important writers who tried the drug route.

As I write, I am listening to a radio program which has "The Sea" as its topic. It is a poetic treatment. Suddenly I am aware that some verses they are quoting are from Coleridges's "Rhyme of the Ancient Mariner" .... I recall the verses from junior-high-school days and begin to visualize myself in a classroom in Pennsylvania, reciting the poem. Is it by chance that I am writing about a "sea of consciousness" and specifically about Coleridge just before the radio is turned on to a program dealing with exactly those same things? This train of consciousness also leads me back in my mind's eye to a beginning English composition class in which I wrote a long term paper about the effect of drugs on English literature.

In **The Doors of Perception**, Aldous Huxley champions the use of mescaline to help intellectuals bound up in western rationalism experience other ways of perceiving, of becoming aware, of being conscious.

I feel tempted to try Huxley's prescription sometimes. Len Baron said at a teachers' workshop that anyone who hadn't experienced drugs could not be very far along in a perceptual sense. Judy said she wanted to smoke with me sometime, that this would be an important opening of my eyes. But I continue to hold back from this experimentation. I don't like the idea of chemicals much. Moving into new approaches to perception and consciousness involves a great deal of fear I would have to transcend first if I decided I wanted to try them.

John Lilly, in **The Center of the Cyclone**, deals with the use of LSD to get into altered states of consciousness. Carlos Castaneda's books describing his experiences with Don Juan involve excursions in "other realities". Don Juan attempts to teach Carlos not just to look, but to **see** realities that transcend those that "normal" perception allows us to see from our customary, "rational" perspective. Castaneda begins his training with the use of drugs, as does Lilly. Later, both Lilly and Castaneda learn to **see** without drugs. Lilly finds that certain kinds of meditation and group process activities (encounter and gestalt) help him. Those are "techniques" I can be more comfortable with, although here, too, I have had to overcome certain fears prior to trying them.

In **The Zen of Seeing**, Frederick Franck finds new ways of perceiving and new levels of consciousness through **drawing-seeing**. This is a kind of meditation in which he sketches, or rather lets his hand move as his consciousness dictates. Greater awareness results on his part. The products--the sketches--become less important than the awareness he reaches. I think the best sketches I have drawn have been done in that way. Lucretia uses this technique with people: look at the object you want to draw, not at the paper. Let the drawing flow. What does it matter if your line goes off the page? Or if others try to judge it as a good-poor drawing. Does it help increase the depth of my consciousness? Do I create a different reality as I draw something: Into my mind flows the image of the Alte Brücke I once drew while lying on the river bank near Heidelberg. I had decided not to carry a camera because I didn't want to look like a tourist. My consciousness, awareness, perception of that bridge is greater than for most things I have photographed or just looked at. Now I am beginning to find that photos can lead me to greater consciousness, too.

> *I walk up Mt. Kenya and there see tiny ice crystals sticking out of the soil in a rose-like pattern. Several months later when I look at a slide I took of this, I think that the slide represents an accidental exposure. I even label it " accidental exposure on trail, Mt. Kenya." Then, later still, I find an article in the Geological Society Bulletin describing "Needle ice in the White Mountains of California," with specific references to the kinds of ice crystals I had photographed but forgotten.*

How about my level of consciousness with respect to other cultures? In January of 1974 and again in June, I traveled to East Africa. I soon felt in myself the same kind of culture-shock I have seen in non-westerners visiting the U.S. I have felt this to some degree in various parts of Europe and even in unfamiliar parts of my own country. But here, the differences were so much greater. As Denis Goulet points out in **The Cruel Choice**, when we from the western world move into other cultural settings with an intent to "help" that culture "develop," we see things that make us begin to question the values of our own culture, too. If we have our eyes and other sensory (and extrasensory?) receptors open, the experience alters our consciousness. The part of our consciousness where our values lie can never be quite the same again.

Charles Reich, in **The Greening of America**, develops a thesis about levels of consciousness in America: Consciousness I, II, III. I have written more about this in the essay on "Personality Classifications" which comes later. Reich's consciousness levels refer to social, political, and human value systems—psychological wholeness, well-being, and use of potential.

In **Seth Speaks**, Jane Roberts, speaking as Seth, writes, "Consciousness is, among other things, a spontaneous exercise in creativity." According to Seth, I can play with changing my consciousness in dreams and intuition. I can change my physical environment by manipulating my dream environment. Seth emphasizes the intimate connection between creation and perception. I perceive reality only in my own context, and my creativity is limited by that context. If I can change the context, I alter my consciousness and I can move to another level of creative potential. Play becomes an all-important factor: "... all creativity and consciousness is born in the quality of play...in... quickened intuitional spontaneity."

> *I find the word <u>insight</u> in my mind. That's a word I like: in-sight. Seeing within? Finding new connections within a flow of events and experiences? As I read Franck's <u>The Zen of Seeing</u>, I came upon his quotation from Ralph Waldo Emerson, "What you are speaks so loudly, I can't hear what you say." We used a version of this quote on a poster we made at ES. But we didn't know where it came from. Out of curiosity I reached up*

onto our bookshelf for a leather-bound book of quotes we keep there. I wanted to see what quotes from Emerson it might contain. I pulled the wrong book down, another leather-bound one: Ralph Waldo Emerson's Essay on Compensation, a book I didn't even know we had. A flow back to the roots of consciousness from which our "creative" poster originated. Chance? Serendipity?

Horningdals Vatn

SURVIVAL, COPING, AND PRODUCING: REFLECTIONS ON SOME CONDITIONS FOR CREATIVITY

I've been trying to commit myself to working on this book now for nearly 3 months. What I have written so far will end up dispersed throughout different sections of the book, I suppose. I jotted a lot of ideas onto scraps of paper and threw them into the saniflush box I'm using as a file. I wrote things down in my personal journal. As I look back at my journal entries, I realize that most of them were written while I was on airplane trips — alone for several hours and with no feeling of obligation to anyone. Come to think of it, a lot of things I've written have been done during the "dead time" of airplane voyages.

One of my most joyful times of writing was on a short cruise in the Caribbean in 1971. I was working on an earlier book, **Risk-Trust-Love.** Virtually all of my physical needs were taken care of. Meals came at regular times. Entertainment was always there when I wanted or needed it. A bed was handy. My whole life of professional anxieties was 3,000 miles away. No one knew me or had any expectations of me, and I had, stored up within me, a whole lot of latent energy and previously "prepared" and semi-organized ideas ready to put down.

Today I am sitting down again, and I think I have finally set the conditions for perhaps a month of productive activity.

> *I sit at a small table in a tiny room on the second floor of the Noss Fjellgaard - an old farm converted to a hotel, near the town of Aa in south-central Norway. I can turn my head and look down Hallingdal - a lovely, deep valley that leads out of the Jotunheim Mountains, the "home of the giants." The meadows are covered with wild flowers. A brook tumbles down near the farm, and a gentle rain has just begun. Mist fills the valley, and I have an incredible feeling of peace, and yet I feel tremendous energy for writing.*

I have just been out for an hour or so pursuing aspects of a couple of geological awareness projects I'm working on. One of these involves taking photographs and gathering information about the uses of native stone in buildings and other structures. Another has to do with gathering data concerning the structure in some of the bedrock. Before its metamorphism, could some of these rocks have originated through volcanic processes? I also continue to work on assembling material for talks on a geological traverse across south central Norway.

My feeling of peace seems to be one important pre-requisite for any production. How do I achieve a feeling of peace and at the same time build up a reservoir of energy and commitment that enable me to function creatively and for a long enough time to bring a project to completion, so that I can feel joy and satisfaction in my product as well as in the process of creation itself? If I am to help establish conditions that will help other people create and experience the joys that go with the creative process and with creative products, I feel I must understand how it is that I function. If I live a rich, creative life of my own I may be able to help others find access routes to the peace and energy they need, too.

I have been in Norway for several days now — yet this is the first one when I have felt able to sit down and write.

> *It is lightening up now - getting very bright. The glass in my windows is very old. It distorts the image of a flowering tree outside the window and of the wild flowers and grass. The breeze is cool on me as it comes in the window.*

My journal has been filling up fast with notes. Even though we were in an atmosphere-rich hotel in Oslo for several days I didn't seem to want to work with any really directed purpose. I felt apprehensive about high prices, where we would get our meals, were the family comfortable, were our tickets for further flights in order, and all sorts of trivial matters related to our physical and psychological survival. I tried to focus some of my awareness and energy on the scenes around me, and I think I succeeded in opening myself up to many things in spite of the worry-energy I was wasting. At times I am primarily a receiver of stimuli, and my whole organism can be tuned in to things around me. At other times I am primarily tuned in to fantasy. These times allow me to play with ideas and with various aspects of memory, past awareness, present awareness, and future expectations and hopes. If I am not aware of the fact of my fantasizing, however, I may close out the present and live in a limited world that draws only from the past.

Just before we came to Norway, I accompanied a small group of geology students on a field expedition to Oregon. Bill and I went along to gather material and information for our own research activities and also to try to help Bruce, Don, Steve, and Jim get started on project activities of their own. Bill and I were along primarily as facilitators. We did have a "production" orientation, but we were primarily being as open as we could to whatever might happen. Bruce, Don, Steven, and Jim, on the other hand had a feeling of an obligation to themselves and to us to focus their energy on some discrete problems for at least part of the time.

During the 10 days I was with the group, they devoted their primary energy to food, drink, where to sleep, keeping their vehicles running, whether or not they liked each other, how independent they felt, and other survival problems. Their concern over not doing much science, in terms of total energy expenditure, began to grow in the days before I left, as they began to cope with problems of survival.

When I first moved to St. Lawrence University in late August, 1972, I was in the middle of an active production and creative period with respect to a number of activities. The problem of moving a family of 5 and a van-load of furniture into a new house, selling an old house, and many others seemed to consume all of my energy. I didn't even care about geology anymore. Or about writing this, or about education, or about anything really except just keeping my head above whatever metaphorical waters seemed to be engulfing me. Administrative problems, the start of a semester, all of these things and many more just seemed to pour in from all sides so that all I could do was put out one brush-fire after another. I was spending all of my time responding to other people's expectations of me and I was losing touch with my inner life and denying myself the peace I needed in order to pour energy into any creative involvement.

Kipp and Alan got involved in an outdoor survival project. When they went out winter camping they tried to keep a journal of their reactions. They found that their intellectual activity diminished steadily as their hunger, their fear, and their apprehension about survival grew. Knut Hamsun provided, in his novel **Hunger**, strikingly documented cases of survival needs taking precedence over intellectual activity and creative activity.

I started teaching at Syracuse University during a summer session. My assignment was to give two full courses in 6 weeks, neither of which I had ever "given" before. My family was in transit, I didn't have a house for them to move into yet, and I was suffering from all sorts of physical-survival problems. In addition, I complicated my own life by putting upon myself some conventional expectations of how I should teach. I stayed up every night until the wee hours of the morning preparing lectures to give to the tiny classes I met with every morning. In general, the lectures were not bad, as I remember them, and I myself learned a great deal in preparing them. But my energy was primarily expended on a survival level rather than on a creative intellectual level. I operated mechanically according to a pre-conceived model rather than dipping into my own potential.

Abraham Maslow developed a hierarchy of needs that expresses some of these relationships. We have certain basic needs (deficiency needs) that we must attend to before we can devote ourselves to growth needs such as motivation to strive for truth, goodness, beauty, aliveness, individuality, justice, playfulness, and meaningfulness. Our basic needs, hierarchically stated, include physiological needs first of all (air, food, water, shelter, sleep, sex); safety and security; love and belongingness; and self esteem and esteem by others. Until we satisfy our basic needs first we cannot deal creatively with our lives, nor can our level of consciousness grow.

Some people learn to turn off some of their more primitive needs and to function at a high creative and intellectual level under conditions that would cause other people to devote all of their energy to survival. It is possible to function creatively under adverse conditions if I can ignore or transcend these conditions. I am convinced, however, that I can deal more effectively with survivial and that I can cope better if I become more fully aware of the nature of my processes. Then, if I perceive myself to be in a predominately survival situation instead of in a situation likely to favor creative behavior, I can allocate energy more in the one direction than the other. I can reduce guilt feelings about not being able to create something when I am aware that a survival problem requires all of the energy I might otherwise have devoted to feeling guilty. On the other hand, when I do devote time to creative activity, I can close out survival problems for hours on end. I want to accept in myself that some periods are optimal ones for creative activity. I can force creative activity sometimes. (It is said that Hemingway forced himself to sit down nearly every day for several hours and to write whether he felt like it or not.) Another thing I can do is to have a number of different kinds of creative activities, related to different levels of the Maslow hierarchy, and I can select my activity on the basis of where in the hierarchy my awareness tells me that I am. (If I really need loving more than anything else at a given moment, let me devote my energy to creative love-making!) I can fight against the natural currents of my life and the conflicts I find myself in, but I can probably accomplish more and accomplish it more joyfully if I listen to my body, listen to my context, listen to my feelings, and listen to my mind before I try to expend large amounts of energy on a given activity.

I believe I can help or hinder creative activity in other people as well as in myself. I want to be aware of where in the Maslow hierarchy the needs of other people I am working with may be. Concurrently, they may become aware of where I stand at any moment so that we may pulse together in some kind of creative, organismic rhythm instead of vibrating out of phase.

How did I ever expect a whole classroom full of students to sit down at one time and take any examination?

How did I ever expect a whole group of people to produce term papers on command by a certain date?

How did I expect any people in a required class period all to be ready to talk about the same subject?

(Do you know that John and Jane just broke up? That Carl didn't have any breakfast this morning? That Amy was sick last night? That George is in a world of fantasy at the moment? That Annette has just reached a creative peak with respect to an art activity and doesn't give a hang about science?)

If I tell you that you must do science with me just because it's 9:10 A.M. and that's the period you're scheduled for science, but you would prefer to do art, then there's something wrong with the schedule. There is nothing wrong with you. There may be something wrong with me for telling you that you must do it, though.

Flexible scheduling (or no scheduling?) in schools, in business, in government, or elsewhere open the way to peak creative activity at appropriate times.

When someone is involved with a personal survival problem I no longer expect him to be excited with what I may have scheduled. My genuine interest in his survival problem may help him gain confidence in me as a facilitator for his or her activities in more intellectual pursuits later on.

I want to arrange my own work as a facilitator so that I am working with peak creative energy as much of the time as possible. There is no good reason for my teaching, selling, or doing social work 5 hours a day Monday, Tuesday, Wednesday, Thursday, Friday. Perhaps 15 hours one day and 10 the next may be the time that I can perform best as a facilitator, with other times off for other kinds of activities. One thing is certain: what is good for me today probably won't quite work tomorrow. This must also be true for other people I work with. Each of them will come to me with different needs, a different schedule, and different expectations each time that we meet. Each meeting is in a new context. What I have to offer will come out spontaneously when it is ready to do so.

TIME

I have discovered I have a hang-up with time.

I like to be punctual—because everyone says, "You should be." In order to be punctual, I developed a "watch fixation." I rolled my wrist over and glanced at my watch habitually. I like to observe myself now when I'm on my way to a meeting for which I know I'm going to be late. As I walk across campus I eat up huge amounts of nervous energy fretting, the whole way over, rather than accepting the given: I am going to be late, no matter what I do. It is even more amusing when I am being conveyed somewhere by public transportation and the bus-train-taxi-plane is running late. There is absolutely nothing functional I can do about it. I might just as well devote my energy to better use than exercising my wrist and my worry glands.

I talked for a long time about removing my watch and forgetting the time thing to see how I would behave and feel. About 6 weeks ago I finally took the plunge at a 3-day encounter-group meeting. I removed the watch as we departed for the group meeting and didn't look at it or at any other clock again until we returned 3 days later. For the first time in years I didn't know what time I went to bed, what time I got up, or how many hours I slept per night. It's a strange feeling to wake up and get up because I'm rested rather than looking at a watch and saying to myself, "It's only 6:00 A.M.; too early to get up now," or "It's 9:00 A.M. and I'm late getting up," or "I must be tired because I only got 4 hours sleep." (Everyone knows you have to get your 8 hours to be rested!) I didn't know the hour when I ate. We had food when we were hungry.

Gunner has a good way of handling this. He had all of the clocks in the lodge stopped at 9:23. As he points out, that way he always gets to bed before 9:30 and he never sleeps beyond about 9:20.

I went without my watch again on our field trip to Oregon last month. We ended up working unconventional hours, but what is magical about the hours between 8:00 A.M. and 5:00 P.M.? Sometimes an important and unique recreational opportunity presents itself at 10:00 A.M. If I don't take it then it may be gone forever.

I backslid seriously on one day. We wanted to get to the bank in

Prineville to set up an account for our expedition and to replenish our nearly empty cash box. I slipped my watch on and drove for town at a high speed. We were flagged down a few miles outside of town: road repairs and a long, slow detour—one of the unavoidable delays that no one could have predicted. I began to fret, fume, complain, and look at my watch every few seconds. Finally we cleared the detour and arrived in town at 2:50, expecting a 3:00 P.M. closing, only to find that all of the banks in town stayed open every day until 5:00 P.M. Gradually I learn that I can't fight time. If I go with it rather than against it I conserve energy for more important tasks.

Time is one of the things I hear teachers and students complain most about. "I can't do labs because I don't have time. You can't do a lab in 42 minutes." "I don't have time to show movies." "I can't take field trips because we don't have time." A humanities professor at my university is constantly asking for re-evaluation of a new university time schedule. "Do they still have the same total number of hours in class for each course?" Quality of experience seems less important to him than clock hours of formal instruction. From students I hear "I didn't have time to finish the test (termpaper, project, etc.)" Several years ago a student in my geology course had terrible difficulty with examinations. He complained about time pressure. On the next one, I allowed him as much time as he wanted. He stayed for twice the normal time and turned in a fine paper. That's one of the things that helped me abandon time-constrained examinations.

We live in a world that runs on time, where people are penalized in various ways for missing schedules. Schedules breed time problems because they are inflexible. When the train is gone, it's gone, and there is little that can be done about it. When we miss each other because one of us was late, we miss the encounter. When I come in late to a film, I miss the beginning and that's all there is to it.

Schools—learning establishments—may be places where we can start to help people accept the flow of time, accept that they will be late, that they will not finish "on time", and accept the fact of missing things as well as getting to them on time. By developing flexible scheduling we may provide ourselves with new dimensions of freedom. In order to enjoy these new dimensions we will have to adopt new attitudes about such things as waiting, missing, and arriving, however. Punctuality may be out of date.

As I think about science, I am sure that attempts to hurry the processes of scientific investigation to meet schedules are counter-productive. It is better to throw out a schedule and begin all over again, than it is to continue with a badly begun investigation just to keep on schedule.

When I commit myself to do something at a certain time, I will try to honor that commitment. But more and more I accept that if something else comes up I am willing to change my schedule. Although it is still hard for me to accept that someone else doesn't do something for me "on time," I realize that I want my attitude toward time and schedules to change with respect to my expectation of others, too.

I find myself taking my watch off more and more. Cricket, Gretchen and William are often annoyed. We have already conditioned them.

I find that many times when I am uptight I can find the reason in a worry about schedules or time. If I first remove my watch, I then can relax. The awareness of my problem rather than the removal of the watch is the critical part.

I am learning now that it's o.k. to work a 4 hour day, a no-hour day, or a 24 hour day. What is important is what I produce, and how I feel while I'm producing it.

TEACHING AS CONSCIOUSNESS—THERAPY

During the past several years psychotherapists have told us many important things about people and helping people function. People called "teachers" have much to learn from what psychotherapists are calling "client-centered therapy."

The label "therapy" may be bothersome to some people in education, business, law, government, and other areas, just as it was to me at first. The word therapy conveys the idea of curing an ailment or a disorder of some kind. We think that therapy is for sick people and we don't think of ourselves or people we serve or work with as sick. Therefore we shun therapeutic approaches and attitudes simply because of the label.

Much that I consider to be good in recent approaches to open education has come from psychologists interested in psychotherapy, however. A.S. Neill, the creator of Summerhill School in England, considered himself as much a counsellor and therapist as a teacher. Carl Rogers is unabashedly a therapist interested in introducing therapeutic techniques into all areas of life. Abraham Maslow, Frederick Perls, Barry Stevens, George I. Brown, Eric Berne, and dozens of others make constant references to the applications of theraupeutic techniques in education as they discuss problems of therapy among neurotic and even psychotic patients. Much psychotherapy today is aimed at helping "normal" people (those whose behavior is not generally considered by others to be significantly "deviant" in any way from "norms") discover greater depth and potential in themselves. Rogers, Maslow and others believe that many hang-ups and problems that show up in therapy sessions with both normal and abnormal people might have been avoided if schools were organized and if "teachers" operated along psychotherapeutic lines. Teachers should be as much interested in their roles as counsellors as in their roles as "experts" in subject matter.

We too often approach learners not as people full of problems and potential, but as a mainly faceless population to which we convey information and ideas. By starting with the subject matter rather than the person we may well close the door to effective learning.

The idea of counselling and therapy as an integral part of the teaching-learning process threatens many teachers and even students. Students, by the time they reach junior high school, have often formed suspicions and expectations about how teachers will behave and they have developed defenses to avoid close personal contact. They have learned to treat teachers as distant objects and authority figures just as they have come to expect teachers to treat them as objects (pitchers to be filled up) rather than as individuals full of potential to be opened up.

At a meeting concerning admission of new majors into our geology department, I expressed positive support for several students whom I felt had great potential and who were, in my opinion, developing awareness and personal motivation but who did not yet have much physical product to show to the committee. Some of the undergraduate committee members as well as some of the faculty expressed the view that our job was not to run a motivation and therapy clinic but rather to "teach" geology and geography. One graduating senior said he felt that perhaps I'd better go off and be a full-time guidance counsellor if I wanted to mess around with therapy rather than with geology.

It is difficult for people who are conditioned by years of sterile teacher **versus** student interactions to accept the notion of a full human interaction (a therapeutic relationsip) being not only compatible with, but even enhancing intellectual growth and the learning of subject matter.

To me it is a matter of having the cart before the horse when my initial interaction with a person is based upon an initial human separation, a status barrier related to my supposed expertise. I want to deal with establishing a process of interaction first. Then exchange of cognitive knowledge will follow naturally when appropriate.

I define a truly therapeutic relationship from my point of view as a **growth relationship.** Perhaps the idea of **growth** helps to get away from the notion of therapy as a cure. I think the ideas of growth and curing are synonymous or at least so closely integrated that one cannot separate them—. Perhaps considering the word **curing** in the sense that it is applied to foods — mellowing and improving the flavor — is a way of avoiding a "sickness" connotation.

In order to be involved in a truly therapeutic or growth relationship I find I must be very much in touch with my own feelings. If I have a sense only of helping the other person and concentrating entirely on him or her I can lose track of what I am feeling in the interaction. What I have to offer when I interact with another person is the accumulation of my feelings, knowledge, and experience. If I am really in touch with myself I can learn to express these things both verbally and non-verbally as I am stimulated by interaction with another person and through the empathy that I feel for him or her. I grow during the interaction also. I am not merely a helper. I am a partner. When I cease to be a partner then I am less likely to facilitate growth and learning in either of us.

ROGERS' CONDITIONS FOR THERAPY APPLIED TO PERSON TO PERSON RELATIONSHIPS IN GENERAL

Carl Rogers describes several conditions he believes to be necessary for effective functioning of psychotherapists He advances the idea that these conditions may also be effective for anyone working with "normal" people in virtually any context.

The first of Rogers' conditions is what he calls **congruence**. This means that I avoid fronts and facades and try to be as genuinely myself as possible. I am congruent I am as fully as possible **aware** of the real feelings I am experiencing at any moment, and I can communicate these feelings as I choose to. I can even be stupid and do very wrong things as long as I am really being myself. All sides of me should be present as they are really there. It is impossible for me ever to achieve complete congruence. I can however, grow in such a way as to increase my ability to be in touch with myself. During the relationship I must take time to get in touch with my own feelings. This means I take time to see what I am feeling before blurting things out. Then I decide whether what I may have been about to blurt out does indeed reflect my real feelings.

Empathy is the second of Rogers' conditions. If I am empathic I will, as Rogers puts it "sense the (other person's) inner world of private, personal meanings as if it were (my) own, but without ever losing the "as if" quality..." If my own uncertainty and problems get tied up in the other person's problem, then I will be less effective. If I am really empathic, I am tuned in to the other person's meanings and should be able to communicate back to him, to reflect to him my understanding. I may even be able to help the person focus on things that he is scarcely aware of in his own experience, but which I sense in him. This is a difficult kind of understanding, as Rogers indicates—understanding without losing my own identity or merging with the other person.

Unconditional Regard, the third condition, would have me hold the other person in an unconditionally positive light as a person regardless of what behavior he is showing and without judging the person in any way. This means accepting the person as he is, without wanting to change him. He must make any decision to change on his own. I find it difficult to accept without making judgements, and yet I feel that this might be the most important condition of all. Real, honest accepting of a person as he is rather than as I would like him to be is difficult, but it may set the stage for the strongest kind of facilitative relationship and for real self-directed growth on the part of another person.

BEING "IN TOUCH" WITH MYSELF IN PERSON-TO-PERSON RELATIONSHIPS

The other day when we were picnicking, William jarred my elbow, knocking a gooey, open-faced sandwich onto my pants. I got furious.

The day before yesterday as we sat outside on another picnic, he dropped his mayonnaise-covered bread onto my bare foot. Whereupon, as I muttered angrily he proceeded to wipe my foot off with grass.

Then, last night in the dark I sat down in a lawn chair on our porch and felt liquid soaking through my pants. It was apparently present in a puddle on the chair-seat—William's bitter lemon, spilled there a while before! My immediate feeling was to burst out laughing—much the same way I had felt when the mayonnaise hit my foot the day before. But instead of a laugh, which I was really feeling, out came an angry blast. Force of habit. When you sit down in a mess that someone else failed to clean up, you're supposed to get mad.

Once I "got my mad on," I really played the role vigorously, too. I wasn't very much in touch with myself. I allowed my real feeling about the situation (hilarity) to be submerged by a conditioned reaction.

I think a lot of my responses to people come out that way—as conditioned situational responses rather than as responses in which I have taken a little moment to feel my real reaction before letting it burst forth. If it had really been anger at that puddle of soda pop, that would have been all right, but since anger was not really in me I don't feel so good about it.

I suspect that many responses of teachers to the activities of learners and bosses to their employees reflect more what they think of as an "appropriate" response than what they are really feeling.

Had I laughed at those situations caused by William's eleven-year-old clumsiness, my reaction would have been totally unexpected by the rest of the family. And we would all have had great pleasure from the moment. And, strangely, that honest response might (my fantasy) have just been more helpful to an eleven-year-old trying to overcome boyish clumsiness than my conditioned (but "appropriate") response (anger) could ever have been.

I think that I may be able to develop better relationships with people as I become more aware of my real feelings about situations and allow those feelings to come out rather than play-acting according to how I think people expect me, in my position, to respond. Better conditions for creative functioning should result both for myself and for others.

ENGAGEMENT AND DISENGAGEMENT

Most relationships are not "instant" ones. It takes a while for us to become engaged with each other. This is true of cognitive things as well. It takes me a while to get engaged in reading a book, doing a study of some kind or the other, writing a paper, sitting down to play the piano, or warming up for an athletic event. A long period of "preparation" leads into engagement in creative activity.

Rich Joko once expressed feelings of regret that he didn't become more engaged with more poeple at some of our larger ESTPP and ES workshops. I feel this, too. Can't there be a quicker union or engagement? Can't our gears mesh faster? With some people, I find that the "vibrations" are there almost instantly. With others, it may take us a while to mesh, or we may never have quite enough time to mesh as people.

This, too, is true of person and projects. Sometimes a physical happening immediately delights me and attracts me to interact with it. This is the stuff of spontaneous reaction. Instant knowing that I want to do something and then doing it! Instant knowing that I want to know someone and then knowing the person!

In the learning environment of schools where I work I may react with a couple of hundred people in a term for greater or longer periods of time. How many of those people can I really become engaged with?

Disengagement is the other side of this coin. During a month-long workshop last January, Lucretia and I worked full time with twenty-five people in a closely personal, art-and-science context. Many of us got very close personally and worked together, too. When this ended, I tried to move into another college term immediately. I still wasn't disengaged from the workshop experience, and I couldn't get engaged in the spring term either.

Weekend workshops are tough things to deal with in many ways. We scarcely get engaged and then we break. Encounter groups are often like that. My nerve endings are all at the surface. I feel all exposed. And then an hour later I have everyday life to deal with, with all of its momentary attempts at engagement and disengagement.

Think of the horrors of scheduled classes and what they can do to people! 9:10 A.M.—time to engage yourself in English. Whoops! 10:00 —stop english, start science! Whoops! 10:50—stop science, start music. I seek environments in which each person can engage and disengage himself when he's ready to. Transition times are individually dealt with. If I need an hour, a day, a week to become engaged in a learning experience, with all of its human and cognitive dimensions, I can take that amount of time.

One thing I am really beginning to know about myself is that I have a poor chance of becoming engaged in something new until I am disengaged from what I just stopped doing. I guess this confirms what Fritz Perls and other gestalt psychologists and therapists tell us: as long as you have too much unfinished business, too many incomplete gestalts hanging around, you won't function very well. What I want to do now is become more aware of what my unfinished business really is. "Where am I blocked?" Then I can deal with it, disengage, and move on. I can't do that according to your schedule. If I push you when you feel blocked, all I can do is inhibit your growth and your entree' into a new phase of engagement that is useful to you.

Behind our hutte - Straumgjerde

TAKING CREDIT

> It is very easy for me to read myself incorrectly afterward even when I have moved in the right way. I mistake what happened for what I did myself. It happened by itself through me. But later, I take credit for myself, as for something that I have done.
>
> —Barry Stevens

The planned versus the unplanned! I suppose I can take credit for the success of something when I have really planned it in advance and acted in a certain way purposefully and with a definite intent to provoke a certain reaction or to cause something to happen. I am sure there must be some things that happen just the way I've planned them and where everything is **right**.

But if I am really responsive to any situation, it is almost bound to evolve differently from the way I had planned it no matter how carefully my plans were laid. Then, if I am really letting me be myself I will respond spontaneously and not according to plan. I am beginning to feel that the spontaneous responses give me and others more delight, pleasure, and richness. I begin to trust the idea of moving into a situation as me with the accumulation of all of my experience rather than as the "trained geologist," "the science educator," or as some labelled category of limited dimensions. It may be that the musician in me will contribute most to a spontaneous response to a personal problem that keeps a learner from understanding the physics of a biological problem!

I was in Giraudoux' play **Ondine** while a graduate student at Berkeley. At one of our last rehearsals I suddenly and spontaneously responded to one of the other actors in a way that I had not done before. Shortly afterward, the director called us to a halt—"Cut!" He told me that whatever I had done in my spontaneous response was "right." I had really "caught the feeling" of the thing. It was as if he wanted me to freeze this moment into my characterization. Perhaps I was able to do so, but this "moment" came as a happening, a spontaneous response. Could I really take credit for it?

I suspect that once I tried to freeze the moment in—to imitate my own spontaneous response, I gradually lost the realness of the moment. Spontaneity produces results that cannot be quite reproduced. The moments must always shift a little. Every performance must really be different from every other one for a play really to be successful in a long run.

The same must be true, I feel, in any facilitation situation I find myself in as I try to help others function. I find that every time I apply a "formula," something that worked with one person, in my response to other people, it usually seems less successful. If, on the other hand, I always respond from the totality of me, I am more likely to make a truly spontaneous response that may be much more helpful than a repetition of an old trick. I've gotten very suspicious of "tricks." I think they may lead to shallow results.

When I have responded spontaneously, however, I don't really want to take credit for the response. If learning takes place for another person I may have been an intermediary, but the learning was really a happening for which I just happened to be present.

> *As I sit in the small chalet we have rented in Sykkylven, along a small fjord in Sunnmöre, I am tempted to take credit for planning our stay in such a fine place. Fortunately, the family reminds me that we really stumbled into a fine situation. There is no credit to be taken by anyone. It happened because we were ready to respond spontaneously.*

According to the present ethic of the schools, everything is supposed to be carefully pre-planned—lesson plans, curriculum, administration, all of those things. As I see the relative success of spontaneous responses to situations, I want to avoid the inflexibility of planned situations in order to free myself and those who are with me from the disappointments of unfulfillable, rigid expectations. Good things do happen if I am truly responsive to the feedback I receive from every action I take. I move by small increments, continually flowing along my course rather than swimming furiously against a strong current.

Sometimes I go home at night particularly pleased with an interaction I have been involved in. As I go over the situation, describing it to someone else and analyzing it, showing delight in what my response was to a problem and how I might have been involved in its solution, I may be tempted to take credit for my helpfulness and, specifically, for a given set of my responses, as if I had planned them all along. If I fall into the trap of this kind of pride I may work against the maintenance of the very spontaneity which allowed the successful happening to occur in the first place.

One area of taking credit is the one in which I hear people talk about "their" students or "their" subordinates. Every time I refer to someone as "Oh, he was one of mine!" I feel uncomfortable. I do not want that kind of possession in the interaction I have with other people. Each of them is himself or herself and I am myself and each of us belongs to no one.

This works two ways, of course. In the case of several students who interacted with me last spring but not with other members of our own faculty or with other students on our admissions committee, one committee member took me to task for not seeing to it that these students, who were more occupied with personal problems than with science, produced more "hard science." But I do not accept responsibility for seeing to it that any "standard" product, in terms of committee expectation, must be produced by any particular person. Spontaneity, credit, responsibility - these are all tied up together in interactions I have as I work together with other learners.

In **My Fair Lady** (and **Pygmalion**, too) Henry Higgins and Colonel Pickering return from the ball at which Eliza Doolittle, the flower girl who has worked with Higgins to become a well-spoken, well-mannered gentlewoman, has shown herself to be a true lady and has actually passed as a duchess. Pickering congratulates Higgins for his success in creating Eliza-the-lady. Higgins willingly takes full credit for Eliza's transformation. This greatly annoys Eliza, who breaks out into a rage. When Higgins asks what's wrong, Eliza says, "I've won your bet for you haven't I? That's enough for you. I don't matter, I suppose." To which Higgins responds, "**You** won my bet! You! Presumptous! **I** won it..."

COUNTING

Twelve days we've been in Norway as of today. Thirty-two more to go.

Three weeks gone out of the semester; eleven more to go. Only five more until Thanksgiving.

Six hours I've slept. Only two to go until it's time to get up.

Six laps of the pool I've swum so far. Only 14 more and I can call it quits for today. One, two, three, four, five, six, seven, eight, nine, ten, eleven, twelve, thirteen, fourteen, fifteen, sixteen, seventeen strokes to make one lap. If it's 15 or 16, I'm pulling better than usual. Oof! NINETEEN strokes that time; I'm getting out of shape. One-two-three, one-two-three, one-two-three - that rhythm feels good.

Two chapters of this damned physics book and I've still got 15 to finish.

Two times I've been over this piece, and I promised my piano teacher I'd go over it 4 times a day - for, let's see - 3 more days. That makes 14 more times.

Three beers - that's all you get!

Count off! One, two, three, four, five, six, seven, eight, nine ....

Forty-two years old! Half way through? Why does each year go faster than the last?

Fifteen pages of this term paper written now, but my biology teacher said it would have to be at least 20 pages long if I expect an "A". How'll I pad it out?

Five hundred and twenty three words. But this abstract for the Geological Society is limited to 250! How'll I cut it down?

Oops, forgot to fill this thing out in triplicate!

Twenty analyses done. Another 4 or 5 and that'll be about enough to get a publication out of this stuff.

William has read 1,076 pages so far this summer. I found his addition staring up at me from his desk:

298 - The Wheel of the School
560 - Papillon
218 - Invisible Man
1,076

Twelve papers this year, eleven last year. I guess my productivity is going up. How can I keep it this high?

Twelve hours of contact a week? Why, in our institution we only have 6 a week!

Thirty students per class, 6 classes per day, 3 preparations.

Thirty days hath September ....

We are proud of our 15:1 student:teacher ratio.

Two students to a room - very few singles available.

6:1 male to female ratio? WOW!

Eleven trout? Afraid I'll have to fine you.

Only 3 or 4 pairs of whooping cranes.

Sixty percent for Nixon: a real mandate!

Ten percent A's, 15 percent B's, 50 percent C's, 15 percent D's, 10 percent F's. Normal!

5 syllables followed by 7, followed by 5. That's haiku.

Da-dah, da-dah, da-dah, da-dah - iambic tetrameter, you say?

Picasso painted how many hundreds of paintings?

Can't you cut down the price to $3.50?

John, you've already had 4 pieces of candy.

I've finished 320 pages of this book, but it seems to be never-ending!

How many more miles until we get there, Daddy?

We're all hung up on numbers and counting things. How often does the quality of what we are trying to make or do - the quality of our lives - give way to numbers? Science and math may be among the worst offenders in the schools, but people in most other areas do it too.

I can stop counting if I choose to. Even though I'm conditioned to keep track of the numbers, I can become aware of when numbers inhibit me. I want to look at things as wholes as much as I can rather than as accumulations of numbered parts. There is little danger of my forgetting quantities altogether. They too have their own special kind of importance. But there is some kind of balance and too often the weight of quantity exceeds the weight we give to quality by too much, and we often mistake quantity for quality.

By my own counting behavior I am sure I affect others around me. William counts a lot because he hears me fretting over numbers. He constantly is asking how much this or that costs. In this I see the reflection of my own worrying about prices. Then, when I reject my own worries and decide not to think about them any more, William is there to keep echoing it so that I seem not to be able to escape the notion. I have begun to stop thinking about time, but Cricket, Gretchen, and William ask for the time several times an hour. This is a reflection of my counting. No, I guess I can't take that responsibility on myself. Our society has a time and numbers fixation and we are all affected by it. I can work to move away from it, however, and perhaps others I work with-live with may come to share my rejection of control of my life by time and numbers.

HABIT, RITUAL, TRADITION

> The only trouble with travelling in a rut is
> that sometimes it gets so deep
> you can't see out over the sides.
>
> —Jonathan

"Rats," I say to myself, noticing by my watch that it's 9:30 A.M. "Too early for my cup of coffee. Have to wait until 10:00!"

I go out to get on my bike. Mechanically I unlock the lock and carefully lock it through the spokes. I had forgotten to lock it when I left it, but my mechanical, unthinking response is to do <u>something</u> *with the lock before I get on the bike. If the lock happens to be* <u>on</u> *the bike as it's supposed to be, I unlock it and I'm off. Sometimes I get fouled up in my own mechanical routines.*

Can't go to bed yet - forgot to brush my teeth.

12:30 - time for lunch!

Fourth of July - today we shoot off fireworks. Too bad it's raining, but we'll manage somehow or other.

10:30 - time for science class, even though we're having a ball reading.

Didn't get my swim today - every time I miss a day I'm afraid I might fall apart.

Only had two meals today. I've got to watch it. Might be bad for me to miss meals that way.

In order to do this kind of math problem, here is the way to go through it. First ....

Always start a term paper with an introduction; then you go on to write the body....

First read through the chapter all the way. Then look back at the words in heavy type and make sure you know what they mean.

We'll have a quiz every Friday ....

We <u>always</u> *end our courses with a final examination.*

Monday, Wednesday, Friday at 10:00 A.M....

The committee will meet every Thursday at 3:00 in case we have any business.

In spite of my desire to be a free person and my belief that I am moving more and more in that direction, I am aware that I have many routines and rituals. I see rituals in Cricket, Gretchen, William, and Lucretia. I see rituals in just about every person I come to know. Routines and rituals of other people whom I think of as "free" become especially apparent when I have occasion to live in community with them for a while.

I frequently allow my personal habits and rituals to bind me and to keep me from taking advantage of unique opportunities. Institutional habits and rituals take the form of traditions and also may conflict with needs and opportunities of the moment.

> *What's so special about bedtime at 11:00 P.M. and rising time at 7:00 A.M.? Supper at 6:30, you say? Every day? Senior week at Commencement each year - even as a disruptive strike raises whole new sets of educational and personal issues? Black caps and gowns again? In 85-degree weather? Final exams in all courses, every semester, all during the same week, all the same length of time? Pre-registration - always? But my interests may change between now and September. All courses will be 15 weeks in length and classes will meet for 50 minutes each, 3 times a week, in one of these little classrooms we will assign to you.*

Sometimes I enjoy letting my day flow along and just watching how many things I do as a matter of habit or ritual, without even thinking about it. Do I always comb my hair using the same motions and in the same order? When I shave do I always begin on the same side? Do I shave every day, regardless? When I brush my teeth what series of motions do I go through? How ordered or random are they?

I remember how I used to do my French as a freshman: read the passage over once aloud without looking up any words – concentrate on pronunciation and meaning without consciously translating. Now read it a second time, writing down all the words I don't know. Now look up all of the words and try to learn the list by heart. Next, do a smooth oral translation into the best English possible, trying not to need the new word list but using it if absolutely necessary. Last, after obtaining a "perfect" translation in my own opinion, re-read the passage aloud in French stressing pronunciation and understanding without translating. Then go over any problem areas again.

Or in science: before going into lecture, re-read the notes from the last lecture carefully. Have advance assignment read. Take careful notes on the lecture. Immediately after the lecture, reread the notes, high-lighting the important parts. Go over the related reading immediately. Then read the advance assignment. Just before the next lecture, reread the previous day's notes....

Those are what you call "good study habits." They'll almost certainly get you graduated with honors, into the National Honor Society, on the honor roll, Dean's list, into Phi Beta Kappa or what have you. And what a grade point average! **So what?** How about that National Geographic Society television program I didn't watch because of my study habits? How about a hundred other unique opportunities for new experiences that can far exceed, in learning potential and in helping me to grow and be aware, my habitual activities.

I look back to some of my days as a student in France. While there, I continued with my "good study habits." What I also did was to reject many opportunities for person-to-person contacts with French students and adults. I don't waste energy crying about that loss, and my experiences were unique and important. But I feel a lingering regret as I become more conscious of how I limit myself by my habits and rituals. I let them inhibit me as a scientist, learner, person.

Note that I don't say I want to get rid of all of my habits and rituals and traditions. I just want to be more fully aware of them. Habits simplify my life and allow me to accomplish many genuinely essential functions in a somewhat mechanical way that doesn't require much energy. But a deep and pervasive awareness of these habits puts me in a position to choose consciously when I want to "violate" a habit or tradition. It also helps me to enjoy and savor my habits, rituals, and traditions more fully rather than taking them for granted.

In **A Sense of Community,** Bill Coulson tells how the well-developed work habits of Carl Rogers help Rogers to keep producing valuable things even when he becomes involved in peripheral events. Don't knock work habits **too** much, and yet don't be dominated by them. Find the point of balance and try to hover near it.

Rituals and routines and traditions can be all right, they allow me to accomplish many functions that are more or less essential to the sustainment of my physical and mental health. I can then conserve energy and use more of my conscious awareness to deal with special things.

There is a risk, though. New rituals can creep in and, unless I have a high level of awareness about even simple and routine aspects of my life I can come to accept meaningless rituals and I can, in a sense, become their prisoner. I can give up some of my independence and right to make decisions by entering into new rituals or holding onto old ones without even realizing it.

It is also easy for me to impose on other people I work with or live with the expectation that they will adopt my rituals without our even talking about it. If I perceive myself as a leader, I may begin expecting others to drop their rituals and take up mine.

Your rituals are just as much your property as mine are mine. You have as much right to yours as I to mine. I don't like it when I consciously or unconsciously expect you to adopt my rituals. If we both **happen** to share a ritual or decide to adopt some of each others' rituals to try them out, then we have a basis for living together or working together for as long as we maintain some congruence or at least for as long as we can be fully acceptant of each others' rituals. If a ritual or routine is set up by an administration to organize us and does not fit with out individual routines, I work to change or avoid these outside rituals that inhibit me and you. I have no right to intrude upon your rituals without your permission, and you have no right to intrude upon mine. Together, we try to negotiate a relationship, to try out new combinations of events. I want my habits to be flowing, negotiable, changing so that my life can be richer and more varied - so that I can experience a greater range of things. I seek to become more and more aware of my routine and rituals so that I may enjoy the useful ones more and decide consciously to reject either temporarily or permanently the ones that do not meet the needs of the moment or of my life in general.

If I accept the routines and rituals of learners who come to work together with me as much as I accept my right to maintain my own rituals, the way that I operate in any learning environment (call it "the school" for most people) will be much affected.

When I say, "Excuse me, that's just a habit of mine," I really am not taking full responsibility for what I am doing. I am blaming my habit. Awareness of my habits will help me in my efforts to take full, conscious personal responsibility for all that I do.

A habit, ritual, or tradition is only an objectionable box to me when I can't see out of it and can't bend it easily. My habit boxes need to have lots of holes and freely swinging doors. What's more, I want a wave of my hand to be enough **magically** to make any given habit box disappear into thin air. Likewise if I choose to create a new one, I wish to do it easily and quickly and let it have gossamer walls.

EINSTEIN'S MEAT HOOK

Ronald Clark reports that Albert Einstein used to receive enormous amounts of correspondence. This included just plain fan mail and all sorts of requests for Einstein to speak, make appearances, support causes, loan money, and write letters of recommendation. When Einstein was deeply involved in working on the General Theory of Relativity he needed to work alone and undisturbed much of the time. How to handle this flood of correspondence? Einstein kept a big meat hook hanging from the ceiling above his desk and he would, when he was particularly occupied, simply hang whole packages of unopened letters up on the meat hook for future attention. A visitor, noticing huge bundles hanging on the hook asked him what he did when the meat hook was full. Einstein answered with a simple, "Burn 'em!"

The president of a large middle-western university, tells of a time some months after he began his job. One morning at 4:00 A.M. he finally finished his briefcase-load of work, much of which consisted of relatively trivial administrative correspondence. Suddenly it struck him that he did not **have** to deal with all of the trivia. His job was in the long run not there to be defined by someone else and for him merely to fill someone else's expectation of what a college president **should** do. He could define his job any way he chose. The next day he began the redefinition of his own job in terms that put him in the position of conceptual leadership that he desired rather than in the position of just responding blindly to every request, however little he was interested in it, that came to his desk.

Every time I begin to complain about the work I **have** to do I find that I **can** indeed select what I wish to do rather than just doing a job because someone else wants me to. As director of ESEP I started out to try to fill other people's expectations. I never did quite get out of the habit of answering virtually all mail that came to me, whether I was interested in it or not or whether or not I felt the energy devoted to it could have been spent more profitably in another direction. But I did begin to redefine the role of project director in some very substantial ways that gave me a chance to be much more active in operational aspects of our programs.

As a department chairman I now get enormous loads of administrivia sent down for "action." I'm just now beginning to realize how many items I can simply ignore. I am learning that I can even say very openly and bluntly to other administrative officials that I'm simply not going to do what they are asking me to do. **I** define my role to the extent that I choose to do so. I have learned that I do not have to answer my telephone, after years of allowing myself to be affected by random intrusions from people who are far away.

I can do this in a normal teaching situation, too. I do **not** have to give examinations. I do **not** have to give grades. I do **not** have to meet groups at standard times set by a schedule. There are very few aspects of my job as a so-called "professor" that I cannot redefine in my own terms. I become much more effective, I believe, in carrying out my real function—facilitating learning and communicating to others about ways of facilitating—when I take personal responsibility for defining my work in the way that I consider best for me. The way I define my function and refine this definition is, of course, affected by feedback from the system I exist within. When I have success in carrying out my primary function, all sorts of eccentricities are then accepted in the way I deal with administrivia.

An important fact for me to remember, however, is that I also accept the right of every learner and every faculty colleague to define his own role in his own terms. This means that we must negotiate a good deal about ways in which we can interact with each other.

Einstein's meathook becomes an important metaphor for me. It says to me that I really can **choose** the way that I respond to outside expectations. When I am really me and when I really define my own role I can contribute more that is really useful to others too.

TEMPO

Lucretia, Cricket, Gretchen and I just climbed up a mountain here at Straumgjerde to look at some waterfalls, alpine meadows, and an old seter (mountain farm) surrounded by sheep. Gretchen and I went tearing up the mountain. Cricket and Lucretia puttered along at their own speed, too. A few days ago, William and I started off in Oslo to walk to a little pond called Bantjern, where we wanted to go swimming. It was soon apparent that William would take an hour or more to get there rather than the twenty minutes I had predicted. We changed our plan and went to another, nearer, pond.

Years ago, in Paris, Jean Conway and I used to walk back from the theater to our rooms. Jean had a particular speed for walking. As he said, "This is my speed. If you want to walk with me, then it can't be any faster than this."

In a field-geology course I once took, the instructor used to take us tearing from one outcrop to another. Just as we had gotten started writing down our detailed descriptions, he would be off again, leaving us scrambling after him in the dust. People in the course kept leaving hammers, hand lenses, and notebooks behind because they didn't take time to pull themselves together. After all, they couldn't let the leader get the impression they were slow. And there were grades to worry about.

One time I went scrambling through the brush after him. As I popped through the poison oak earlier than he expected me, he was standing over me with a big grin on his face that seemed to say, "Let's see those guys scramble through **that** thicket." As soon as he saw me his smile changed back to the usual frown. "Don't want to let them know my game, after all!"

Every now and then I find myself unconsciously setting a fast pace more or less to show off. I don't like it when I discover that motivation in myself. Setting my own tempo up just to impress someone else serves neither of us.

At other times however, I realize that I have a kind of natural pace in my own work. I am interested now in an apprenticeship kind of relationship with learners who want to share expertise I may have - a working together to solve a real problem rather than a teaching of something where I am merely leading someone through something I already know. In these cases I want to follow my own natural tempo. That is my own working process in action. The other person must decide whether or not to come with me or to leave me (either ahead or behind depending on the "sign" of the tempo difference). There are no penalties for not going at my tempo. We recognize that we are different.

Sometimes I alter my tempo because the working relationship or the collaboration with another person may be more important than anything else. In this case my tempo is altered because of the new rhythmic factors I feel vibrating as I work with another person. I may be able to slow to a snail's pace if I value some particular aspect of our relationship enough to want to do so. Or our physical and psychological health may depend upon staying together.

Last year, on a trip to Italy, Lucretia and I visited many art galleries. Lucretia's tempo is often very different from mine in many aspects of our lives. She was spending what seemed to me excessive time in each gallery and I ended up waiting, frustrated. Then I suddenly developed a new approach of my own to the galleries. I began to study the renaissance paintings for the way in which their painters portrayed earth features. How carefully were they really looking at cliffs, mountains, rocks, rivers, the sea? How conscious were they of the things I see? My whole tempo changed and often Lucretia was left waiting for me. A redefinition of my interest and approaches led to a change in tempo that made our association more congruent.

Gary Boone, Don Thompson, and I once collaborated on a study of some feldspar crystals. I have a rather slap-dash tempo sometimes and wanted to plunge ahead in our analytical work at great speed. Gary is an extraordinarily meticulous person who would putter around endlessly with details of our analysis procedure. I'm sure we grated on each other sometimes because of our different tempos. But we had important things to offer each other in the collaboration and we had respect for each other's differences that allowed our research to proceed in such a way that we obtained imaginative and useful results.

I am less inclined to wait around for other people than I once was, and I do not really want them to wait for me either. On our field expedition to Oregon last month two of our group members were inclined to sleep very late, while 3 or 4 of us were generally up early ready to go work on more volcanic rocks. We had no particular desire to waken the others and impose our tempo, but we had things we wanted to do. Finally we simply started leaving on our own when we were ready. A natural split into groups with different tempos occurred.

Some people will choose not to work with me because my tempo may be too fast or too slow for them and the nature of our interaction does not produce the new composite rhythm that makes it comfortable for us to work together.

I want to be aware of the tempo factor in people as I interact with them. It is important enough that we must develop some kind of a minimum match before we can work together on any long-term basis. It is essential to me that learner or colleague not be constrained to work with me if my tempo is too fast or too slow for her or him. I also am feeling freer to reject a working association myself if our tempos mismatch too greatly.

In a situation where students are assigned to work with me for a given length of time, I want to provide maximum freedom for them to develop activities at their own tempos with no penalties for not moving the way I do. Whenever possible I want to be able to facilitate a change of advisors or facilitators so that people need not feel bound to me or to someone else where tempo differences inhibit our working together.

Six feet three inches tall, slim, hair-line receding, sort of blondish, prominent blond eyebrows, sometimes with a beard covering a mouth that gives away emotions and feelings at times, still pretty young looking, fairly bright, laugh a lot in crowds, write reasonably well, pretty good "teacher,"....

As I write this, certain things I think about me come to mind and I find myself hedging about putting them down. How much of my real self-concept am I willing to share with you? How about this part:

not really at ease in crowds, timid about initiating a relationship when I am an unknown person in the company of strangers; not as confident of my ability as a "hard scientist" as I think I should be; attracted to girls I work with, but afraid of imposing or being a "male chauvinist" (or is it fear of being rejected?), shy and unaggressive about it; hesitate to make the first move when it comes to initiating or deepening a relationship but eager to have relationships form and deepen; not as well organized as I'd like to be.

I wonder how much of what I'm putting down in the first draft of what I write I will leave in for you to read? When we are face to face we may decide to share much of ourselves with each other - to move rapidly below the surface. I always hope for this kind of sharing with anyone I work with and even with many people I meet only casually.

It's easy for me to share fairly superficial things about me with others, but I frequently hide much of real me. A few sessions in encounter groups have helped me to "come out" more.

How do the opinions of others affect my self-concept. Rich once mentioned to me that I sometimes come on at first as pretty aloof. Some others tell me that I come on too strongly. Do I seem to hide behind my intellect? How I "come on" is of course not just how I am. Instead, it is how I am to someone else, so that all of that person's perceptions and experience of people are wrapped up in that.

T. B. thanked me after a meeting for putting her at ease when we first met at a workshop for teaching assistants. That was positive feedback for my self-concept. When I was getting very hot under the collar at a department chairmen's meeting, Wendell Brown wrote me a little note: "Cool it!" This was feedback that reminded me of my impetuosity at times and of my failure to **listen** to others. Chalmer Roy has often reminded me just to listen sometimes when something that starts out like criticism is coming my way. "Hear it out first, and let it settle a while before you respond," is the message. When I heed the advice I find that often the criticism ends up taking care of itself without even any need for me to respond. Sometimes all a critic is really doing is expressing a generalized resentment. He neither seeks nor expects a reaction from me. At a conference in Massachusetts, involving college and secondary school science educators I was taken to task by a psychologist from Colgate for my lack of introducing a more structured program. He ended his criticism with the question, "How do you feel about **that**?" My response, after a long pause, was, "I accept your feelings." This response had a positive effect on both him and other participants who later spoke to me. My more usual defensive responses have effects that leave me in a far less comfortable frame of mind.

My self-concept has all sorts of peculiar ins and outs that I don't readily share with others. It constantly changes in its details and sometimes even in more important ways as I look into the mirror of other people's perceptions of me and as I experience new things and become aware of my reaction to them.

Generally, I have had a positive self-concept. I have an active motivation to do things. I am persistent in working toward goals I set for myself — perhaps too much so. Sometimes, I miss opportunities for new spontaneous experiences that could be important in helping me grow and be more self-actualizing. I am a drudge sometimes.

A good self-concept is essential to any person who is to grow in any substantial way. Evidence from the Coleman Report bears this out statistically with respect to how children from various backgrounds perform in school. Children with a good self concepts generally cope. Those without, don't. Susie Lusk visited the children's court in Boulder a number of times. After several visits she came back to us with the observation that "kids who have either a good home life or a good life in school seem to be able to make it. The kids who come to juvenile court in deep trouble seem to have had neither." I interpret her comments about "good life" as relating to the young people's self concepts primarily. The Jencks Report further confirms the important role of self-concept in learning.

The way we affect people's self-concepts in the educational system are sometimes blatant, sometimes subtle. The evaluative emphasis of schools constantly reinforces learners in certain directions and discourages them from following directions in which they may be equally or even more capable. We condition students to depend upon the outside world to tell them whether they are capable or incapable rather than learning to evaluate themselves in terms of their own real likes, dislikes, and potential.

I was always successful in school - at least as far as the grading game was concerned - except in math. I remember grade school teachers giving me a bad time about story problems. In tenth grade I got caught for cheating — the only time I can remember even having tried during all my schooling to get an answer from someone else during a test. I avoided all math as an undergraduate, because my self-concept included a statement that said, "no good at math." When I later entered graduate school I was told that I'd have to build math background. From a conceptual point of view the calculus seemed as if it ought to be interesting and useful. But the evaluative, time-limit approach, bolstered by my own poor expectations for my ability in the area, caught me up and I had a miserable time. I had problems with certain areas of chemistry and physics also, and I am now convinced that my image of my ability in math was my worst enemy. Since then I have done a lot of math, physical chemistry, and physics related to my research in science. Once I got out from under the extrinsic, test-based evaluative conditions that reinforced a poor self-image and low self-confidence I found myself competent in these areas.

I now feel that I can do just about anything I set out to do. I know that if I am willing to invest enough energy and effort I can ultimately learn to do moderately well.

Large numbers of students have come to me over the years and said, "I'm bad at science and I hate it!" before we have had any chance to interact and before they have even started a course of study. They come to satisfy a science requirement and are already defeated by their expectation of poor performance or failure. In conventional courses most of them have done badly on tests because of their poor self-concepts. Last year I worked with a special group of students in geology who "certified" in advance that they hated science and did badly at it. We worked to redefine the whole notion of "science" in terms of aspects of their self-concepts that they already felt **good** about.

George, a recent graduate is now a typical example of a first-rate "hard" scientist with a very strong mathematics and statistics emphasis in his work. Yet two years before he graduated he had a miserable concept of his own abilities. He had done badly in normal course work and was ready to drop out of school. Just at that time we changed the operation of our group to a student-centered mode of operation. George was placed in the position of being able to plan all aspects of his own program and to assume total responsibility for his own learning, to claim credit for any activities he chose to engage in, and to evaluate his own work. At the end of the first term of activity in this new mode, he called all 5 members of our departmental faculty together and informed us that we were going to discuss his progress. We declined to judge him in terms of conventional grade-scale factors. After a long discussion he decided to claim all A's for his transcript. As he left us, he said, referring to his roommate, "I don't know what Mike will say when he hears about this. Everybody knows I'm not an A student." Now this particular person knows he **is** an A student on anybody's measurement scale, but what is most important, he now has a sense of his own potential.

Connie, who was interested in art and who "hated" science was turned loose in our student-centered program. She did very little at first and asked to defer recording an evaluation until she had done something she felt comfortable with. We consented to this deferral, as we always do for anyone who wishes to stretch an experience beyond the normal boundaries of a term. She returned some months later and showed me some good work she had done on the geology of several national parks and including a number of excellent sketches she had prepared. When the time came to settle upon an evaulation for the record, she wanted to take a low mark at first. We talked at length about this. She admitted that she had done badly in several other courses, and if she gave herself an A in geology her roommate and friends would say she had done this just to get out of academic probation. She finally did opt for an A, which her work was well worth from even a conventional viewpoint. She seems now to have developed a better concept of herself.

If I look at every transaction I have with a learner in terms of how it might affect self-image and the ultimate actualization of real potential then my interactions with learners are very different than they would be if I made flat, out-of-the blue judgements of learner's tangible, paper-and-pencil product. In many instances I have seen an apparently trivial piece of product open the door to a new self-confidence that could have been denied had I imposed a negative judgement. As one girl said in a self-evaluation statement she gave me, "This may appear to be something that would be more appropriate for a third-grader to hand in than for a college student to submit, but what is important about it to me is that **I did it all by myself. I have really made something that is all mine and it seems to me as if this is the first time in my life.**" The experience she had, regardless of what "level" any outsider might assign to it, was of first-class importance to her. More and more I find myself declining to pass judgement on another person's **experiencing.** Any product is a shallow and superficial reflection of the experience that went into the process of producing it.

If I truly wish to help people unwrap and become aware of their own potential, I want to facilitate their building bigger and better self-concepts. One of the most important ways of doing this is by deferring judgement.

APPETITE AND HUNGER—MOTIVATION

"Give me some structure so I'll have at least some idea what to do," she said.

This girl, coming to work in our "open" science community, was showing signs of what Eric Berne has called "structure-hunger."

"I want **you** to guide me. I refuse to guide myself," said a boy after finishing a semester of work with us.

He was showing a hunger for recognition.

Each person in a learning environment comes in with various cravings and appetites that he needs to deal with in some way.

After Harvey Blatt visited our group he wrote us that we had an extremely "hungry" group of students. He saw them as hungry for information, cognitive material and ideas on techniques and problems. One of the things Harvey liked about our learners was their active quest for knowledge. They were, he said, highly motivated to learn. This is without any real extrinsic pressure being applied by our faculty, too. Intrinsic motivation seems to be present in many of our people.

The hunger and appetites people bring to us when they join our science group include many varieties. One hunger I see a lot of is exploration-hunger, an appetite for wide-ranging exploration. Some people can deal with this appetite through reading. Others must move about physically. They must travel. I want to legitimize both of these. The traveller's hunger is, technically, a little harder to legitimize, because our administration feels that studies for credit must mainly be out of books and labs. But we go ahead anyway and arrange sub-rosa off-campus programs. Some of our people are travelling cross-country on bicycles. A large number receive credit for independent travel in Europe and elsewhere abroad. Some are off on apprenticeships in various laboratories. It's too bad that we have to "sneak" these experiences in because our administrators are so hung up on the need for the experiences to be "supervised." But at the same time we are working through ponderous administrative channels toward more open legitimization of these travel experiences. In the long run, my experience is that teachers and facilitators can allow virtually anything, any kind of freedom they want, and as long as no **substantial** trouble results from the practice, administrators will not stop it.

The hunger to skip around—to be a dilletante—is an important appetite of many people who want a bite of this and a bite of that, but who don't choose to delve deeply. Dilletantism is a quality that many teachers scorn. I feel that this is to the detriment of individual learning processes. Alvin Toffler writes of the need to experience new things, to skip about, to change jobs and activities frequently.

An appetite for depth is found in some learners too, once they get into something they simply have to follow more and more deeply. Dean is most interested in learning geology. He wants to go to the moon in the worst possible way. He has centered enormous energy on his study. He has also explored a variety of peripheral material so his general background has also grown while he has at the same time worked to satisfy his strong appetite for in-depth study of a single major area. He is becoming a scientist with both breath and depth, although his approach to the subject could at first seem narrow to an outside observer.

Carl Rogers, writing about his work with psychotics, expresses the view that, "working with a lack of conscious motivation in the individual is more difficult than working with the problem of psychosis." He extends this view to normal people as well, although a normal person who is not motivated to change would not seek help from a psychotherapist. In a sense, students in schools, and especially in public schools where attendance is mandatory until age 16, can be compared to inmates of a mental or penal institution. They are not there by choice and may have no hunger for what they perceive that the school can offer them. The same is true for colleges. Here, no laws compel students to attend, but strong parental and peer pressures may effectively have the force of law in compelling unmotivated people to attend. I accept, thus, that I may be confronted by some apparently unmotivated people who approach the learning situation anywhere from kindergarten through grade 20 with hostility and fear.

Still, every person has needs and hungers. I want to become aware of the real hungers individual people bring with them when they enter a learning environment in which I am identifed as a paid facilitator. Then I want to accept the hungers that are already there and work with the person on her or his terms toward acquisition of cognitive knowledge. If I assume a hunger for knowledge about any given topic when there is none, I am doomed to disappointment and the learner will continue to be apathetic. "Why aren't you interested in this fascinating stuff I've prepared for you?" is simply not a viable approach.

Some people have hungers that involve other people—hunger to control others for example. I feel the necessity of recognizing such hungers in others. I want to work against such hungers once I have discovered that they exist. I do not accept any person's attempts to control another person and to try to use either psychological or physical force.

Motivation to learn, change, or grow is an intrinsic property with respect to any person. You can't "motivate someone." He or she is the only one who can **become** motivated. Yet most curricula operate on the assumption that you can, through requirements, push someone into a state of motivation.

I believe educators **can** set up environmental conditions within schools which foster the identification and growth of motivation. Once motivation is present, the best thing I, as a facilitator, can do is to keep out of the way, participating in the work of learners and communicating to them my feelings about their work when they request such help. I can also produce and organize various kinds of learning packages that will help in the acquisition of appropriate skills that people of all ages and backgrounds may wish to acquire, once they are intrinsically motivated to do so.

An essential way of helping to stimulate the generation and growth of motivation is to avoid establishing subject matter requirements. To the unmotivated learner these become blocks to the development of motivation. I can provide invitations to involvement, but if these appear in the form of expectations that students **should** participate, even "invitations" lose their effectiveness as soil in which seeds of intrinsic motivation can grow. I used to think that I could plant seeds of motivation. Now I begin to think that the seeds are pretty much in the person already. I can provide soil and fertilizer. I do accept, however, that someone **may** get a totally new idea from me and that this can become a basis for intrinsic motivation. This is the reason I still like to show my own enthusiasms and interests as publicly as possible. Still with the richness of today's public information and stimuli from the media and the world at large, the basic seeds for motivation are present in most learners before they even enter school.

THE MYOPIA OF INTOLERANCE

Several times on preceding pages I have mentioned my desire to accept what I discover in other people as part of them and to go from there. I shall often repeat this litany of acceptance.

Even though I accept intolerance as a basic trait in many people I cannot help regretting its existence. Sometimes I think that I really in the long run do not want to change people. The litany of acceptance tells me to accept them as I meet them. On the other hand, as long as I claim to be interested in education I at least tacitly accept that I **do** want to change or at least to participate in their process of change. I subscribe to George Leonard's view in **Education and Ecstasy** that there is no education without change in people. I confront people with my impressions of them as intolerant if I feel intolerance in them. If they choose to remain intolerant then I may choose to avoid them except when administrative necessity brings us together.

I regard intolerance as a kind of myopic condition—a nearsightedness. There must be some metaphorical set of corrective lenses that could be prepared for intolerant people. If I want to be a real facilitator of learning I will try to help people find those glasses. One way of working on it is by confronting them with my perception of their intolerance when I observe it. Not from the point of view of saying, "You should be more tolerant," but rather from the point of view of saying, "I see in what you have just done (or said) a lack of acceptance and I feel bad when I perceive this." I want to express my opinion and feeling as information about something that is within me rather than as a suggestion to them.

In the long run, change within a person only occurs when he is motivated to seek ways to change. He has to put on his own pair of glasses if he wishes to see beyond the range of his uncorrected, myopic vision. Once he wants to change, then I will be glad to offer feedback, a listening ear, or whatever else we decide together might facilitate the change.

If I am really open, then I can even accept closed minds! Acceptance does not, however, mean that I need conceal bad feelings that the closed mind induces in me. It only means that I will not worry about trying to open up such a mind until the person involved is motivated in a direction where he or she wants me to participate in the opening-up process.

Open-mindedness and acceptance go far beyond life styles, and acceptance of me regardless of how I am. They go deeply into religion, politics, and all cognitive areas. They apply to art, music, dance, the environment, and to everything that people can possibly have conflicting opinions about. Because much of my recent experience is in science, I offer some examples from that area.

At a recent workshop involving 40 earth scientists a staff member suggested an attempt at water-witching (dowsing). Many "good" scientists have a preconceived idea that water-witching is nonsense. Nonetheless, several of us agreed to try. The most competent and serious, younger, research-oriented scientists were among the first to say, "let's try it." Some of the people who refused altogether turned out to be among the relatively inactive scientists in the group.

The history of science and modern science journals are full of controversy between those with closed minds and those with relatively open minds to new ideas and approaches. I especially recommend regular reading of the "letters" section of the weekly journal **Science.**

An interesting study of tolerance versus intolerance can be found in the controversy over whether or not the biblical version of the creation should be required to appear in every science textbook in California that mentioned the Darwinian Theory of Evolution. A great deal of opinion was printed about this during 1972 and 1973 in **The American Biology Teacher, The Journal of Geological Education, The Science Teacher, Geotimes, Science,** and other journals, The extent of intolerance on both sides of the controversy is well worth examination by anyone interested in problems of open-mindedness within the cognitive areas of science.

All major scientific controversies lead to a feeling of stress in people whose belief systems are affected by the particular confrontation of ideas. Under stress, unusual aspects of people's personalities are apt to show up in public and in print. Then we have good opportunities to study the effects of the myopia of intolerance on the growth of ideas, on the way people interact, and upon the quality of our lives. When I become aware that I am afraid of criticism or that I am expressing criticism of others for their "faults" rather than expressing as a fully-owned part of me my dislike for what they are doing, then I want to go looking for my acceptance glasses!

FREEDOM

Freedom is being equally distant from all 4 walls.
—quote from somewhere

I advocate open and free alternatives in ways of learning. The implication is that I am really a free agent to make my own decisions and that I want learners working with me to enjoy this same freedom. In **Beyond Freedom and Dignity**, B. F. Skinner calls into question whether or not we have any substantial freedom at all and proposes that our behavior is mainly controlled. We should seek to improve the nature of these controls and make them less aversive rather than working to develop feelings of freedom. True, all sorts of controlling factors may surround me, but I prefer to operate under the assumption that each of us has powers of decision that enable him to be freer than he could ever imagine. I can increase my feeling of freedom and thus my **real** freedom by becoming more aware of possible constraints that surround me.

A network of constraints surrounds me. These include the purely physical needs that I must satisfy in order to survive, as expressed in the Maslow's hierarchy of needs. It is interesting how rarely teachers usually take into account Maslow's hierarchy. Many students are simply "not free" to deal with schoolroom pursuits on certain days and even for prolonged periods because of lack of satisfaction of more basic needs identified in Maslow's hierarchy. Even if we don't think in terms of Maslow's hierarchy, constraints do surround us no matter how free we feel. The law says you go to school until you're 16. If you don't go, aversive contingencies such as reform school and detention homes can be imposed. (A talk I recently heard suggested, however, that perhaps 2 million school-age children in the U. S. manage to avoid school without punishment.) I must work to live. Life in a commune where I could raise my own food and become "self-sufficient" would be as limiting to my freedom to do exactly what I want to do as an eight-to-five job in the city. A whole set of social contingencies conspire to reduce freedom.

But let us assume that these basic personal needs and social "obligations" **are** satisfied and then examine how free we really are. Imagine a day when you can get up in the morning and say to yourself, "what do I **want** to do with myself today?" If I have real and complete freedom, then anything **might** be possible.

One of the first things that can limit me in my choices is the whole range of my previous successes and failures, however the perception of each act as a "success" or a "failure" was established. I know that areas in which I have been told that I "failed" in the past according to one judge's criteria have been viewed as successes by other judges. In any case the shaping of my perception of what I can succeed in is apt to affect my choice of what I want to do with myself today. I am likely, as are many people, to elect to do something at which I have succeeded in the past and been reinforced for doing (either by internal feelings of joy or by external praise.) The degree of real freedom I feel affects my willingness to try something I have never done before or to try something at which I previously failed. If I really want to learn to ski because of the culture it opens up to me, I can tolerate many falls.

Chris Samples told me that at the Jefferson County Open Living School in Colorado the teachers noticed lots of activity by children in their "free" environment, even at the very beginning of the experience. Soon, however, they became aware that the students were actually just repeating past successes. Another example is the case of Jake, a strapping college athlete who worked with me in earth science. Jake, age 19, said that he wanted to make a model volcano as a project. He was, according to our agreement, free to pursue any activity he chose in any way he chose. I asked him if that's what he really wanted to do, or was he just doing this to have a "project" done to sooth his own felt-need to do something and to try to express his involvement in some concrete way. He finally confided that he had done a similar project when he was in the first grade, that it had worked out pretty well, and that he had been complimented by his teachers. It was apparent that he was trying to recreate that old success. He was allowing his freedom to be constrained by previous activity.

In Jefferson County, after a couple of months the students ran out of things to do over again. They began to get bored with making another papier mache volcano or cutting up the 23rd frog or singing the same 3 songs or doing the same kind of math problem. They entered a period of apparently aimless activity, afraid to try anything really new, and tired of repeating more of the same. Finally they started to risk new kinds of involvement, and gradually the whole tone of the school has grown to one of risking entry into the unknown.

A new set of limits emerges, however. How many things are there to do that I've never even thought of before? The possibilities and combinations are obviously proportional to the degree of freedom I have to interact with other people and with materials. In truth there are no limits in terms of sheer numbers of possible activities. We do, of course, reach physical limits inherent in our own bodies and in our world. Advocates of **Jonathan Livingston Seagull** or of **Seth Speaks** may argue that any limits can ultimately be exceeded or at least that we can profit for entertaining that belief.

My values and prior social conditioning (which is there whether I like it or not) become a set of limits also. Given all the factors of my life, how likely am I to decide that I will go out and commit a robbery just to have a new experience? I grow through having new experiences, but I will probably limit the scope of these experiences. How likely am I to take drugs, to rape someone, to cut off all my hair, to put on a silly costume and go into the college president's office, to spontaneously jump on an airplane and go somewhere, to burn up a ten dollar bill? These possibilities are common subjects of explorations by philosophers. They are even more commonly explored by each of us in fantasy and in dreams. The things each of us tries in the privacy of her or his mind are incredible, but we test very few of these out in practice.

André Gide created a character named Lafacadio, who tried to establish his freedom at one point by pushing an old man out of a moving train, killing him. The act was done with no motive other than to experience killing a person and getting away with it.

A group of art students at one northeastern university painted their bodies and marched into the Dean's office. He severely reprimanded them.

Galileo wrote down a large number of fantastic ideas about the universe. He looked beyond the limits. The Inquisition imprisoned him for the rest of his life.

A. Wegener proposed in the early 1900's a fantastic story of drifting continents. He died with most of the scientific world still laughing at him. Now nearly everyone believes that his basic idea of moving continents is correct although the mechanism he proposed for their movement may not have been.

George Plimpton, a journalist, plays football with a professional team, boxes a champion, and commits himself to a huge range of unusual activities for the sake of having new experiences and exercising his freedom.

Some travelers always go to new places just because they have never been there before. Some people order the item on the menu they've never heard of in order to find out what it is.

On the other hand, doing only things that are new is also limiting. If I do only things that are new, I develop no real competence in anything and I reject the very experience of expertise — which may be based on drill and repetition of a single set of activities.

Being with other people helps me to see possibilities that are beyond things I could imagine by myself. Yet I am limited by their presence at the same time. Some activities demand the presence of other people - competitive and team sports for example. I can also let myself be controlled by how others react to what I do.

Lucretia and I did a month-long workshop called "Art and The Earth." We worked together with 2 dozen college students. Each of us was free to define both "earth" and "art" in his or her own way. Then we agreed that our experience during the month, as much as possible our **total** experience, would consist of having these two things interact intensely. We also agreed to get together a couple of times a week to share the results of our exploration and creative activity. I entered this experience with the intent of getting up every morning and dealing with the question, "What do I want to do with myself today?" My success was only mediocre. I did engage myself in a whole range of brand new activities, but I also soon found old compulsions, displaced supposedly for the month, creeping in, saying, "How about me?"

I like to think of myself as enlightened and daring. But then I have to look back with sober eyes at how few **really** spontaneous things I have done. My habit of prior planning limits my spontaneity.

There are also external contingencies of **context** that limit me. I want to paint today, but there is no paint available and I don't know how to get any. I want to swim, but the pool is closed and the river is frozen over. I want to ski, but it's July. I want to make love, but no susceptible women are around. I **can** get around these limitations given persistence and resources. If I truly set my mind to skiing in July, I can go to the Southern Hemisphere, go up into some of the high snow fields in the northern Rockies, or even switch to skiing on plastic nets that are now available in some areas. Each of the problems I mentioned above can be solved if I want to devote enough energy and imagination to it.

I have to find my limits to find out how free I really am. Len Baron recounts that whenever someone makes a suggestion to do something or whenever he thinks of some new potential experience he watches his own reaction. If he feels tense or defensive about becoming involved or if he hears something about himself that makes him feel defensive he knows he is near a limit. The awareness of a nearby limit gives him a chance to explore the nature of the limit and then he can make a conscious choice as to whether or not he will go beyond it and on toward some further limit in an ever-expanding sphere of freedom to act.

There may not be freedom to do all things, but there is wide freedom to choose within any set of constraints, and beyond this is the freedom to test the limits and generally to push them back. A more ultimate freedom is the freedom of fantasy where we can begin to explore endless new possibilities.

EXPECTATIONS AND TIME — THE SAME OLD CHARLIE!?

Consistency is a virtue of small minds

—Old Proverb

"You didn't used to do that sort of thing! You used to be such a nice person. Now you're different somehow. What ever **happened** to you?"

Many people have an expectation of stability in other people. I suppose I do, too. I know that I grow and change in various ways each year. My behavior changes; my views change. Yet when I meet an old friend after a separation of several years I still expect him or her to be more or less the same as when we last met. I have changed a good deal in my views about education. Often I meet an old acquaintance who used to share my former, relatively conservative views and expect him still to hold these same views. Frequently I find that he has changed in the same direction I have and we rediscover each other at a new level of consciousness. Sometimes I find that we have changed in opposite directions and we are unable to communicate at all.

I'm finally getting to accept that people are not stable, but that all of us change in one way or another. Each meeting becomes an encounter between two different people with new experiences. The best way to share these experiences, I find, is always to expect newness, freshness, and difference rather than sameness and stability.

"The same old Romey" is a phrase that makes me wonder if I am stagnating.

I have discovered an interesting thing about my work. When I enter into a new position, my colleagues, who generally don't know me at all or know me only a little easily accept any behavior, habits, and attitudes I bring with me. I can introduce many changes quickly and easily into the system I enter. I can be bold with little risk. Everyone says, "Oh he hasn't found out that we don't operate that way here" or, "Oh, he's just learning the ropes so you have to expect him to make some mistakes." But if I persist, the changes I have introduced into the system mainly become accepted, without the rest of the group really knowing that it has happened. They are too busy with their own routines to worry about, "the new man," who is, in any event, carving out his own niche.

Within about a year or two, however, my immediate colleagues have developed a set of expectations about how I will react in certain situations. They get so they "know how to handle me." (And, incidentally, I think I get so I "know how to handle them," too.)

But if I continue to grow and change at a faster rate (or in a different direction) than those around me, then it becomes more difficult for me to introduce systemic changes. "The honeymoon is over," is what I often hear, meaning, "We have now stabilized you in the eye of our expectations."

The last several years of my own experience have been marked by what I consider rapid change. I think this change may have been relatively easy for me because I have changed positions several times. I have stayed in education, but I have changed groups.

After completion of undergraduate work as a language major I had several years of work in the Navy. People developed expectations that I would become a government bureaucrat with a bent for languages. Or perhaps I would become a language teacher. This was followed by several years of graduate school in geology, during which time people developed expectations that I would behave as a conventional, research-oriented college teacher. For my first real job, I was hired to teach both geology and science education at Syracuse University. I had two very different sets of people to work with in two different contexts. I did education-oriented things with the education faculty and science-oriented things with the science faculty. When people in one group saw me in the other context, they were always surprised. "I didn't know you wasted your time doing **that** sort of thing." (To which I might respond, "I didn't know you wasted your time gardening, either!")

After 5 years at Syracuse I went abroad on a research leave to Norway. When I returned, I found everyone expecting me to behave in the same way I had before I left. A year's absence, with my activity oriented in very different directions—this time of almost straight, hard-line research—had led to evolution in a very different direction. Yet I found at Syracuse tremendous inerta that I could not seem to overcome, so fixed an image did people have of how I **should** behave due to the gradually evolving image of me my colleagues had formed during my first 5 years there. We were able to push through channels a rather dramatically improved program for the education of secondary school science teachers, but only at the cost of enormous energy spent in committee hassles rather than on the substance of working with students. It seemed impossible to make any substantial dents in the united front of the science departments. My own courses continued to evolve strongly and rapidly in new directions of personalization and student-centeredness.

I then moved to work at ESCP with a mandate to develop new programs to supercede that project, which was in its terminal phases. Even though this was with a "new" group of people, they already had substantial expectations of how I might behave because of earlier consulting work I had done for them and because they considered that I still subscribed to most of what I had written in **Inquiry Techniques for Teaching Science.** I learned, to my surprise and delight, that the stabilized images **I** had of the group of people I was going to work with were also out of date. The immediate project staff and I were moving strongly in similar directions and we made a quantum jump in the way we operated. Almost overnight, as a group of **new people** encountering each other, we transformed the direction of our projects. We were able to do this because of the **New Man Effect,** I feel. By the time the Institute had caught up with us, our new directions were firmly implemented at a new level.

Of course, as often seems to happen, we again reached a plateau of stable expectations. We found that we had to push harder and harder to make smaller and smaller amounts of progress.

After three years with the AGI group I moved to St. Lawrence University where again, as a new man, the community at large has tolerated what would seem to be outrageously unconventional approaches. After only a little more than a year of full time involvement there I began to feel the system closing down and stabilizing its expectations of how I would behave. More and more I hear the phrase, "but last month (last week, yesterday, at our last meeting) you said..." I change constantly and it is hard for systems and groups of people operating through normal "democratic," committee-oriented groups to understand this and to accept a rapid rate of change.

John Gardner speaks of the need for a constantly self-renewing society. In this kind of society, the one stabilized image would be the expectation of difference and continuing change rather than stability. In such a world change and rapid evolution would continue to be easy even in a single organization. Organizational pressures would not "clamp down" in terms of expectations that make it increasingly difficult for changing people to move ahead. Inertial factors would be reduced in the more or less frictionless response of a flexible operating procedure within the organization.

Even in a single organization I can build opportunities for growth experience outside of the organization. In academia, research leaves, sabbaticals, summers, and academic "holidays" provide these opportunities for special experiences far-removed from normal habits. My research leave in Norway did this for me at Syracuse, as did 3 summers of activity with ESCP before I joined that project on a full-time basis. So did a dual appointment. People on dual appointments were regarded as somehow different. We were fully accepted by both faculties we belonged to and yet, when we did "odd" things as we changed our own procedures, each faculty seemed more acceptant than they were with people who were entirely "their own." Each faculty seemed to feel, "He's just trying out some stuff he got from 'over there.'" And this somehow made changes in us "duals" more easily acceptable. It gave it a kind of organizational sanction.

John Coleman, the president of Haverford College, took a leave in the spring of 1973. Without informing anyone except one son about his plans, he went off to work, at 51, as a common unskilled or skilled laborer, whatever jobs he could get. He told none of the people to whom he applied what his real business was, but represented himself only as a middle-aged former salesman out of a job. He values the lessons he learned in several months of such vital new experiences as a unique way of being in touch with himself and with the world. The old tales about kings going out to live incognito among the people involved a similar approach to extending knowledge through experiencing personally the life styles of people who occupy different roles in society.

Somehow I feel that it is important for me to get away often from the fixed expectations that surround me in any given role I am identified with. The danger of being identified too long by others with a single role is that I might get to believe that the role and I are indeed synonymous. Any time I really believe that **I am** this role I am constrained to an unacceptable degree. I do not want to be just "a first-grade teacher," "a bank president," "a college dean," "a geology professor," "a humanist psychologist," "an athlete," as any of these narrow roles is generally defined or even as more widely defined due to the way I might fill the given role.

Perhaps Toffler is correct when he proposes that each of us should change his job dramatically no less than every 5 years if we are to avoid the traps of fixed expectations, of stable behavior, and plateauing of behavior and systems as opposed to constant growth and change.

I keep hoping to communicate to any group I am in that the only thing they can expect of me is that tomorrow I may be very different than today. I do not want to waste energy justifying or explaining changes. Nor will I be surprised if others change. Any expectation of stability on my part (in terms of my duplicating past behavior) are likely to lead them to disappointment. Any attempt to predict how I will respond on the basis of my past behavior will probably lead to disappointment. I want to respond as spontaneously as possible to the situation I find myself in. Input into my responses will include the sum total of my past experience and my perceptions of the new situation. But I want my response always to be spontaneous and fresh rather than just a duplication of what I did before in a similar, but still different situation.

++++

After reading part of **Risk-Trust-Love**, Bud Holland mentioned to me that I appeared to be inconsistent in some of what I said. Then, suddenly, he smiled and said, "But I guess that's the way we really are!" Do you refer to people as "consistently" good students? Some of the most "creative people" often appear very inconsistent and unpredictable. I suspect that a lot of the so-called consistent people may be offering us only a partial view of themselves. Whenever a person appears inconsistent to me, this is related to my expectations of him rather than to him as he is. Each person is basically consistent within himself in terms of his own interests. Any judgement of inconsistency I make is unlikely to be useful in helping another person learn, grow, or create.

How about the person who plays a consistently good game of tennis or does consistently well in theater work, or who can always be counted on to be there to help in setting up the lab? I guess we do need people who can be counted on to fulfill commitments. But I think we tend to expect a cross-the-board kind of consistency in schools rather than a self-directed, personally initiated consistency based on the learner's own, personal, self-generated commitments. I cannot cause someone else to be "committed." Commitment is an intrinsic property that lies within each individual person and cannot be imposed. Interest in one area and the satisfaction of doing well in it and feeling good about it often lead to the notion, "I may be able to do well in this other area, also." If I ask learners to be "consistent" in many different areas at once, many of them outside of their own general interest areas, I may be leading them to experience a feeling of powerlessness, a feeling of "I can't do it." I want to avoid looking for consistency in other people, based on my expectations of them. Learning and creativity occur best when low-risk exploration is favored. Exploration is trying things out. Trying things out makes behavior appear inconsistent. Unabashed inconsistency may, when legitimatized in a learning environment, favor learning, discovery, and the development of creative power. Consistency is sameness. Growth requires risk, exploration, false steps and therefore inconsistency.

EXPECTATIONS AND EXPERIENCING OF PLACES

On a first trip abroad at age 19, I went to France to study for a year. In spite of all the publicity pictures of Paris, the wealth of literature describing Paris, and even the reading I had done about Paris I was stunned by the place when I arrived there. Somehow I had formed no particular mental image of what Paris should be like, and I could thus accept it as it was only 5 years after World War II when there was still much evidence of the ravishes and decay of the wartime situation.

I have been struck many times since then by the lack of preconceived visual images I seem to have of places I am going to visit — even in the time of wide-screen movies, multiple color-slide shows of trips that friends share with me, and a lot of reading I do. Only last year, on a trip to Italy for which I thought myself "prepared" I was again struck by the general freshness and unexpectedness of vistas.

I find that I work this way to a large extent in geology too, I don't get much interested in the geology of various areas or in the geologic relationships until I physcially visit the place. No matter what I've read in advance, I'm always wide-eyed at the sensory impact of a real place.

From a personal, visual image I can go back and follow literature about the place and then begin to build knowledge and understanding about the place. I need physically - in all the dimensions of my perception - to **experience** a place before I can do much with it in terms of building a continuing interest.

Then I think about the way schooling deals with places. Children are asked to learn geography, science, history, art, literature, and many other things that relate to places. I wonder how many people share my need for direct experiencing as a pre-condition to interest. The more I ask, the more I find.

I am glad that I seem to defer my expectations of place in this way. I like to be stunned by direct experience. It's exciting to me to go into a place and to be totally taken in by it, to be able to stand there or sit there dumbly, mouth agape, just drinking the place in.

Somehow I want to open things up to others who want to share my joy at direct experiencing, with minimum obstructions from advance expectations. This wish clearly has an effect on the way I work with people in a learning environment. I wish to leave the road open to a very personal kind of self-directed inquiry for each person I encounter.

Another problem involves how to keep a fresh view of familiar places. How can I let my awareness and consciousness of a given place continue to grow so that each time I look at it I see more of it rather than seeing only the things I saw before. Each place has in it the substance for infinite exploration and delight if I can only see.

WARMTH

Warmth has been a primary quality of people who have been important to me. It's something that can't be put on. There aren't any recipes for becoming warm with people. But I guess maybe it starts with listening to them, trying to focus my awareness on what they are really saying, encouraging and accepting their expressions of feeling. People whom I have felt to be warm have been patient with me and gentle. I don't know for sure if I can know when I am "warm." Warmth is probably a summation of many other things of which I can be aware — such as whether or not I am listening, whether I am feeling relaxed and patient, whether or not we feel free to talk about our emotions and feelings together.

I think I can recognize when I am being cold with someone. When I feel this way and don't like it I can express this awareness and then we can work this feeling through. When I seem aloof, I'm probably off in my fantasy or intellect somewhere.

Warmth is a quality of an interaction more than an abstract quality of a person. When I feel warmth myself in an interaction I think the person I am with must feel it, too. The supportive quality of a human and physical environment where I feel warmth helps me to risk saying wild things. Out of wild things come new ideas and approaches. I want to seek warmth in other people because it supports me. If I find warmth in them — and everyone has his or her warm spots — then maybe I reflect warmth myself.

ACKNOWLEDGEMENT

I used to get embarrassed when I felt warmth toward other people. When I felt that I was getting a "crush" on a student or a co-worker I resisted it and tried to suppress the feeling. This led to a tremendous life of fantasy on my part—dreaming about closer relations with people and afraid to admit this to anyone else and perhaps even to myself. But images in dreams don't lie! I sometimes even found myself avoiding some people for fear I would really slip and let them know how much I liked them.

All sorts of tacit rules circulate among male faculty members in many schools about how "far" they should go with female students. "Always keep your door open," some people say. Whew! I remember times when I was so preoccupied with trying to control and suppress my feelings about the beauty and warmth of girls visiting my office that I must have been very mechanical, awkward, superficial, and unresponsive. I tried to force myself to attend to their academic problems, but I certainly didn't feel very integrated about it all. It was just as difficult with attractive male students, too. If I admitted really liking males might this not be taken by others as some kind of homosexual attraction? Heaven forbid that!

So I built a little uncomfortable cocoon to try to isolate myself from some of those feelings.

With little children, it is easy and acceptable to acknowledge love and a physical feeling of warmth. It's somehow acceptable to hug a six-year old or to put your arm around an eleven year old. But as soon as puberty hits, there's a whole new dimension of sexuality that enters. Not only is it there in the eyes of other people and how they might interpret my behavior, but it also really is there in me, too. As much as I might try to deny it from within a cocoon of anglo-saxon-protestant-puritan morality, it is there.

Fortunately, people would sometimes acknowledge mutual physical attraction that they sensed between us and warmth could begin to grow between us.

When I was working with ESEP, we all began to realize how our failure to be open about these kinds of feelings inhibited our relationships with each other and with learners and reduced the quality of physical products, publications, and of the cognitive learning we could facilitate. If cognitive learning and affect (emotions) are all really tied up together in a **whole** person, then reluctance to admit and work with close feelings reduces the possibility of experiential learning in all cognitive areas as well as in human relations.

We were working at the time primarily with graduate students and in-service teachers. We had agreed to try to get down to the real roots of some educational problems. Many of these teachers, who ranged in age from their early twenties into their fifties, shared the discomfort that I was experiencing without being aware of the reasons or of how we might reduce our discomfort. Some high risk-takers in our group began to express these things openly. Before we knew it we were involved in a process of informal, non-manipulative encounter like that described and explored so widely by Carl Rogers and his colleagues.

In a recent letter to me, Don McCarthy said he was sorry I hadn't expanded more in **Risk-Trust-Love** on some of the things that had helped me make the intellectual and fuctional transition from basically "conventional" educational practice and role-concepts into open education in which expressions of personal feelings become important. I think this shift into an open sharing of emotional concerns probably did a great deal in providing the kinds of experiences that are part of the foundation of the things I value and want to practice now.

In the Boulder group we began to work in a more conscious way to explore and express awareness of our emotions and feelings and their relationship to learning and creativity in science. All of a sudden it started to become more important to me to acknowledge my feelings so that I could start out in a more honest way with another person.

That's risky, because sometimes I get rejected. But at least it's out in the open a little more. It becomes important to me, when I feel that I want to touch another person, to either admit the feeling openly or to move ahead and try it.

At a recent encounter group with a number of teachers I experienced a warm feeling toward one of the men in the group. Wayne is a sturdy basketball player. As we parted, having expressed warm feelings verbally, I made a motion toward him, but was hesitant. He then moved to me, and we embraced warmly as he said to me, "Man, when you feel like it, **do** it regardless of who is around." I also felt a close attachment to Val. We expressed this feeling to each other both verbally and physically. I have the same kind of warm feelings about a number of people in our geology and geography community. Every time I have risked acknowledging this we have felt better together. Our relationships become relationships of greater ease, and the possibility of supporting each other intellectually as well as physically becomes greater.

Barry Stevens tells about Wes Westman's interaction with an attractive young, psychotic woman. She had had unsatisfactory interaction with a number of psychologists and when the new man arrived she was suspicious and guarded with him. Finally, she blurted out "You want to go to bed with me, don't you?" Westman looked at her, took a moment to get in touch with his own feelings, and responded honestly, "Yes, I probably do, **but I don't think I will.**" The woman, reassured by his honesty (as opposed to that of others who had hastened to lie, "Oh no!"), opened up to him in such a way that a truly useful therapeutic experience could follow. Martin Duberman writes, "...eroticism in the classroom receives too little attention. Sexual feelings are always present — between teachers and students, between students and students — always affect the texture of so-called intellectual transactions and are always ignored.... the feelings exist, and the way they can influence "discussion" can never be weighed nor their source of energy tapped, if the pretense continues that they don't exist."

I don't want to pretend that I can separate feelings about sexual expression of love and some kind of "heart" love. Some psychologists seem to suggest that these may be two different kinds of things. I feel they are on a continuum of some kind. When I hug or kiss a girl I would be deceiving myself if I pretended I was not experiencing sexual feelings and desires. Holding hands-an initial touch - is not so terribly difficult for me to risk. An arm around the shoulder easily follows as does a hug and then a kiss. I won't pretend with girls I work around that I don't have sexual feelings about them.

William Bryce-Douglas discusses community and celibacy as experienced by nuns and priests. He explores with "religious" (nuns, priests, and brothers) their feelings about sex. Many have this feeling of continuum. They begin to feel freer to express sexual feelings and to acknowledge sexuality as an important aspect of their relationships with some people. But they also accept that they can make a decision **where** on the continuum they will stop because of some commitment they may feel that leads them to avoid completion of a sexual relationship. As a married person, I have a similar feeling of commitment that I may choose not to break. As Wes Westman said, "I probably do, but I don't think I will." When I can say that, I may be more truly free than if I carried a sexual desire to completion without being in touch with the rest of me.

Then I think, "Is that just a cop out?" Am I a prisoner of my narrow WASP morality and upbringing. To be truly free **shouldn't** I follow any desire? But that WASP morality - even though I didn't choose it - is still a part of my fabric and if I fail to be in touch with that part of me then I am perhaps not really free either. To follow the **Playboy** morality may be as much a restriction as to follow a monastic morality.

Acknowledgement of attraction and the consequent direct dealing with sexual as well as other feelings allows me and many people I know to feel more comfortable and more free with each other. We can decide that right now we just want to hold hands or to hug or kiss. But we can choose not to go beyond this level for now. No promises about future behavior or limits, but dealing with **now**. Acknowledging longing, but acting in the context we find ourselves in as we **choose** to act. Taking responsibility for both our feelings and our actions.

Whether you sense it or not, writing this has been a risk for me. Will I dare include it in the book? I think maybe so. I'm feeling bold today.

Acknowledgement of dislike or of bad feelings is probably very important, too. I do this very hesitantly, myself. I mainly prefer to be silent or to avoid someone rather than to say, "I don't like you very much." Yet **if** I can acknowledge feelings of dislike, then we'll have a basis for choosing whether or not we want to try to change this, to do something so we may come to **like** each other.

Recently I have gotten to thinking about how my initial feelings about people may be colored by the visual effect they have on me. I may be much more attracted to a person I find visually attractive than to a person who seems plain or visually unattractive. I'd almost like to try meeting some people completely "in the dark" (literally so). How would I react to voice cues? Fritz Perls worked a great deal in gestalt therapy with the quality of peoples' voices. What differences would there be in my initial impressions of people if visual cues were unavailable to me? If we were in contact by voice alone? Or by touch alone? There are so many aspects of relationship to explore and become aware of. And they're all related to intellectual and cognitive possibilities and growth, too. They affect our consciousness and how creatively we approach problems.

THE ASH LAD HYPOTHESIS AND OTHER IDEAS ON CREATIVITY

THE ASH LAD HYPOTHESIS

> There was once a man who had three sons. When he died, the two eldest decided to go out into the world to try their luck; but they wouldn't take the youngest with them at any price.
>
> "You, now," They said, "you're no good for anything but sitting and holding the pine torches, poking in the ashes and blowing on the coals!"
>
> "Well, well, I'll just have to go by myself, I will," said the Ash Lad...."
>
> —The Golden Castle That Hung In The Air.

> To the princess.... "Now you're mine," said the Ash Lad, and so he got her, and half the realm and kingdom into the bargain.
>
> —The Princess Who Always Had to Have The Last Word.

In Norwegian folk literature, the askelad or Ash Lad serves as the male counterpart of the Cinderella of German folk tales. He is a pervasive youngest brother found in dozens of folk tales such as "The Ash Lad who made the princess say, 'You're a liar;' " "Taper-Tom who made the princess laugh;" "The princess who always had to have the last word;" and "The Ash Lad who had an eating match with the troll." These have appeared in the collections made by Asbjornsen and Moe, which have been widely translated into English. A similar day dreamer also appears in Russian folk tales.

In a typical story involving an Ash Lad, the boy concerned is the youngest of several brothers. Often the family is poor and the sons must go forth to work their own way. Or occasionally one of the local kings has an ailing daughter who needs to be cured or cheered. The King offers her hand to any man who can solve her problem. He reserves death or terrible physical punishment for those who fail. The elder brothers, usually portrayed as strapping, big, active fellows venture forth, eldest first, to seek fortunes, princess, or both. Meanwhile, the Ash Lad sits by the fireplace, dabbling in the ashes with a stick. Parents and brothers discount him as a lazy n'er-do-well doomed to spend his life lazing in front of the fire. The older brothers, praised for their compulsive desire to win fortune or princess or both usually show a trace or more of avarice and a penchant for self-agrandizement.

One by one the elder brothers depart with their parents' blessing. In some stories, along the route they may pass an old man or woman begging for money, food, or help. The elder brothers always refuse. They invariably fail in the tasks that arise and are either tortured and punished or eaten by trolls. Fortunes and princesses remain out of their compulsive reach.

Meanwhile, the Ash Lad, seeing his brothers gone, asks his parents' blessing so that he, too, may go out into the world. The parents refuse time and again. "You haven't a chance," they tell him. The Ash Lad goes back to the ash pile to dabble but keeps returning as a gentle persuader. Finally the parents give in. Some stories show him leaving with the barest crust of bread instead of the ample provisions the doting mother sent along with her older sons.

In stories when the Ash Lad meets the old beggar he always shares what he has. As expected, the beggar turns into a wizard whose magic or cleverness lead the ash lad to success. In other stories the Ash Lad's own native ingenuity, applied in the calm, reflective manner we have come to expect from him, helps him to pass all tests, slay all obstructing trolls, gain the fortune or princess (and usually both), and live happily ever after. Sometimes he even sets his parents up with a comfortable retirement and may even save his brothers, if they haven't already been eaten.

I believe that the Ash Lad represents an important metaphor for our life styles and education in the compulsive age we live in. The ideas I shall discuss below represent what I shall call the **Ash Lad Hypothesis**. This hypothesis can be briefly stated as follows:

> Dabbling in the ashes may get you to your goal
> before you'd think so!

Another way of looking at it is to state that a relaxed, intuitive, spontaneous, gentle, aware, and generous approach to problems may lead to a solution before an institutionalized, rigid, formalistic, procedurally-oriented approach.

In modern education we started a number of years ago to move into what has been termed an activities or process approach to learning. If a student isn't physically active and obviously busy doing a pre-planned activity of some kind he can't be learning very much. The same thing holds true for the way students behave during lectures, films, and demonstrations for that matter. If they're not taking notes, they can't be learning or retaining much.

If they don't ask questions they must be dull or asleep. Teachers have come to hope for strongly participatory education characterized by 6 or 7 hours a day of solid, non-stop, visible, classifiable, active behavior.

The current emphasis on performance or behavioral objectives and on behavioristic approaches to learning such as those so strongly advocated by the followers of B. F. Skinner is a sign of our infatuation and preoccupation with easily observable and measurable changes in children. As educational systems move more and more in the direction of accountability to narrowly defined and closely specified, sequential, performance objectives we point with pride to the increased level of superficially observable activity. Students are taking more tests, writing down more things, doing more experiments. Even while they watch films teachers expect them to take notes. William, who was 9 at the time, had a particularly stimulating teacher-aide whom the children loved just to **listen to** and watch while he did demonstrations. The regular teacher forced the children into note-taking and testing. William came home one evening and said, wistfully, "I wish we could just listen and watch. I have to work so hard on the notes that I don't hear what Pat says and can't really watch the neat things he is doing." Classroom behavior of students and teachers gets more compulsive. Therefore they must be learning more, the argument goes. They are "behaving" actively and visibly in response to carefully applied external stimuli. The extreme of this stimulus-response reinforcement system is seen in computer-assisted instruction. The computer asks a question, the student responds, and the computer immediately reinforces a correct answer or diagnoses a wrong one and sends the student back for another round with the concept, fact, or problem being taught.

As for me, I have tried to move away from performance objectives and from required, sequential, linearly programmed instruction. I am trying to implement strongly "humanistic" learning environments of the types that derive from the third-force psychology of Abraham Maslow, Carl Rogers, and Fritz Perls. I make programmed instructional materials, including even computer-assisted ones, available in the learning environment just like I feel free to make any other resources from workbooks to libraries available. I try to facilitate virtually free access to the outside world. But I do not require that they be used.

However, as I work with students I become aware of the extent of my own remaining hang-ups with respect to activities approaches. For a while I gave up lecturing almost entirely because I didn't want to "encourage" students to "cop out" by being passive spectators rather than "active" learners. I still feel pleased when lots of students show up in our optional laboratory sessions and are "active" without prodding. The more compulsively active they appear, the more I feel they may be learning something useful. (But then the Ash Lad hypothesis presents itself before me. Is compulsive activity the main road to creative activity, to growth, to the treasure?)

I have encouraged my colleagues to give up more and more of their lecturing and demonstrational activities, feeling that these may give students too much chance to "cop out" of their responsibility for their own learning and therefore deprive them of their chance to be **active** (as I define active) and to learn through experience.

Maslow discusses the differences between spectating and experiencing, emphasizing the superiority of the latter over the former. Carl Rogers also glorifies experiential learning, and I follow him enthusiastically in this. In my own life, I carry this into athletics — where I practically refuse to watch, but am a regular participant; into theater — where I would rather play a bit part in an amateur production than see a Broadway play; into my scientific work — where I may forsake advance preparation through reading, going to talks, etc. in favor of plunging into a research situation and experiencing what the rocks have to say to me directly rather than through any intermediary. Carl Rogers writes of "outwaiting" class groups, — sitting silently with them until they generate their own activity without his starting it. He agrees to participate but not to lead authoritatively. Maslow describes the same process. I find myself trying it too. (Then I think of the Ash Lad hypothesis and its ramifications.)

On the other hand, Maslow also makes reference to passive states of reception that form an essential element of some eastern religions. When a person enters such a state he tries to exclude all conscious analysis and opens himself to whatever is going on. Awareness exercises of the type described by John O. Stevens indicate some ways of sharpening tacit perception. Polanyi also stresses what he calls tacit learning. All of these represent behavior which cannot be observed by an outside observer and form part of the fabric of intuitive and preconscious activity that may be going on in the Ash Lad.

The academic department I work with has instituted the idea of a student portfolio as a means of long-range student accountability. In this portfolio the student maintains whatever products he wishes to have represent him to the outside world and to people within the department who do not know him particularly well. The contents of the portfolio are limited in form and in content only by the student's imagination. The department's governance operates basically through committees having as many or more students as faculty. The group decided that admission to the major should be a matter for a portfolio review committee to oversee. The committee at first took a strict approach in which they rejected or admitted only provisionally (with later reviews specified) applicants with little in the portfolio. Consequently, students who had in some instances spent only one or two terms in work related to the major were expected to provide substantial **product** for evaluation. Perhaps a quarter of them showed little other than a letter of intent and interest. When interviewed these people frequently described their activity as "browsing," becoming aware, or, from the point of view of our Ash Lad, "dabbling in the ashes."

My awareness of the proposed Ash Lad hypothesis now leads me to a revised valuation of the role of spectatorship in learning. Watching, followed by imitation has always been a way in which the young have learned. During our time of compulsory public education and the "college education ethic," however, we seem to a large extent to have created a serious dichotomy with respect to spectative behavior of the "dabbling-in-the-ashes" variety, daydreaming and what may appear to be random, non-directed play with materials on one hand, and required, spectative activity and required "activity-oriented" behaviors surrounded by a matrix of accountability on the other.

I no longer worry about the student who fiddles around for months or even years before beginning to develop completed products for display and judgement. But I now move another step and attribute new value to presentational events — lectures, demonstrations, and other formal and semi-formal events **as long as these are optional and as long as the student is not required to be accountable for what transpires in such events.** I have in the recent past actively discouraged students from attending large numbers of formal lectures. "A few, ok, but **many** means you're avoiding the task of seeking things for yourself." Now I am more open to metaphorical "dabbling in the ashes" of more different types. Each person should be free to spectate as long as he chooses and to engage himself in a more directed manner whenever he chooses. You can't program a relationship between intuitive play and the onset of self-directedness. If we try to force a learner into our kinds of compulsion before he chooses to seek the princess we may be turning him into troll-bait - just another carbon copy of us at a time when there are new challenges to deal with, new obstacles to surmount en route to the treasure.

In schools, we expect visible activity and worry when we don't see it. The conventional school expects production immediately and allows little or no real time for play, browsing, spectating, and exploration. The expectation is apparently that forced production under threat of failure will lead to commitment and that this will increase exploration and self-directed creative activity. I see no evidence for that order of events.

Some students, especially older ones, who are well conditioned to produce for others and on command may have forgotten how to play, receive, and browse. Awareness-training possibilities might be offered to them. It would be a pity to lose them to the trolls.

Although I have used the Ash Lad hypothesis mainly in the context of education in this essay, I believe that the same principles might be applied in almost any other area as well.

SOME STAGES IN LEARNING AND CREATING

As I observe people learning and creating, and as I examine my own processes I perceive several more or less distinct stages that people go through. I want to write about these under the following headings: **play, exploration, involvement, commitment, rigor.** Organizations in general give short shrift to the first and second stages, with supervisors in any organizational hierarchy or teachers in schools generally expecting activity in the last 3 stages. People who linger in the first two stages are punished, held back, and sent along with records that indicate low potential, disruptive behavior, and previous failure. My observations lead me to feel that people who spend no substantial time in the first two stages function and learn in a basically superficial way. Theirs becomes a non-experimentive and often non-functional kind of performance. Yet they may be rewarded for this because of their success on supervisors' reports or, in schools, on trivial examinations and because they are quiet and do as they are told. These are values that are much favored over play and exploration, which may appear to be disruptive in a conventional organizational environment. What is wrong, I say, is not the play and exploration, but the inflexible environment that identifies these behaviors as disruptive rather than accepting them as fundamental in the producing or learning process and making a place in which they can occur without bothering others.

PLAY: THE PAPER PLANE HYPOTHESIS. Most people acknowledge that young children learn and begin to function primarily through play. I have enjoyed watching a baby discover his toes and play with them, learning more about the relationship of one part of his body to another. You must have seen young children playing with blocks or forming words with blocks or magnetic letters. They play with sounds, too, as they learn speech. **Sesame Street** capitalizes on a structured variety of play that to an adult seems repetitious and drill-oriented. But to a small child all of the visual and auditory effects lead to playing in which the child participates actively. When he tires of it he goes off and does something else.

In kindergarten, the main activity there **may** still be play, although it often becomes a more regimented play "to help socialize the child" (get him to obey teachers?). By first grade at the latest he usually hears, "Now it's time to get down to business. There's a time for work and a time for play, and here is where we work." The play component is abruptly terminated as a learning activity accepted by the school. Children, of course, continue to play, but teachers call them down for it, punish them for it, and try to relegate play to separate times. The relationship of work and play is rarely explored, and the two become increasingly separated.

It has been said that "play is the work of the child," but we too often forget about this concept or consider that it ceases to apply after age 5.

A funny thing happens, though! Many creativity "experts" such as W. J. J. Gordon, Cal Taylor, and others now believe that creative activity originates mainly in play. When they get adults into their workshops, they have to teach them to play all over again! I feel sad when I realize how much playfulness I have "forgotten" and how I now want to learn all over again the art of silliness, word play, body play. Most adults accept the idea of "foreplay" - but even that seems to have developed its set of rules and manuals on "how to do it." We have schools of recreation where play is circumscribed by rules. As for free play, most of us have forgotten about that pretty much by the time we get to high school. "Horsing around," it gets called, and we try to keep it out of the real "school" part of school.

I find that I consciously have to shuck off whole layers of inhibitions before I can engage in any very satisfying kind of free play. There is much free play in my fantasy, still, and free play is a regular part of my dreams, so I know the tendency and the resources to play are within me.

I've just begun to realize that the people I can best relearn playfulness from (or who can best help me strip off the conditioning that blocks my natural playfulness) are young people I spend time with in the learning environment. When I join them in play rather than trying to control, direct, or block their play, I regain some of the playful qualities and ability to explore and put things together without set goals that I now feel are essential to any really fresh creative activity I engage in.

The play I write about here is play in which the player has no goals in particular. Imagine that, - no goals!

To me, curiosity and play go together. Curiosity often arises out of play and in other instances it can lead to exploratory play. If these two factors are absent from any working or learning environment, the environment is likely to be sterile. At one major university's geology department, their new building included a balcony overlooking a large interior lobby. Many of the graduate and undergraduate students began using the balcony for paper-plane throwing contests, held amid great merriment. The department chairman and several senior faculty members quickly cut off the activity as "unbecoming a serious science department." Many students from there told me of the sterility of the relationship among people who inhabit that building, too.

Recently, one group that got seriously interested in paper plane play organized a massive paper-plane contest. The results of their play are reported in a magnificent book on the dynamics of paper planes. In our ES material we called one assignment: **Kite Flight.** The assignment is to go fly a kite! We wanted to legitimize this kind of play. For that reason I think an appropriate name for the hypothesis that **non-goal-directed play can lead to important cognitive learning and to the growth of creative power is THE PAPER PLANE HYPOTHESIS.** Some of our geology community students at St. Lawrence have gotten into paper plane play and midnight bike rides through the hall in our building. I knew that things were beginning to "work" in our group when some of the students hung a swing from the rafters of one of the "serious" labs and began to use it, too. Another group, who labelled themselves "The Quantum Jumps" began to stage impromptu comic scenes in classes and corridors. The group includes some of our most imaginative and promising scientists, too. In playing with sophisticated equipment in unusual contexts they end up discovering new uses for old apparatus. At the graduate school of a large southern university, a group of graduates identified themselves as "The Midnight Skulkers." As such, they prepared outrageous hall displays and performed other acts to make good-natured fun of the overseriousness of some of the faculty and other graduate students. Their activities helped in loosening up the department as a whole (although they got into a certain amount of trouble with some departmental administrators) and a general improvement of creative flow within the group.

At the farewell banquet of a conference we held for earth science educators a couple of years ago, Jonathan produced a batch of water pistols. A spontaneous water fight occupied part of an otherwise "serious" meeting. Play deformalizes. It facilitates the emergence of realness in people. Facades drop. Better and deeper working relationships become possible.

When the chairman from a rather formal department visited our group last winter he reported to some people, on his return home, that we had a "kindergarten" going. His comment makes me happy-sad. Happy that we are at least approaching the playful quality that I want to see here. I know that, from a cognitive point of view, our people are doing high quality work, so no apologies are necessary from that point of view. Sad, when I see an influential person in a big department full of good people reject informality and play in such an out-of-hand manner. (Incidentally, a senior research fellow from abroad who accompanied this particular person was much impressed in a positive way with our kindergarten!)

In general, the spatial organization and informality of open schools like the Jefferson County Open Living School, the St. Paul Open School, The Wilson Campus School and others do have a kindergarten atmosphere. That's one of the things that worries people most about open schools. At any given moment a substantial number of members of the community, teachers and students alike, are at play. Some students may play for days on end and then suddenly enter a period of intensely productive study. The efficiency of time devoted to "conventional" study is greatly improved and enhanced. In any case, what is important is that all of the cognitive things that are learned in a conventional school are also learned in the "play" school, too. An important difference, however, is that in the open school, people don't forget how to play, and they don't learn to build facades and walls around themselves. They retain and build creative power and their sense on self - both of which, to me, are far more important to productive and satisfying lives than the coverage of factual and conceptual materials.

Non-goal-directed play involves much apparently random activity and messing about. It is highly spontaneous and its outcome cannot be predicted. The player does what feels right. It may involve a great deal of random physical play. In small children this is seen as odd, jerky movements or sometimes rhythmic and flowing motions that occur without advance planning. A little involuntary motion may produce an interesting feeling, catch the person's attention and then be greatly exaggerated and explored. I remember, as a 13 year old, flipping my hands back and forth in an odd figure-eight motion as I walked. Once my sister asked me why I was doing it. The "Why?" destroyed it for me and from then on I never did it without being self-conscious and looking around first to see who was watching me. I tried it again the other day. The motion still has an interesting feel to it. When I do it I can visualize whole scenes connected with other things I was doing concurrently while I played with this motion, at age 13. **(Does repetition of such** "childish play" represent an access route to the retrieval of information, ideas, and feelings stored deep within my biocomputer?) Any attempt to get people to explain or analyse playful behavior can destroy the play. A person draws a doodle for the sake of the doodle, not necessarily to represent anything.

The doodle may or may not grow into something during the process of its creation. I once saw a 5-year-old playing in a cardboard box at the Wilson Campus School; he was running back and forth under a table, growling. I asked him if he were a tiger. He said he didn't know. I was analyzing. He was "just playing". My intrusion probably sidetracked his game. Better to have joined him in the play, without comment, or just to have watched without speaking. Children do this to each other, too. In the cartoon, **The Family Circus**, a little girl says, "Mommy, Jeffy won't pretend he's drinkin' my tea! He doesn't know how to use his magic-nation!" Jeffy, in the background, has his gun raised in the direction of shadowy tigers, bears, giraffes, and kangaroos, an imaginary menagerie that inhabits his room.

Play requires no justification or explanations. It defies analysis. At its best, it simply **is** and needs to be left alone to run its course.

Between stints of writing this section I am also reading **Catcher In The Rye** for the first time. It's quite by chance that I have picked it up. Cricket happened to borrow it from a friend in Oslo, and I have been attracted to it, through hers and Lucretia's chuckling. When I tire of writing this, part of my playtime goes into reading it. Holden Caulfield shows a great deal of playful behavior, as, for example, when he suddenly and spontaneously breaks into a silly tap-dancing routine in the men's room as he talks to his roommate. Or he is apt suddenly to pounce upon someone for a playful wrestling match. Just as I see Gretchen and William pounce on each other now and then. Holden Caulfield keeps analyzing or at least describing his behavior, and he usually ends up with, "That's just the way I am," by way of a justification. Jim, the young history teacher-hero of Kingsley Amos' **Lucky Jim** confines his face-making to his own room and to times when he thinks others can't see him. Society doesn't really understand face-making!

Play can also show up as quiet manipulation of objects.

Yesterday as Lucretia and I sat on the terrace together having a glass of sherry she suddenly asked me why I was blinking so strangely. She had caught me at a random game I often play without thinking about it. (Perhaps this belongs in the next stage I will describe — exploration — but the analysis I am developing is not meant to be a rigid one anyway, and there are no strict boundaries. Its goal is to help me become aware of and more acceptant of the way we learn and create. Classification of behaviors into these categories is thus not an end of any great importance. It becomes a means of facilitating awareness and learning.) I have just named this game "Three Dimensional Framing." To play it, I close one eye and then, using the other, I frame a scene through a window or between two branches, or through any nearby grating. Then I close that eye and open the closed one. The scene changes within the frame because of the parallax effect resulting from the difference in the location of my eyes. With both eyes open I get a third scene which now has depth. A very silly game, but I play it often. Perhaps it's too focussed to be really random play, but I do it spontaneously and without thinking. Actually, it turns out to be a fairly sophisticated game in perceptual psychology if I move up into higher stages of analysis. Partly, the level of any activity will differ depending on how I approach it. I can approach a sophisticated subject in a random, spontaneously playful, and non-goal-directed way or I can approach it in a rigorously analytical way. Play also occurs as daydreaming, where the activity is internalized rather than externalized. I think most of us, at all ages, engage in a great deal of fantasy play. I know I do. For many people this fantasy-play comes out in dreams if nowhere else. Maybe we never quite lose our playfulness; we simply repress it.

In any case, non-goal-directed play is generally thought of as having no acceptable place during regular school or business hours. You're supposed to do that during recess, or during lunch-break or possibly coffee-break. In many junior and senior high schools and in other organizations non-goal-directed play is not acceptable anywhere on the premises. In schools, "passing" between classes is supposed to be in an orderly fashion and play is discouraged by hall monitors.

In science, play is almost never tolerated in a laboratory area. Here again, the problem can be redefined in terms of the way the lab is set up rather than in terms of the destructiveness of play. If play is defined as important in the process of creating and producing then the lab environment can be set up to accommodate it.

There is a wide range of kinds of play all the way from totally random play up through games that have more or less definite rules. Listening in a casual way can be a kind of play. Imitative play is yet another kind. I include them in this first stage in learning as long as they are dominantly random and not specifically goal-directed.

At a creativity and production workshop we held in Valley, Wyoming we went through some exercises in synectics (group creativity techniques). A large component of synectics, in the early stages, involves play. Bob Tannen, who led us, kept pushing us away from our goals, many of which were so much a part of our natural consciousness that we didn't even realize we were still pursuing the same old goals. We **thought** we were playing randomly and simply were not aware of our orientation toward goals until Bob's perceptions from outside helped us to sharpen up our own awareness of our processes. We gradually became somewhat freer. However, when Bob left the A2Z Ranch early one morning before anyone else was up he left us a parting note scribbled with a magic marker onto a big sheet of newsprint paper. The note consisted only of a list of totally weird nonsense words. The point was clear to many of us. The translation was, "When you can do **this** as part of your "work," you will have learned in a functional way what random play is all about." He was also saying, since we had not yet generated any such real nonsense, that in his opinion, we had a long way to go yet.

EXPLORATION. Goals enter the picture to some extent when the exploratory stage begins. There isn't any clear or sharp break between stages. These flow into one another so that some tentative exploration may occur during what appears to be play and may then be abandoned for more random play. There may be a great deal of rapid shuttling back and forth not only between play and exploration, but even up into the areas of involvement and commitment. Rigor may even show up for short periods.

Basically, I see exploration as a more focused variety of play, in which relationships between objects are examined in a somewhat purposeful way. A baby who lies there and manipulates and examines a single toy for an extended period of time may be genuinely exploring it. Listening attentively for a while is a kind of exploring as opposed to casual listening. Seeing what happens when I try **this** is exploratory in the sense that I mean here. This kind of behavior is accepted in schools and other organizations to some extent, but people are still inclined to say, "Why don't you stop just fiddling with those chemicals and get on with some more systematic work.

The way we use the word "experiment" gets me sometimes. Usually it means to follow the prescribed steps in a lab book. Such an activity with steps prescribed by some-one else has little to do with experimentation in the true sense of the word.

Curricula and job plans don't provide time programmed for play and exploration. How can you really program them in? There is no real way of predicting how long will be needed. Each person requires different amounts of these activities, different times, and this changes for different kinds of activities. The mood of any given person on any given day comes into the picture, too, so that there are just too many variables involved for a program to handle. Only the responsiveness of the teacher - facilitator - manager and the nature of the relationship between him or her and the "subordinate" can legitimize these two early stages of learning.

Duke Ellington's mode of creating music provides an interesting example of transitions through play, exploration, and involvement in a coordinated team. At an Ellington rehearsal, John Lissner saw Ellington chatting about the arrangement, allowing playful interruptions, sitting down at the piano to finger seemingly random chords, fiddling with his hat. After an hour or so, Ellington grabbed some music paper, studied it, and started to hum. One by one, the other musicians started to play soft things back at Ellington, who was still humming and singing. Then, the musicians would grope around, repeating sections, polishing, rejecting, under Duke Ellington's guidance. A copyist then transcribed the piece. A new work had been collectively improvised.

INVOLVEMENT. This stage represents a time when a person becomes absorbed in a substantial way in a problem or exploration. At this stage, his behavior, from an extrinsic point of view, appears to be purposeful and even intense. The person seems to be concentrating on what he is doing. His tongue may either figuratively or literally appear to be held between his teeth as he concentrates. This is the first stage that is really fully tolerated in most schools and organizations. We seem to expect people to be involved in "their" work (translation: the work we have assigned) in a substantial way all day long. Presumably play and exploration are relegated to the hours after school, or work—to extra-curricular or "outside" activities.

People learn to go through the motions of involvement and yet to be off in the land of free play as far as their actual primary attention is concerned. I remember so well doing this myself. As an example I remember writing essays about things I was interested in, while appearing to take notes on a lecture on some completely different subject. My teachers were always pleased with my involvement. I got so I could look at a lecturer or speaker in a most attentive and complimentary way and yet have 90 percent of my mind off in the land of fancy. The 10 percent was tuned in to the lecturer ready to alert the rest of my mind and convey the necessary information to it in case a question was directed my way. In labs I could always manipulate the apparatus in a very purposeful way while actually far away. Have you ever gone to sleep with your head propped on a microscope? Amazing how involvement can be faked. Yet we reward people for the external appearance of involvement and thereby invite dishonesty and fakery. It's easy to appear busy. The building of facades is encouraged by the refusal of supervising people to accept as valid the earlier stages of the creative process and the process of learning even the "basics."

At ES, we allocated the equivalent of one full day per week for our staff members to do whatever they pleased. This day could be taken in any kinds of chunks, distributed in any way people chose. We encouraged people to treat this as some kind of play-time, perhaps to be related, in their own terms, to our project activities. Our production actually **increased** when we established clear permission to engage in a more personal kind of play, exploration, and involvement. The quality of the creative product also improved. People worked more effectively and efficiently both individually and as a group. They brought to bear on our tasks greater diversity and more new ideas from more different sources than ever before. Students from the University of Colorado who worked with us found themselves "learning their basics", too, in addition to functioning in a creative manner on higher-level problems as well.

COMMITMENT. At this level, I develop a question I really want to deal with. I make a conscious decision to spend some real time and effort on what may be a long-term basis. (I do not wish to exclude short-term commitment, but I think for purposes of this analysis that the long-term idea is more useful. Again, we are faced with the needlessness of actually drawing lines between categories of the learning and creating process, which actually flow into each other and among which there may be a great deal of shuttling back and forth in actuality.) From an external point of view I can be seen to devote a lot of real time to a project or an activity and some concrete results are generally available for inspection. Perhaps the production of some concrete results is what distinguishes activity at this level from that at the preceding levels. So-called commited activity which is not preceded by some play and exploration may end up shallow and unrooted. What appears to an outsider to be committed effort may still amount only to doing problems to please someone else. Real commitment, preceded by personal involvement, leads to substantial personal cognitive growth and to growth of creative powers. Note the difference between the intrinsic qualities these stages need to produce efficient functioning as opposed to extrinsic valuing of what we think is going on in a person we may be observing.

RIGOR. To me, there is a time for rigor. This time is when a person chooses to devote himself to an intense, analytical, developmental, or creative process. A lot of teachers talk about giving a rigorous course. Rigor, in this sense, has no value to me. Rigor makes sense only when it is intrinsic, and this comes from within each individual person. What **I** do as a teacher or facilitator has very little to do with whether or not a learning experience is rigorous. If, by rigorous, I mean **hard**, then all I need do is present material in the dullest, most uninteresting, and most rigid way possible. This will guarantee that it is unpleasant and will therefore seem hard. The same thing applies to any other work as well. People need to find intrinsic meaning and worth in what they are doing and they need to be partners in determining how they will do their jobs if they are to devote themselves to their work in optimum fashion.

I have seen some interesting developments along these lines at St. Lawrence.Some of the science majors in other departments have referred to ours as the "gut major" because of our lack of "rigorous requirements." Yet learners work in our labs far into the night, long after the other science labs have closed down. "All you people do is have a good time." Outsiders can't conceive that pleasure and work can be melded together in the unity of a full, absorbing experience when the "work" arises from an intrinsic commitment on the part of the learner. Our rigor shows up in the articles that sophomores, juniors, and seniors publish in professional journals or write for themselves as progress reports, and in the data they have gathered and analyzed because they wish to satisfy their own curiosity rather than to fulfill an assignment. I am not sure that a truly rigorous approach is possible in response to outside requirements unless an intrinsic commitment is present. Real rigor becomes labor of love rather than something that is hard. Most of the best scientists don't think of their own work as hard.

I recall many language-haters expressing astonishment at the way I devote effort to language learning. "It's so hard. Isn't Russian 'harder' than French?" The fact is, I don't regard any languages as "hard." "Hard" is a state of mind rather than a property of a discipline. I work at language from an intrinsic point of view. I work at certain aspects of science from an intrinsic point of view. They are not "hard" for me and yet someone looking in from the outside may say, that's good, rigorous (=well documented and explicated) work. The external value judgement of rigor is also very subjective. Readers who pick up this book and approach it from the viewpont characteristic of the editorial policies of the **Journal of Research in Science Teaching** may find it totally lacking in rigor. I hope they **do** find it lacking in their kind of rigor. Yet some people in the Association for Humanistic Psychology may find it too much preoccupied with classification, analysis, and explication and therefore too rigorous (rigid, or hard.) As Jonathan says to me sometimes, "You're still not out of your head." I'm working on it. I'm not sure yet how you get rigorously out of your head. I guess it's by abandoning any attempt to analyze stages of learning or creativity and by simply letting them be - letting it happen as it does in the freest and most open way possible. I feel that in this book I am speaking to at least some people whose awareness of learning processes (my own included) might be enhanced by this kind of analysis.

There I go justifying again. But I still want you to see my processes working. This is how I continue to jump back and forth as I wrestle with myself to accept a more free-flowing acceptance. Perhaps you feel this process in yourself, too. I want to lay my processes out in front of you so that you will know I don't feel super-confident.

* * * *

The more intellectually advanced a species the more basic the need for the simplicity of play.

- from Dean (as recalled from Star Tre

ART AND ESTIMATION

Several people were working together last week on a problem that involved skills in estimating percentage of various mineral components in rocks. Jim takes a very "hard science" view of his activities. Annette is in art and looks at things mainly from the view point of esthetics. She immediately was struck by the concept of certain rock textures and the way that they show negative and positive space concepts she was using in an art group. Jim seemed uninterested in this "side-track." When it came to actual percentage estimation attempts, Annette was the most accurate estimater in the whole group. Suddenly Jim became aware that the mode of perceiving that Annette was developing as an artist made her a better and more quantitative observer than he, the "hard scientist," was. Jim, by integrating the viewpoint of the artist, may be a better scientist. Annette may be closer to a good scientist (if this is proportional to ability to observe) than many "science" majors!

THE POTTER'S WHEEL

After opening up the curriculum of a beginning geology class, I found a number of students coming to me, wondering what kinds of options involving art might be available. Several people expressed special interest in pottery. At the time, we had no real capabilities in this area. Nonetheless, I told them that anything of this type they chose to do was all-right but that I would not be able to give any really active help — only encouragement — if they wanted that. I did know of a book called **Keramos** and I recommended this. Kriwanek shows the beginning potter how to find natural clays, how to beneficiate them for use in making pots, how to use natural materials for glazes, and many other useful ideas and techniques.

At first some students obtained access to pottery wheels and to help in the art department. But their use of the facilities was often restricted. One girl, a senior, found a friend who was a production potter and paid her to take lessons and work in her studio. Both girls ended up collecting and using natural clays. It became apparent that pottery-making is an excellent access route to the study of occurrence and origin of clays ("scientific" matters in anyone's language).

I finally decided to order a potter's wheel and clay for our geology department. Careful shopping allowed me to get the basic parts - fly wheel, vertical metal rod, and upper wheel for a little over $100.00. Trouble was, we would have to make the stand for it ourselves.

The pottery wheel and about one hundred pounds of clay soon appeared in the department. I told our interested "potterologists" that they would have to build a frame and set the thing up themselves if they really wanted to use it. I would not have time, energy or interest to deal with that problem. Almost immediately, some of our people who viewed themselves as "hard" scientists began to ridicule the "potter s" in various subtle and not-so-subtle ways. Notes of ridicule and sly comments began to appear on blackboards and notes on the walls or attached to the crate in which the wheel awaited its assemblers. Three girls and one freshman man decided to assemble the wheel. None had any experience in carpentry. They solved the problem of acquisition of materials and got some help in assembly from some of our majors who take a broader view of the all-inclusiveness of "science." These students were practicing a kind of inventive empiricism toward which many of our "hard scientists" have as yet shown little inclination.

One of the girls, Becky, was one day involved in working on the stand when some of the majors were especially cruel in their remarks. Becky dissolved in tears after they left. She was involved in a very important kind of personal growth - having taken personal responsibility to do something unconventional and totally new to her and to carry it out in somewhat hostile surroundings. She almost abandoned the project at that point, but she realized that she had freedom to proceed and that she had full permission and faculty support as well as support from numerous classmates and less "narrow" majors. So she and her associates continued their work. As a matter of fact, Becky later developed a very secure feeling around the department and spent a good deal of time there doing work for her other areas of interest as well as geology-pottery. When the wheel was nearly complete one of the antagonists put a photo of a potter's hands working at a wheel on the apparatus with the words "bull shit" prominently displayed across it. I became very angry at this, but Becky took it right in her stride.

Since that time other students, including some serious potters, have begun to help and have rebuilt a sturdier stand and have made arrangements to organize working sessions with some experienced potters to help. This activity is now accepted and valued.

Incidentally, the presence in the department of the potter's clay has had other effects as well. Another student (Tom) is constructing scale models of oceanic rift and subduction zones in his studies of continental drift and plate tectonics. As he developed his model materials he found that some of the potter's clay was exactly what he needed to simulate plastic materials of the earth's mantle. The interaction of Tom and Becky working in the same group and using the same materials in different contexts is bound to affect both of them and all of us in such a way that we are more likely to recognize odd combinations of relationships and to integrate our knowledge and understandings more completely.

Several potters have already moved into readings on the chemistry, structure, and general mineralogy of clays and the chemistry of glazes.

Now that the wheel is really operating, even our "hard" scientists have begun to use it.

Casual onlookers have long suggested that creative people have a basic lack of rationality. Some people, among them a good many scientists I know, go so far as to suggest that there is a linkage between neuroticism and creativity. Lawrence Kubie in **Neurotic Distortion of The Creative Process** proposes that neuroticism actually hinders the creative process and shows that excessive rationality actually leads to a type of neurosis just as does excessive irrationality. Science is often thought of as a basically rational enterprise. In parts of this book I am trying to document and also to show my own feeling that intuition and fantasy play important roles in the generation of some of the most fundamental scientific concepts. Many of the journeymen of science limit themselves, perhaps because of a lack of confidence in their own complete organisms and intuitive powers. They rarely take the risk of advancing ideas that are not, in their opinions, all tied down. The risk-takers are willing to advance concepts that they find intuitively attractive, knowing that any idea will be tested and tried over and over anyway and that science and knowledge grow in the long run, make quantum jumps as it were, only through the advancement and subsequent acceptance or rejection of various outrageous hypotheses that cannot at the time they are advanced be substantiated widely. Advancement takes place largely through the conflict generated by what many self-designated "rigorous" practitioners consider to be irrational ideas.

Kubie presents a diagram to illustrate his idea. I have used Kubie's idea as a basis for Figure 1.

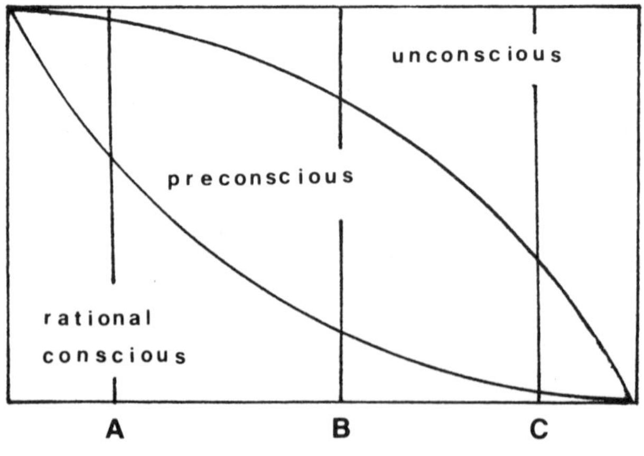

The domain of the rational conscious represents states of mind in which people reason, justify, and analyze a great deal. They avoid expression of feelings, which they are likely to distrust. Their mental processes restrict them largely to what they consider hard facts. In the area of the mind represented by this domain lies the information that we have ready and conscious access to. We "remember" these things with little effort and can call them up easily for use. The area labeled "preconscious domain" represents the tremendous storehouse of perceptions and ideas that are accumulated in the backs of our minds, out of reach of normal rationalizing, analyzing, and conscious thought. This can be thought of as a hidden reservoir. Within this storehouse may be records of greater than 80 or 90 percent of our experiences and knowledge. Usually, conscious, rational efforts to acquire information stored in this "area of the mind" fail. Parts of this information pop randomly into mind (the rational conscious part) when a certain context allows it to do so. The preconscious domain is very unpredictable and undependable. Information can be retrieved in some instances through hypnosis, recording and analysis of dreams, and by certain free association tricks and games that are being pioneered by the Synectics group and others. In Einstein's case, involvement in music was a method of mobilizing the subconscious (the preconscious as here discussed) to help solve particularly tricky problems.

The so-called "unconscious domain" is the dwelling place of records of experiences so far repressed that they are effectively inaccessible. Reflections of them may emerge in our feelings and intuitive behavior, and they appear irrational and emotional. This is the residence of very deep feelings of many types that defy rational explanation.

Consider 3 people with different characteristics and how they might fit into this scheme. Person A is represented by the vertical line near the left boundary of Figure 1. Most of this line lies with the domain of the rational conscious. A small portion of the line lies in the so-called preconscious domain, and the rest lies in the area labeled unconscious domain. The person represented is likely to reject feelings and emotions almost entirely, to conceal his own emotions. He is likely to have limited access to the immense storehouse of information in the preconscious areas of his mind. He is apt to have a large and well-developed store of information available for "rational" discourse.

> I just thought of an interesting point. If the amount of information in his preconscious is 90 percent of his stored information and experience, and the amount of information in his rational domain is only 10 percent, then he has access to a total of perhaps only 15 percent of his total information, even though he may be able to call up rapidly and easily what he knows rationally. This is a small amount.

Person B is represented by a vertical line near the center of the diagram. Here, the preconscious area (the residence of the intuition) is shown to be very large in terms of his access to it. He still has access to a reasonably large storehouse of rational knowledge and the length of line representing effects of his unconscious emotions and feelings is just about as long as that for his rational consciousness.

> If he has access to a much greater percentage of his preconscious (90 percent of his total stored and potentially retrievable information) and still a reasonably well developed area of rationality, he may have far greater potential for creating new ideas than is true for Person A, the super-rational person.

Person C is represented by a line at the far right and represents a mirror of Person A, full of repressed emotions and feelings that are largely uncontrollable and with small access to both rational (conscious) and preconscious knowledge.

In Kubie's view, both people A and C are potential neurotics. Person C is almost certain to be "disturbed" in the psychiatric sense. Person A, in his compulsive rationalism will be unresponsive to emotional aspects of life and people and may be excessively cold and analytical. Person B would seem centered and well-balanced.

It is tempting to think of the ideal scientist as a highly rational person, therefore approximating "A." And yet, person A has access to a much smaller total percentage of his stored experience than does person B. He has fewer resources to call upon through his basic lack of trust in his intuition. Highly creative scientists probably would be represented by lines near the one for person B, but perhaps slightly to the left.

We might think of the typical artist - a Van Gogh who slices off his ear in a fit of madness perhaps as represented by a line like that for person C. Kubie rejects this idea and feels that highly creative artists are also generally centered in terms of the diagram. Perhaps a highly talented artist might be represented by a line near that for person B but slightly to the right of it.

In short, the highly creative scientist and the highly creative artist are likely to have similar personal characteristics in terms of rationalness, emotionalness, and easy access to a large and well developed intuitive sense. This idea is confirmed by students of creativity like Frank Barron.

The excessively rational scientist is likely to be neurotic, uncreative, and limited in his intuitive powers. The excessively emotional artist is likely to be neurotic, uncreative, and limited in his intuitive powers.

I hypothesize that we do not necessarily occupy a fixed position in this scheme, I believe it is possible, through various kinds of creativity training to shift positions on this diagram. The effects of psychotherapy are well known in getting people out of one or the other extremes represented here. I want to have better and better access to more and more of that preconscious area of my own intellect. I want my intuition to increase in power so that my science and my art will both benefit and so that I can be maximally creative. Creating is a thing I like, and I want to do more of it. It makes me feel good to do something-make something that I like. I can choose where I wish to be within Kubie's hypothetical scheme. Awareness of these relationships can be a tool I use to enhance my own growth.

I can also help learners who work with me be conscious of their potential power and know that they can choose, too. Each of us is responsible for himself and the ultimate use of his potential.

LUCK AND DISCOVERY

In assessing the role of serendipity in science, James Austin discusses the connection between chance and creativity. His classification of chance includes the following:

CHANCE I — pure blind luck where an idea or a relationship simply falls into our laps by accident.

CHANCE II — luck which results from a lot of general movement, exploratory behavior, and activity. If we keep moving and everything around us is in some kind of movement, too, then we increase the chance of having random ideas collide to produce a new idea.

CHANCE III — luck in which a clue appears by chance, but only a certain background and training make it likely that a relationship can be seen. This is the kind of luck referred to in Louis Pasteur's statement, "Chance favors only the prepared mind." (I wonder, contrary to the conventional idea, if the "preparation" needed might not really be a generalized kind of aware openness rather than a technically sophisticated background?) A classic case of the appearance of Chance III might be seen in Fleming's discovery of penicillin or in some of Pasteur's discoveries.

CHANCE IV — luck which results from a person's general habits and derives from intense contact with relationships in a certain area of interest. Mary Leakey discovers **Zinjanthropus** and one of the Leakey sons discovers **Homo habilis** after Louis Leakey has worked for thirty years around Olduvai Gorge. Or, an example used by Austin, Don Marcelino de Santola, practicing his hobby of archaeology one day, takes his daughter with him to a cave that had been previously discovered by a hunting dog. As Don Marcelino putters about as usual, searching the floor for artifacts, his daughter looks up and discovers the now-famous prehistoric drawings on the ceiling of the cave. That Leakey and de Santola were involved in these discoveries was not a result of Chance I, II, or III. Nor were these kinds of luck completely responsible for the fact that the actual discoveries of the key skulls and of the drawing were made by associates rather than by the "primary investigators." The discoveries resulted instead from a long-time pursuit of certain unique personal interests. The rest of the Leakey family, Don Marcelino's daughter — to what extent did their involvement in these discoveries depend upon Louis Leakey's or Don Marcelino's own musty "hobbies?" Distinctive and perhaps even seemingly eccentric habits, life-styles, hobbies, and behaviors seem to lead to Austin's Chance IV.

I experienced a lesser but more personal encounter with this kind of luck while studying the geology of an arctic island in Norway. I talked a lot with my family about things I was looking for. It ended up being Lucretia and Gretchen who discovered the relationships I was looking for, one day while they were out fishing. My interests in those rocks must have been involved in their discovery. My arcane research project and our odd, arctic life-style led us into, and promoted the chance discovery of these special relationships. The importance of community and of not being overly concerned about getting credit, personally, looms large in Chance IV.

DREAMS

Dreams become fundamental access routes to creative activity and increasing levels of consciousness. Jung, Freud, and other classicial psychologists have long recognized this. But their emphasis was more on seeking subconscious causes for emotional and psychological problems than on recognition of the role of dreams in creative behavior. Fritz Perls and the gestalt psychologists, on the other hand, use dreams as access routes to deeper levels of feeling and cognitive activity. Using even a small segment of a dream often provides help in **unblocking** an emotional hang-up (without worrying about "causes") or in retrieving "forgotten" information (what is stored at levels below those of the rational consciousness.) Many people find value in keeping dream journals in which fragments of dreams provide keys to the "hidden reservoir" of stored information. Merely glancing at a partial script of a dream fragment may start a train of thought and free up ideas, recalled sensations, and mental images. If a large part of creative activity depends upon the number of ideas and bits of experience that we can retrieve, how then can we improve our information-retrieval capability? The more fragments of information, feeling, experience we can call forth at any moment, the greater our chance of creative responses.

William Fry provides suggestions about how to use dreams for retrieving information and ideas and for activities that involve synthesizing, problem-solving, and creating. His suggestions include uninterrupted and leisurely, prolonged sleep. "Recreational" and creative-problem-solving dreams apparently occur after earlier dream cycles devoted to mental "tidying-up." Things like too many blankets may inhibit "creative" dreaming. Alcohol and drugs, contrary to Aldous Huxley and others, would seem to decrease the chances of using dreams because they diminish the amount of dreaming that takes place. Emotionally exciting or physically exhausting activities before the sleep increase the amount of restless sleep and thereby decrease the quiet sleep needed for using the dream-brain in problem-solving. Any attempts to force things will likely doom the chances of success. Possibilities of success seem to be enhanced if preparations —

concentration on the problem, seeking information, etc. — are made several hours or even days in advance. Creative processes need time to simmer. Then, just before going to bed, the prospective dreamer should review his or her conscious thoughts about the subject.

Not in connection with dreams, as such, but along the same lines of trying to put distance between one's self and a problem, Wayne Park, a mathematician, once told me that at times he feels a strong need for complete "down time" — complete rejection of any kind of conscious intellectual activity. Out of these times, he says, come some of the most creative things that he produces.

GESTALT PSYCHOLOGY AS A ROUTE TO CREATIVITY

Fritz Perls has defined a "gestalt" in the following way: "...an irreducible phenomenon. It is an essence that is there and that disappears if the whole is broken up into components." However, using an auto engine as a metaphor, Perls also shows that the motor is one gestalt, but the unassembled parts are another gestalt — "maybe merchandise, or junk, or potential engine — according to the context, the background in which they appear." Gestalt **therapy** involves helping a client become aware of unfinished business, of unfinished "gestalts." It involves channeling of energy into the **now** as opposed to the **then** of either future or past. Once a person has his awareness tuned in to himself and to the possibilities of the present moment, rather than dwelling on the past or present, he is in a position to be most effective in making decisions and taking fullest possible responsibility for himself and his actions.

> *At the present moment, I am aware that I am not attending to my writing very effectively. I am able to write, but I am so aware of several other things going on around me that I stop frequently to observe the preparations for serving of drinks on the BOAC 747 aircraft I am now sitting on. I am aware, too, that I am living in a fantasy, thinking about a gin and tonic I will order in a few moments. So I am using energy rehearsing my order. Nope! They just rolled the beverage cart back to start at the back of the aisle and work forward, so the energy used in rehearsing was a waste. But the momentary anticipation provided some pleasure nonetheless. I enjoy the pleasure, the disappointment, the continuing anticipation. William, sharing my fantasy, just jumped up and ran after the cart, hoping to get a bitter lemon. He, too, will have to wait. I was about to make a decision to give up writing for now, but since the cart has moved away, my energy flows back into the writing. Although I now focus better, I am aware of opera music*

coming through my headphones. The singing is in German, which I like to listen to, but I allow myself to concentrate more on the writing. As I write, my head bobs to the music, and my foot taps. A man from India sits next to me reading the London Evening Standard. I have a gay and joyful feeling. That means it's a good time to write more about gestalt. And I can stop to focus my energy on that gin and tonic followed by dinner and... but I'm aware of moving away from the <u>now</u>. The now is a knife edge I want to balance on. The more aware I am of my mental excursions into the past and future, which detract from my full enjoyment and awareness of the <u>now</u>, the more easily I can decide whether or not I want to focus consciously on now or to pursue a fantasy of past or present. When I'm fantasizing, I want to give full energy and attention to the fantasy so that I can more fully savor it, too. Is it a blending, an integration of past, present, future that I am seeking?

Obviously the business of science depends enormously on awareness. If I am to function as a scientist — and as a person helping others to learn about science — I want to have my awareness continue to increase in power. Once the level of my awareness stabilizes I am probably dead as a functioning scientist or science facilitator.

The quality of my "science" on any day depends greatly on my awareness at the moment. As I look at field notes from previous research I can detect evidence of when my awareness was particularly high or low. At the time of some observations I wasn't very aware. Many times I have had to go back and repeat measurements later. I am sure I have used data that were not very good or complete because I lacked awareness of my own processes of functioning. In places, my notes show these changes in awareness level. For example, there are squashed black flies and mosquitos preserved in my notes, occasionally accompanied by an angry scribble, "Goddam bugs!" Also the number of notes and their detail change with the time of day, so that at certain periods my observations have been few and of relatively low quality, while at other times they have been many, detailed, and of high quality, accompanied by lots of interpretive notes and questions. I can look back in memory's eye to times of low awareness and see myself bull-dogging along, forcing myself. Thinking that I **should** continue in spite of my wandering attention. The "shoulds" that always lead me to continue are related to the perverse "work ethic" that I have often, in moments of low awareness, allowed myself to follow. Blindly continuing, often to the detriment of my "science," was, in a sense, irresponsible. I failed to take full responsibility for myself and operated as I thought someone else expected me to do.

> *The drink cart finally arrived and I courageously abandoned my writing, using my energies to best advantage!*

In graduate school, Jim McLelland and I were in a field course with all of the other new graduate students. Once, as we walked from one area of rock outcrop to another, we were busily talking about what we planned to do when we finished our graduate programs. Garniss Curtis, who was leading the group, came up behind us and growled that if we didn't pay more attention to what was going on right then, what we were walking over, we'd probably never get our degrees and then we wouldn't have to worry about what we were going to be doing! He had caught us with our awarenesses down!

At a University of Colorado conference at Estes Park, Jonathan joined us as a consultant. At the time he was working in the Gestalt Institute in San Francisco. During the group meeting he time and again brought to our attention his awareness of what the group members seemed to be doing - what their process was. He was more interested in that than in the supposedly important questions we were considering. The group was helped by his focus on their process because, in the long run, that was really what the conference was all about. How could the teacher education faculty and the cognitive-area departments develop a new program integrated in its operation both among the departments and, as important, with a group of cooperating school districts. The problem was a whole new focus for the University's teacher education programs in all areas and the innovation required was primarily one of human relationships and group process. The group tried to avoid this issue, but Jonathan's awareness helped to focus upon the real issue. At one stage during the meetings, Jonathan mentioned to me that, besides letting his awareness flow on the group process, he was also focussing on his own process, learning more about his own functioning. (He was engaged in a process of **shuttling** back and forth between his inner awareness of self and his outer awareness of the larger group.)

Many kinds of awareness exercises are used in gestalt therapy. Some can be done profitably by an individual interested in developing his own awareness all by himself. Some require a partner or even a group. Exercises involving people working together become important to me, although I am often timid about proposing them. I still fear "looking silly" to others by trying things that seem so far removed from "science." Gradually I gain confidence as I find that these things **work** as ways of helping stimulate individual growth in myself and in others I work with. Equally important, they seem to enhance performance and functioning in the cognitive areas of science.

Much scientific hypothesizing is really a kind of fantasy. Consider the whole question of organic evolution, for example. No one was around to see all of the things take place that we often accept as "fact." We have woven a web of circumstantial evidence that supports a **belief** that animals and plants have evolved in a certain way. Explanations of the origin of the universe can never be considered as more than fantasy trips of some kind or other. There can never be **proof** that any explanation proposed is **The Truth**. The geological ideas I work with are likewise fantasies about things we **believe** happened eons ago. Fantasizing is thus an important part of the scientific process, and we never know for sure which fantasies may eventually be supported by substantial bodies of information and evidence. When this support is discovered such fantasies can become accepted as "scientific hypotheses" rather than as fantasies.

In trying to emphasize the role of fantasy and to provide experiences in fantasy I have begun to try gestalt-type fantasy exercises with beginning science students. I started with an exercise Bob Samples and Bob Lepper told me about. Later, after I had tried the exercise, I read descriptions of similar exercises in John Stevens' book **Awareness.** At the same time I was much interested in the "passive-reception" ideas described by Abraham Maslow. These involve elements of Zen. The person involved tries to avoid all conscious "thinking" and makes himself into a passive, unjudging and unthinking receptacle for whatever stimuli may come his way. So I thought I might try a "passive-reception" exercise along with a guided fantasy. It took me fully four weeks to work up enough nerve to try it, so apprehensive was I about the possibility of **failing.** (More and more I realize that nothing is really worth trying unless there is risk of failure. It is only through accepting risk of failure and indeed of failing that I grow.)

As the group of about seventy five arrived in our sterile-looking, but comfortable amphitheater I told them that I had some unusual exercises—experiences—I wanted to try. I wanted the group to know in advance what I wanted to do, in general, so anyone unwilling to commit himself or herself to the exercises fully could leave and not disturb the rest of the group.

For the "Zen" passive-awareness exercise I asked the group to empty their minds as completely as possible and to give themselves as fully to passive reception and acceptance as possible. All stimuli were to be accepted, ingested without internal verbalization, analysis, classification, reasoning, hypothesizing. I wanted them to focus totally on each instant. I proceeded at that point to show a random group of slides on one screen. On another I projected images of thin sections of rocks through polarizing filters. All of this was done to low music of the **Moody Blues.** As I showed the slides I tried to let myself be carried along by the movement of the music and the changing colors of the projected thin sections and color slides. I found myself playing with focus on both projectors, moving in and out of focus. I remembered seeing the well-known American potter, Paul Soldner, give a "slide-show" at an "environmental craft-in" held by the Colorado Artist-Craftsman's group at Steamboat Springs, Colorado in summer of 1971. In this, Soldner played with slides of his own pottery in a similar way, but without music and with only a single projected image. I attended similar visual "happenings" led by Aidron Duckworth, then an instructor in sculpture at Syracuse University. So happenings of this type are not uncommon in the arts. Many of the slides and thin sections I used were directly from and of earth materials. The particular songs of the Moody Blues I used had environmental and evolutionary connotations.

The group was totally quiet and passive throughout this exercise.

After this, I moved on to the fantasy exercise, first allowing a chance for any people to leave who were unwilling to commit themselves to the remaining exercise, which I sketched out for them. Below, I have written out a rough transcript for the fantasy. You might like to try it yourself. If so, have someone read it to you slowly, with long pauses where each of the series of dots appears. (You can also simply read it and give yourself time between instructions to create your own fantasy.)

I would like to take you on a trip into fantasy now....First I want you to become perfectly relaxed....Allow yourself to integrate the whole feeling of your relaxed, aware body. Now, I want to take you on a trip into your fantasy. I want you really to see, feel, and experience the scenes I suggest. You and I, just the two of us, are standing on a hill....We are in a grassy meadow....There are flowers all around us....See those flowers....Smell their fragrance...Feel how they touch you....Ahead of us is a path through the meadow....I take your hand and we start to walk along the path together....Down the hill....The sky is very blue....The sun feels warm....Puffy white clouds in the sky....Cool breeze.....As we go down the path we come to a hedgerow....Feel the hedge brush against you....Now there is a stone wall....Let's sit down on a wall together for a moment....Breathe deeply to get your breath....We get up now and walk on down the path....There is a little stream in front of us....Listen to it....Let's go over the narrow little bridge....We continue through another meadow....Through a woods....Ahead of us is a big hill with a huge rock ledge on top....We start to trudge up the hill....The path gets rocky....There are shrubs and low trees around us....Climbing gets difficult....Let's stop a moment to breathe....Let's go on now....The rock ledges loom ahead of us....There is a big hole in the ledge...It's a cave....We move on up to the entrance of the cave and stand outside for awhile....Now we enter the cave....Inside the cave, you will find what you actually came all of this way to get....I want you to go find this, whatever it is, and to do what you want with it....Now I'm going to leave you here in the cave to do what you wish with what you have found. When you're done, I want you to go back, by yourself, to our starting point. When you arrive back there, open your eyes, so I'll know you're back.

After I "left" the group at the cave, it took some members of our group as much as ten minutes to "return" and open their eyes. (In more informal environments some people may take a half hour or more.) People who "got back" early seemed to respect that others were still off in fantasy, and a delicate, gentle, comfortable silence prevailed in the room. Some of the toughest-looking people in the group took a very long time to return, including some people I knew to be football players. Then individuals simply talked gently and quietly about what they had experienced. People had found all sorts of objects in the cave, many of these related to past experiences of high personal significance. Some had refused to carry out some of the steps I suggested. One girl, on trying to get back, realized that she didn't know the way. She started back to the cave to find me, so that I could help her. Then she turned around again, realizing that she really **could** find her own way, and she did make it back **without** my help. People had formed various images of the place and these were different since the instructions, although seemingly specific, left large areas open for personal embellishment and creation. For days people kept coming in to talk more about aspects of their personal experience.

I'm supposed to lead a fantasy group tomorrow night, too. I wonder how it'll go? It's always a little scary. But I have confidence that the group will be supportive and that people in it will care enough about each other to be gentle and accepting as they hear each other open up and as they open some deeper parts of themselves to others.

Several summers ago before I had ever heard the word "gestalt" I traveled on a rubber raft together with a number of earth science teachers on the Green River in northern Utah. At times when we were in relatively calm water I would lie on the edge of the raft, basking in the hot summer sun. One day I imagined myself a small pebble or a grain of sand being carried down the river. I responded to currents, to irregularities of the stream bottom, to collisions with large and small stones and sand, to animals, to the temperature. I found myself washed up on beaches, eroded again, and carried further. This was a fantasy I carried with me for several days - a fantasy that led me to see and feel things about the river that I would not have seen or felt otherwise.

Now I might make this kind of idea into a suggestion for others: Become a rock, a trilobite, a moss, a mushroom, and explore what it is like to be that object or organism. Really **be** that object or organism and pursue the fantasy at length.

At the time we were writing the ESCP textbook, **Investigating The Earth**, I decided to insert a life history of a calcium atom as a way of illustrating the way matter is recycled through the earth's multiple processes. It turned out to be a fairly "cute" example, I felt at the time. It was included, only slightly chopped up by editors, in the final version of the book. I think now it would have been more useful as an exercise for people to **do** rather than as an illustrative story to read. Becoming involved vicariously in a process of any kind in a guided or unguided fantasy can lead to great personal and scientific insights.

Jim McLelland and some of his advanced geology students went home from an ESTPP workshop determined to play-act the crystallization of molten rock material for their petrology class the next week. I never heard whether they indeed did so, but I liked the idea and may try it myself soon.

Some significant scientific insights have emerged from such fantasies. Kekule, in discovering the nature of the benzine ring, for example, dreamed and imagined himself a snake swallowing its tail. From this metaphor he derived the notion of a ring structure as opposed to various "chain" models that were currently in vogue. The discoverer of hemoglobin owed part of his conceptual leap to imagining himself to be a red blood cell. So the game is not a silly one at all!

Don Rapp runs a group exercise he calls **Information Intermix.** In one science-oriented exercise he asked different students to play different roles. A girl became "beach," and two men in the group were "ocean" and "land." The group interacted verbally and physically, exploring their relationships to each other. At one point the girl became depressed and wept. She felt so tortured as the zone of conflict between water and land that she had great difficulty coping. More than scientific lessons came out of this exercise, but science was a part of it, too.

At the end of these kinds of exercises, I have often asked people just to sit quietly and to explore their own and each others' feelings about all aspects of the experience. As a participant I have wanted to reflect and to share in this way. All of this can help to develop deeper personal relationships and to allow spontaneous and functional communications systems to emerge in a group as well as creating a climate for creative activity.

SYNECTICS

Synectics is another "technique," developed by W. J. J. Gordon and G. Prince, that helps set the creative process in motion and develop. At a recent ES workshop, 30 of us got together and decided to use this approach, demonstration-style, to try to solve a human-potential problem. Gunner had spoken about the importance of helping teachers have "full buckets." By this metaphorical expression he meant that a teacher must be a full and complete person in order to pour out his own potential so that it affects his students.

In the game, John became our "client." The idea is to get the creative potential of the whole group to help the client find a solution to his problem. In this instance, John wanted to find out, "How can I find out what's in my bucket" or, "What is my real potential as a person and a teacher and how do I find this out?"

A synectics "excursion" involves trying to find new viewpoints. The figure in this chapter shows the flow of the excursion I shall describe. In order to do this, the group leader tries to create tasks whereby the group is focussed away from the actual problem, in the hope that new ideas will emerge from the preconscious of the group members. If the group becomes too preoccupied with the direct solution of the problem, they are likely to lose access to the preconscious and come up with trivial or ordinary solutions. A synectics excursion allows the group to generate wild ideas that may later fit into novel solutions. In this particular excursion, we explored analogies and metaphors of various kinds. At the first stage we attempted to find analogies from the area of astronomy, a field that was as far away as possible from the real thing we wanted to deal with. In working through "Astronomy" we came up with the notion of the Big Dipper, and I, as leader, then asked the group members to do a gestalt psychology exercise in which each person was asked to "become" the Big Dipper and to express his or her feelings about what it is like to be the Big Dipper. The phrase "honey dipper" came up, and then I asked the group to find analogies for "honey dippers" from the world of biology. Among the words presented, someone advanced the idea of "latrine." From a latrine we moved on to another synectics technique known as "book title." In "book title" the group is

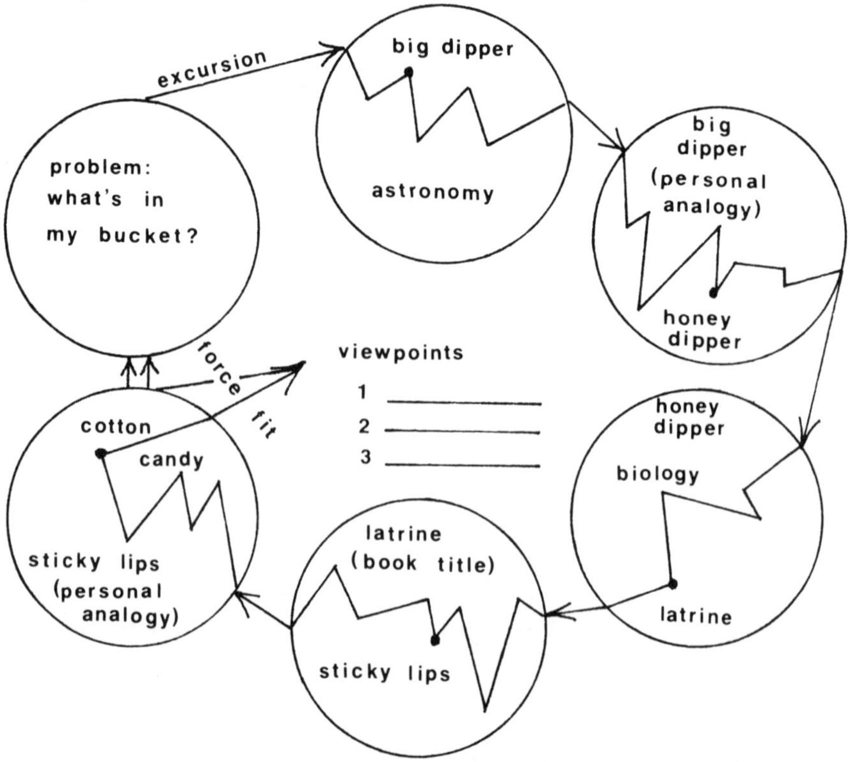

requested to give book titles that capture the essence of the word or words concerned but also present a paradox. From this paradox we advanced in another stage of the excursion to the idea of "sticky lips." At this point I asked the group to do an exercise in personal analogy, pretending they were sticky lips and telling me how they felt in that capacity. After the presentation of several more words over a period of several minutes, I then told the group that the time had come to go back to our original problem. We then entered into the most demanding part of a synectics, exercise, called "force fit." In the Force Fit stage the idea is to take the last idea that we have come up with or that I as leader have chosen and to try to use that idea to come up with new viewpoints about our original problem. I selected the words "cotton candy" as the words we would force fit. The group was asked to force fit whatever they could about the cotton candy into our original problem, "What's in my bucket?". As the group talked about possible ways in which the notion of cotton candy could be related to the problem, our client was asked to listen closely and to select from the suggestions things he felt related to the problem he had asked us to help him solve.

Obviously, there is no true "solution" to a problem as broad as "How do I find out what my real potential is?". However, a number of viewpoints developed which the client found useful. Among these were the following: "You expect taste (in cotton candy), and the end-product is something very different;" "Potential (cotton candy) is weak and easily dissipated;" "Even though it looks like fluff, the essence is really there;" "I find my essense--do I feel or accept what they tell me?" "There is the possibility of an expanding bucket (potential) without fear of change in shape." Although these did not present a single "solution", they did provide for John an access route to new insights about himself. The group helped him to feel more comfortable with the idea that he had a great deal of potential to offer his students. In a human-potential problem such as this the synectics group has a therapeutic function for the participants as well as providing new ideas. In more product-oriented groups, targets such as "How to invent a better can opener?", or "What should the name of this new book be?" lend themselves to more definite solutions. At ES, most of our final products and many of our intermediate ideas were arrived at through synectics-type processes.

CREATIVE ACTIVITY TRANSCENDS THE DISCIPLINES

The **Notebooks of Leonardo Da Vinci** provide remarkable insights into the ways this painter-sculptor-inventor-scientist-technologist worked and what the nature of his creative activity was, with its ever-changing face and the way he brought together different kinds of experience. Unfortunately, he was so creative and experimentive that many of his works of art never really "succeeded." The paint ran or cracked, or something happened to the plaster. His inventions didn't work. His contributions to basic science were largely ignored, and he was widely criticized by many.

In magazines like **Art News** there are regular features such as "Rauschenberg paints a picture." In these we sit, figuratively, with the artist and through an interview participate vicariously in what he actually does while painting a single picture.

This has been little done in science. I find myself wanting to go out and talk to "successful" scientists I know of and to see if I can get them to talk about how they really work rather than about their work and ideas per se. That's what we always talk about at professional meetings: our results rather than the processes involved in our activities. I am especially interested in trying to find people who are willing and able to trace the development of their ideas. What things from their past experience can they identify that ultimately led to their big and more important creative ideas. How orderly or disorderly was their process? To what extent does intuition enter into their work? One thing I know is that some of the most creative scientists I know now are hardly what you could call orderly people in the way in which they live and work. I used to think that science was all orderly and precise, but I know now from personal experience that it is far from that in the way that many highly competent people practice it.

Some scientists become willing to talk about their ways of working: People like C. P. Snow, J. B.S. Haldane, Aldous Huxley, Albert Szent Georgi, and others. But now I'm spilling to you an idea for something I want to do in the future- gather information of this type from scientists of whom I have a particularly high opinion because of the creative lives I **subjectively** judge them to be living. In the meanwhile, lacking the information to give really detailed stories about lots of people I'll provide a little about a few.

Clyde Wahrhaftig of the University of California has long been interested in the study of land forms. He's not a "famous man" in the Einstein or Nobel-Prize-winner sense. But he is a highly competent geological scientist whose work has been acclaimed to at least the extent that he won the Kirk Bryan medal of the Geological Society of America in 1965. Prize winners always get a chance to make a talk, accepting their awards, and the acceptance speech is later published. Clyde elected in his speech to discuss the history of the paper, "Stepped Topography of the Southern Sierra Nevada, California," for which he received the award. The award-winning paper shows a neat organization of ideas, logically set out in order to support Wahrhaftig's hypothesis. In the acceptance speech, though, Clyde points out that the ideas themselves did not come to him in anything like the tidy way in which they are presented in the published article. He traces the origin of individual parts of the paper back over a period of 20 years, going clear back to his days in graduate school. As he describes the moment of creation of his actual idea, one day in the Sierra Nevada he was driving around in a jeep with several students. Suddenly, apparently out of the clear blue sky the idea burst forth in an intuitive flash. When he sat down to write it up, all of those pieces that had accumulated in the conscious and preconscious parts of his mind fell into place. Where small parts of the picture were missing, he was able to go out purposefully and gather the additional supporting information he needed. Then all that remained to be done was to organize these ideas into a good logical sequence, and the paper was born. It appears cold, logical, precise, and scientific in the Geological Society Bulletin. In fact it was created in an intuitive and highly "artistic" way.

A footnote in another journal provides a clue about variety of actual contributions to scientific work. In a paper with the forbidding title, **"Ridge Transform Fault Spreading Pattern in Freezing Wax,"** Douglas W. Oldenburg and J. N. Brume state, "The discovery of the ridge transform fault phenomenon in wax glass was stimulated by a seminar given by Dr. G. Thompson and by the fact that the family of one of us ... was making candles at home at the same time..." The origin of many scientific ideas is not necessarily in a hard, coldly empirical and experimental approach. Perhaps more often really significant creative ideas are arrived at through a wide-ranging awareness of many facets of the world and through a wide range of kinds of experiences, many of which would appear at first to have nothing whatsoever to do with science or with a given subject at hand.

These descriptions make me wonder more and more what value the common teachers' statement, "All right, now let's get down to business!" can possibly have. The routes to creative business — to the business of learning and discovering in a creative and worthwhile way — are so many that I decline to reject any possibilities!

James Watson in **The Double Helix** documents extensively the intuitive, irregular route through which he and Crook invented the idea of the double helix as a model for the structure of D.N.A. In the description he also hints at how the straight, scientific approach (in the usually understood sense) may actually have prevented some of his colleagues from coming up with the idea first. They were so hung up on rules that they failed to accept what to Watson became the obvious.

At a recent professional meeting, I had supper with Walt Keller, a grand old man among geologists. In our conversation he discussed his approach to work. He said that he always sits in on a lot of the scientific talks given. He said something like the following "If I find 2 papers that are in my field and that mean something to me, then it's a good meeting. I also go to lots of others and just listen. Sometimes much later, even years later, something I heard in one of those sessions and didn't pay much attention to will fall into place and mean something."

Walt went on to talk of his master's thesis, published as "The Green Spots in The Red Beds." When he first started, he mapped a whole "new" area only to find out that someone else had been there before him. So he started all over to concentrate on the "green spots." These spots seemed to be of academic interest only at the time. However, in 1949 it was found that the green spots were related to the presence of uranium deposits of the Colorado Plateau area, and all of a sudden Walt's work was viewed as very creative and important.

Some of our students were starting to run x-ray diffraction patterns of minerals and of rock materials, always starting the goniometer (a device for measuring angles) at 15 degrees rather than at 3 degrees. When Bill Elberty learned of this, he asked **why?** A myth generated by a previous instructor 3 years earlier suggested that no useful information could be obtained below 15 degrees. This became an unwritten rule that students just accepted without question. It turns out that much valuable information can be obtained between 3 degrees and 15 degrees after all.

Creativity originates largely in the breaking of rules!

There may be a unique moment for creating any particular product. If I were writing this particular part of this manuscript in Canton, N.Y. it would lack all of the aspects of awareness brought to me by the presence of a Norwegian fjord in my front yard. It would lack the inputs of the Fjordane gneisses, rocks I have been "messing about with" in between writing times in the sense described by David Hawkins. The effects of the glaciers hanging off of Brekketinden, a lovely mountain across the valley, would be missing. When we came here, I purposely left all of my note files for this book at home. I took only a rough outline. I felt that note materials might actually hinder me in the writing by making me a slave to December's ideas — or February's. The writing seems to be flowing right along — perhaps it's too informal for you, but I don't apologize for that. When I get home, I'll go over those note files and some new things will be inserted. Furthermore, I'll spot new holes that would not be there if I hadn't written the draft right here, sitting in the side yard with the hot noon sun on my shoulders, feeling glad the clouds and fog of last week have cleared up. When will a rock outcrop I look at (or a seagull, or Barry Stevens' **Don't Push The River** or a corny Norwegian love story in **Norsk Ukeblad,** or William's **Donald Duck og Cie,** which we are reading together in Norwegian) suddenly speak to me and say, "Here, my patient friend, is proof positive that I was once a volcanic rock. Now go out to other parts of the world and use these new criteria I've shown you to extend knowledge about ancient volcanism." Or maybe I'll get another message. Or, more likely none. Perhaps my interest will shift and I'll not even care about that anymore.

Look at the random ways in which Leonardo set down his ideas in his note books. Or look at John Steinbeck's notes for **Travels With Charlie.** These are models to me - good ones for creative activity in art, literature, music, and science.

Unfortunately we understand little about how the creative process really works. Some people limit the notion of "creativity" in their minds to art and literature. Once we understand that "discovery" in science is not really so much finding what is already there as it is putting together a bunch of ideas and data to create concepts, it becomes easier to view sciencing as a basically creative process, too. Hypotheses and theories don't jump forward as god-given explanations of reality. They are made up by men as verbalizations. They please us by helping us to understand, and appreciate, from an aesthetic as much as from a utilitarian point of view, the world we live in and the nature of our lives. They help us in our search for meaning.

Elsewhere I have defined creativity simply as the combining of old ideas and observations, sometimes with addition of new observations and information, to form something that is new to us. It is the invention of a new and previously "hidden" connection. Each of us, either explicitly or tacitly, creates new effects, ideas, and sensations within himself all the time. The very nature of our minds is such that they wander and combine and recombine ideas and new information that we receive. Even the most "controlled" of us, the person who always seems to follow someone else's instructions and who never seems willing to try anything new must occasionally, in the secret recesses of his own mind if not out in the open, "have an idea." The "having" of an idea is to me an act of creation.

I can choose to live a "creative life," devoting much of my energy to trying new things, having new experiences, and trying somehow to record, express, or communicate about these in some way. Likewise I can choose to define my activity as not very creative or as un-creative. By doing so, I choose a path of dependency on others.

Whether or not people "out there" define my creations as important to the world at large is largely irrelevant. Many cases are known of musicians, writers, painters and other people in what are conventionally thought of as "creative fields of endeavor" whose creations were thought of during their lifetimes as "uncreative trivia" but who were later judged to be important creators. There are numerous cases of people in this category in the sciences. Mendel's work in genetics was largely ignored in his lifetime. Wegener's ideas on continental drift were dismissed as nonsense. On the other hand, work valued as highly creative during a person's lifetime may later be judged to have been trivial.

I can let people's judgements of my activities limit the things I try. I become their slave and lose a great deal, denying my own potential, when I do this. I can sometimes profit from listening to what other people say about my creations and activities. I can use this information as feedback but I want to feel free to ignore, reject, or use this to alter the direction or style of what I do.

I can think of myself as creative and of my work as worthwhile and enjoyable regardless of how others may judge it. The creative life makes me feel good about whatever I do. I can be a creative cook, carpenter, geologist, science educator, actor, dancer, painter, whatever I wish. The process of living in what to me is a creative way, is what I value especially. When I take this attitude and choose to live this way, unhindered to any great degree by outside judgements, my products become freer and positive judgements from outside may come my direction. If I am really living creatively I probably am also relatively unaffected by critical **acclaim** of my work too. I can't deny, though, that I'm always glad when I learn that someone likes me, how I live, and what I do. Perhaps I can gradually grow self-confident enough so that I don't need to be "stroked" (positively reinforced) much.

In a paraphrase from Shakespeare's **Julius Caesar**, John Dyer and Frederick Dyer suggest, "The fault, dear colleague, is not in our bosses, but in ourselves, that we are not creative."

As I look back over this section and what follows I find it interesting how my outlines led me to try to treat knowing, inquiry, discovery, science, teaching, learning, and the creative processes separately. My outlines said to do it that way and I sort of tried. But I kept combining titles in various different ways. And even then they all just kept flowing together. I also couldn't keep the "nature of people" out of it. As for myself, I guess **me** got all over the thing.

Writing term papers, theses, and articles I have always found myself being told to (and later believing this "rule" and doing it on my own and even coercing other people into doing it — remember the 15 degree rule for the x-ray machine!) combine ideas into a logical order rather than blurting them out as they occur to me. In so doing, I'm told and I have told others, if I write a paragraph on A, then one on B, followed by one on C and then another on A, I should then combine the two on A so that I don't make my readers jump back and forth. Furthermore, if it later seems more logical to have C precede A, then I should shift things around. **Logical** is supposed to be what I am to drive at.

But my mind doesn't work that way. That's **not** the way I create. Creativity is a process and it's this process I want to convey. Maybe I'll just leave it all jumbled up the way it came out. Maybe that way it'll really convey what I mean. One of the modern poets (was it Alan Ginsburg or Alan Watts?) apparently used to write tight, much re-worked poetry. It was technically very good, but there wasn't much feeling to it. Finally he began "blurting." Now, apparently he won't change a word from his first attempt, so afraid is he of losing the emotional impact that his "blurts" now have. I'm sure there must be a balance point between absolutely spontaneous creative products and things that have been reworked to the extent that they are emasculated and destroyed.

But I'm beginning to think that the balance point, for me at least, may be much closer to the first intuitive blurt than I ever thought before. In over-editing may lie the death of my own uniqueness. In playing-it-safe in research and stating only the obvious and totally acceptable may lie the death of all gems of new ideas and life for science, too.

> To the extent that a person makes, invents, thinks of something that is new to him, he may be said to have performed a creative act.
>
> —Margaret Mead

> An art that produces **effective surprise** - This I shall take as the hallmark of a creative enterprise.
>
> —Jerome Bruner

HUNTING FOR ROUTES TO KNOWING

KNOWING

> Even in order to understand, we have to invent, or, that is, to reinvent, because we can't start from the beginning again.... anything is only understood to the extent that it is reinvented.
>
> — Jean Piaget

> Knowing is a process, not a product.
>
> —Jerome Bruner

> There are two modes of knowing, those of argument and experience.
>
> —Roger Bacon

A popular misconception holds that knowing and knowledge are simple and can be measured and judged in easy ways. A substantial proportion of time in schools is devoted to preparation for various tests of knowledge, helping students demonstrate "knowledge" to the outside world with its compulsion that people should be accountable for knowing certain things. Many professional examinations, civil service examinations, and other such devices serve to filter people into or out of various occupations and control their advancement.

Gretchen just finished her New York State Regents examination in biology the day before we left for Norway, where I am writing this. Yesterday we talked about this examination. All multiple choice questions. Although she passed it with no trouble, she couldn't even remember the **questions** from most of the examination, much less the largely trivial, information-centered answers. As a sometimes research-oriented scientist I am amused at the kinds of things people who write standardized tests look for as evidence of knowing! Come to think of it, I guess I do know a little bit about the way these committees operate, having once chaired a committee that prepared one of the New York State Proficiency Examinations. If you pass that one, it gets you several hours worth of college credit, and shows no real evidence of what I consider to be real "knowing" of earth science, so trivial, low level, and information - and definition-oriented are the questions.

In this essay, I want to ramble through a number of areas that concern "knowing." I want you to see me ramble as I conceive the essay, too, because the process I am going through in writing it is part of the very knowing I am talking about. Furthermore there are a number of **ways of knowing** and **degrees of knowing** something. I can never know anything completely unless I fuse with it. Even then I may not know it completely, for I cannot claim ever to know myself. The more I explore myself, the more of me I find. This is true of any other object I want to know also. The more I explore it the more I find in it.

Merely experiencing is a way of knowing. Unfortunately it is a way of knowing that many people reject. "If you can't express it, you don't know it," they say. Detailed analysis and description on paper is a way of knowing. Loving is knowing in an intense, tangible, and yet verbally inexpressible way. How many poets and novelists have tried to express loving in how many different ways? To me, all ways of knowing are acceptable. Others may discover new ways of knowing through me and I learn new ways of knowing from every person I interact with deeply in any way. Everything that expands me increases my knowing if I can allow my awareness to flow out from my experience. It can be expressed for outside consumption or retained within me. Either kind of awareness and experience is equally acceptable. I decline to judge the knowing of another person either in kind or degree. Knowing is an intensely personal kind of conscious or preconscious experience that may not be expressed at the moment of knowing. It may linger in inner recesses perhaps never to emerge, perhaps to emerge right then, at the moment, and perhaps to emerge only much later, in another context, as part of some later act of creation or intuition.

I only **know** something in any way that is really meaningful to me when it becomes a functional part of my perceiving-responding - exploring - feeling - interacting - producing apparatus. Memorizing a list of terms and reproducing it on a test the next day is one kind of temporary knowing, but I do not feel that this kind of knowing is necessarily something to be courted or aimed at. Yes, information does enter me and it **may** prove useful. Everything that passes into me through any of my senses is part of my knowing. But focussing on that level of knowing may let my awareness of more important learnings get rusty.

> *The harsh squawking and crying I hear outside my window says to me, "seagulls at work out there - probably fighting over a piece of fish." The "bleep bleep" is from an oystercatcher. A dim roar in the background comes from the cascade through which the lake at one end of Sykkylvsfjord empties into the salt-water part of the fjord. The word "fjord" has real functional meaning to me*

because I am next to one. I am experiencing it in the fullest way. A "moo" across the way identifies the wearer of the cowbell I just heard. Or was a sheep wearing it? That would make it a "sheepbell" I suppose. The grass and branches are all bending to the north. South winds predominate in this fjord and affect the weather. I wonder what that has to do with the amount of precipitation and with the fact that this particular valley is invaded by several glaciers? The mountain peaks here are alpine in their appearance as opposed to the relatively flat-topped peaks in much of the dissected plateau further south. I wonder if, when I drive around the fjord this afternoon to look at some of the rocks, I will find some lenses of eclogite which Inge says are there. Gretchen just brought in a snail shell, partially bored by some small sea creatures. Yesterday when William cleaned the huge cod he got out of Stromme's net, as a reward for helping pull in the fish, he found the stomach full of tiny starfish. I didn't know cod ate starfish! When I cooked the cod last night I intuitively knew when it was done, although I'd never cooked a cod before, because I remembered how it flakes into big, firm, but tender, slabby fragments when I've eaten good cod in restaurants. Day before yesterday, William got a copy of H.G. Wells' <u>*The Invisible Man*</u> *to read. I've wanted to read it now for 15 years. Ever since Howell Williams mentioned that the Invisible Man got to be invisible by making his refractive index equal to that of air and then you couldn't see him any more. I think of that and use the anecdote with students interested in petrography. Perhaps it will tickle their imaginations and help them remember what happens to the appearance of a mineral grain when you immerse it in an oil of the same refractive index as the grain. I think I will reproduce this and pass it out this fall to people in optical mineralogy. Another gnemonic device of Willie's comes to mind - that hypersthene is "as pink as a maiden's blush - (long pause) - but then none of you fellows would know what that looks like." William just came in wanting to know the Norwegian word for "sinker" for his fishing line. He has "forgotten" much of the Norwegian he learned as a 5-year-old. Much of it had become non-functional over the five-year period since we were last here. Now he needs a sinker. He used his dictionary to find the word. We worked on the proper pronunciation and the rest of the sentence he needs to obtain the weight. Now he has borrowed a kroner to go buy it. The rate at which he is gaining words is phenomenal.*

I could continue with this account of what comes into my mind as I shift my awareness back and forth between what I feel, see, smell, taste, and touch here and how these things are integrated with my past experiences — combined to form new realizations and complex perceptions. I am astonished at the range of what I know and by the way what I know enriches my perception of the now I am living in and how both give me ideas for new things I want to do, experience, create. Science, literature, living, joy, art, poetry, music, all are tied up in a complex package of knowing and wanting to know.

I never know what piece of knowing may be important to me and so, more and more, I eagerly accept as many new perceptions as I can possibly get. New elements come in at each second and each one that I am aware of has a chance of striking an old chord and perhaps helping me dredge up some old piece of information or experience from 1, 5, 15, 40 years ago.

I do not "put down" as useless the information Gretchen was required to learn for her regents' exam in biology. Just as I don't put down what I know about the mineral hypersthene. What I put down is the fact that Gretchen was "required" to learn the order of biome, ecosystem, population, and niche and that I was required to memorize 100 minerals and their properties. The mineral properties that are part of my functional repertory are the ones that I work with regularly in my research and as I work with other learners. The cute gnemonic device about the maiden's blush is part of my mental picture of a remarkable person — Howell Williams — and was not learned in any forced way, but rather because it struck me.

Functional knowledge that is part of my operating repertory is knowledge that for some reason or another **I feel good** about. When I think about information and "knowledge" that is really **not** functional in me (such as many areas of mathematics that I was forced through and held accountable for on someone else's terms and in a strict way) I realize that it is material that I had bad feelings about during the acquisition period. I think that knowledge supposedly "acquired" (and it's acquisition "demonstrated" by passing appropriate cognitive tests) under conditions of constraint, force, and accountability with threat of failure and penalty, may actually be doomed to non-functionality. Unpleasant learning experiences may actually **inhibit** later recall or ability to use the very information whose acquisition was once "demonstrated" under rigorously controlled conditions.

Recall cannot be divorced from the dimensions of the experience during which learning was acquired. At times I find I am having difficulty recalling something that I can feel "out there" in my mind just beyond the range of my consciousness. If I can recreate in my mind the feelings I had as I learned the material, everything comes flooding back to me in a wave of **functional** knowledge. (If the feeling was a bad one, I hypothesize that such recall may **not** be possible. I'm not sure just how one would test such a hypothesis, but it would make a fascinating study.)

It is well known and has been amply demonstrated that we perceive many times more things than we are consciously aware of. A person brought into a room he has not visited before, removed from the room, and asked to list all of the objects he can remember from the room may be able to list on the order of 50 objects. The same person, under hypnosis, may be able to increase the number of objects that he can report as much as tenfold. Police officials have been able to use hypnosis to help witnesses recall how criminals were dressed, what they looked like, what vehicles they were driving, etc. — all kinds of information that could not be recalled under normal questioning.

We have conscious access to only a small proportion, perhaps as little as ten percent or less of the things that we actually perceive, that somehow or the other **enter** us. Our ability to learn even while asleep has been demonstrated on a number of experiments involving taped messages. Some colleagues of mine have greatly accelerated language learning through use of some of these sleep-learning techniques. The fact that subliminal advertising (brief messages appearing on a movie or TV screen for such short periods of time that we are not even consciously aware of their appearance) is now forbidden is further evidence of how much more quickly and tenaciously our minds and memories work than we "know."

Michael Polanyi has written at length about the extent of things we can know and yet not express. I am fascinated by the fact that I can sit down at the piano and retrieve from my fingers a complex piece of music. When I think of the astonishing problem of having 10 different fingers going 10 different ways and each one "knowing" just where to land and when to create a group of sounds written several hundred years ago by Bach or Telemann, I am astounded at the capability of the organism that I am.

When I am in a theatrical production I become angry with myself when I have trouble mastering lines. I seem to be able to learn them perfectly, to repeat them on cue without error. And then I march out on the rehearsal platform and they're all gone! Gradually as I integrate movement, business, **meaning**, lines, relationship with other actors (both as the people they really are and as the people they become in the play,) light, sound and other aspects of the total experience of play-acting, the lines — even very complex combinations of speech and movement — begin to fall together and flow out from me into a functioning characterization. Incredible capability of my mind and body to be able to integrate all of these factors at once, in a way that is beyond analysis.

Sometimes attempts to analyze how the organism works can actually be detrimental to its functioning. When a golfer gets too much concerned about exactly how he is swinging rather than swinging "naturally," he may lose his touch. **The Inner Game of Tennis** discusses the use of Zen to free up the organism for better tennis-playing. I once read about a fine concert violinist who began analyzing his technique. He became so involved with how he was playing that he ceased playing effectively. For a period of about 5 years he had to leave the concert circuit because he couldn't get through the pieces he had chosen to play. When he **did** regain his "concentration" or whatever had been missing, his spontaneity, he was able, however, to play far better than ever before, with a whole new depth of feeling and an incredibly refined technique. It may be dangerous to analyze some of the things we do out of our enormous reservoirs of tacit knowledge, but if we persist in analysis, once we begin it, the reward may be very great. We may lose our functional ability totally in the analysis or we may raise ourselves to new pinnacles. It is important to know the risk before we try to analyze some of our tacit knowing too deeply.

Janos Starker, the cellist pointed out the problem of child prodigies. "When I picked it (the cello) up (after a year's absence from any practice) I played like a blind man. What happens to the bird who sings and doesn't know how it sings? That's what happens to child prodigies. They wake up and ask themselves dangerous questions about how they do it — and have no answers. I nearly had a nervous breakdown. Consistency is the difference between the professional and the amateur. I was grown-up and could no longer depend on instinct."

How do we learn to keep trusting instinct?

Some months ago, after I had proposed a special short course I was called before the course committee to "justify" my proposal. I had declined specifically to state any requirement as far as an explicit product of the course. Essentially, I said that each person could produce what seemed appropriate to him or her. I even said that a lack of any concrete physical product would be acceptable if that seemed appropriate to the individual learners. Several committee members expressed the feeling that if you can't say it or put it down in writing or in sketches or music or something you haven't really experienced it and you can't really know it. This attitude denies the existence of tacit knowledge, which is an essential aspect of knowing. Experience alone and in itself is enough to make a learning experience that I as a facilitator of learning, am willing to "certify."

I am increasingly pleased with the growth in overall functional knowledge which I sense in people I work with under conditions of no constraints (or at least lowest possible constraint that I can recognize and perceive at the present time in my life.)

In truly functional knowledge I agree with Fritz Perls that there may actually be a metaphorical fusion of me with the object of my knowledge. An extreme case that comes to mind is a graduate student who returned from a day of research and saw his wife sitting in her rocking chair, rocking their newborn son. Superimposed over them was a huge, colorful, interference figure similar to the one he had been observing under his microscope that afternoon. In a sense there was a metaphorical fusion between the graduate student and his work.

I recall awakening once on a bus, at 3:00 A.M. as I returned from a field trip in New England, where we had had to leave our disabled car behind for repairs. As the bus went over a bridge in Albany and I saw the street lights extending along on either side of us I had an uncanny feeling that there were rows of atomic nuclei in a crystalline lattice and that I was an electron moving along through the lattice. I experienced an acute feeling or fusion with an area of great interest to me.

Feeling at one with something I am doing or learning is an important aspect of truly functional and meaningful knowing.

SCIENCE AS A PART OF KNOWING

> ...why should (science) be so often condemned...as unimaginative, mechanical, routine? In part, the scientists themselves are to blame. Intent on emphasizing that experimental method which is their badge of authority, their professional distinguishing mark, they have deprecated their own imaginativeness. They have wrongly supposed—exactly like their critics—that the exercise of the imagination and the experimental method are essentially opposed to one another: They have failed to understand that science is the wedding of the two.
>
> —J.A. Passmore

> We must learn to live with a science which by limitation in its logical structure must remain an open system of knowledge subject to change and continuous correction.
>
> —J. Bronowski

The idea and practice of science has been much maligned in recent years. Scientists and science teachers must accept a large share of responsibility for this. Myths in the minds of many people represent science as a monolithic, powerful block of human endeavor in which most scientists are pretty much in agreement about the nature of their enterprise. The fact that the term "scientific method" is used at all is one piece of evidence for this. Most people who have done much research work realize that there are as many "scientific methods" as there are scientists and new problems to be solved.

The enterprise of science can hardly be called any kind of united block in which there is anything even approaching consensus about anything. In general, scientists are a pretty independent and often outspoken lot of people. They organize themselves into various professional organizations, but each of these is very different from each other one in many significant ways. In addition some capable scientists shun these organizations, so unwilling are they to be tied to organizational positions. Paul Brandwein has defined science as "The art of intelligent failure." Percy Bridgman stated that science is "doing one's damndest with one's mind, no holds barred." For me, then, science is anything I choose to make it!

One problem with science at the elementary and secondary levels and even in many colleges is that the large majority of people "teaching" science have never been really involved in doing science. In general they have worked through books and lab exercises prepared for them by someone else but few of them have actually participated in any personally-originated inquiry. Most have done their "science courses" as a set of prescribed requirements. Few spend their weekends or summers in pursuit of more understanding about the world we live in. (Incidentally, this holds true for other areas than science, too.)

On the other hand, I have known many teachers who are not necessarily involved deeply in the pursuit of new scientific insights but who nonetheless seem to understand that science has no special status or significance but is simply part of the normal human hunger to know more and to understand, enrich, and extend our experiences. Still, this more open state of mind is relatively rare among science teachers, and this may be because too many science teachers are willing to **believe** what some scientists say and publish that would seem to limit science.

T.S. Kuhn discusses how textbooks systematically disguise the creative way in which scientific revolutions occur. They describe the outcomes, the conclusion of important changes in ideas, but they rarely undertake to describe the process through which the old ideas were discarded and the new knowledge became accepted. Old scientific ideas become "non-persons" in the same way that a discarded Soviet politician disappears from Soviet history books. The textbooks are rewritten as each new idea takes its place, and the older ideas and the evidence of conflict between the old and the new, prior to acceptance of the new, disappears.

Historical detail, according to Kuhn, would clearly identify and give status to "human idiosyncracy, error, and confusion." The pretense that science evolves in an orderly way whereas music and art do not may be a prime factor in concealing the similarity of creative processes in science and in the arts.

Kuhn describes the difference between "normal" science, the kind which operates from textbooks and prior generalizations, and the kind of science which leads to significant advances represented in what he calls "scientific revolutions." Revolutions—major changes in the base from which "normal" science operates—result from highly intuitive behavior of a few people who **do** science but don't get bogged down in existing theory and practice. How, then, do we develop science education in a direction that encourages people to seek the anomalies, the things that **don't** fit, rather than seeking contentment in the security of old ideas and concepts. People with a broad view of science as an enterprise may help us transcend the limitations of science as it is currently represented to so many people.

I take a liberal view of what science is all about. In Russian, the work "nauka," which we translate as "science" actually includes essentially all areas of scholarship. Thus the study of literature and other academic areas that we do not normally include as science are lumped together with physics and chemistry in the Soviet academic image of science. (This is not to suggest, incidentally, that there is no communication problem between Soviet physicists and chemists and their colleagues in literature and history!) In the U.S., we get very sticky about whom we are willing to unclude in our definition of "science." At the Institute for Advanced Studies in Princeton, for example, controversy continues over whether or not to expand the group of sociologists they hesitantly and at a late stage included within their institute. For years, The National Science Foundation more or less excluded social scientists from among the groups they supported both in research and in educational grants. Now they have begun to remedy this situation, and sociologists, psychologists, and anthropologists are beginning to get a small share of support.

Even within the so-called "hard" and natural sciences there is a pecking order. The physicists may talk down to the chemists, the chemists condescend to the biologists, and the biologists turn their noses up at the earth scientists. Interdisciplinary research activities, are helping to break down some of these barriers, but a feeling of caste and of "relative" worth still exists in the scientific, educational, and research "establishment." Only through a basic change of attitudes from kindergarten through graduate school and the research institutes and in the public media can we change this attitude.

One tale has it that the earth scientist, close as he is to the dirt and the foundation of things wishes he were a biologist. The biologist, working with life processes, wishes he were a "harder" scientist—a chemist. The chemist sees the need to understand more basic laws and envies the physicist. The physicist wishes he could abstract things further and quantify them better. He envies the mathematician, the most "pure" of the scientists, who works only with abstractions. On the other hand, the mathematician, high in his ivory tower, looks down from the sky onto the earth and begins to hanker for more knowledge about the earth. And thus the circle goes.

People who divide and limit the role of "science," in my opinion, work against many useful things that "scientists" can do. As soon as someone applies the word "scientist" to me, that can become a way of society's trying to limit what I can do and say. "This is not a subject upon which scientists are expected to be able to contribute. You people, with your emphasis on simplifications and abstractions, can't deal with the real-world problems of people!'' That attitude is what gets Linus Pauling in trouble when he expresses opinions on political and sociological matters. ''Why doesn't Dr. Spock keep to his pediatrics! What does a pediatrician know about ethics, politics, and grown-up behavior?'' Some people in the sciences agree with Linus Pauling's right to his opinions but feel that he has no ''certified expertise'' which permits him to say in public what he does. (''Go get a second PhD in political science, Linus, and then we'll listen.'') It's OK for Johnny Carson or Jane Fonda to make a political statement, but ''fellow scientists'' should tend their own gardens.

The ''scientists'' do that to non-scientists, too, however, when they decline to explain and justify their requests for research money on the grounds that, ''You laymen just wouldn't be able to understand how essential my study may ultimately be to mankind.''

Science has recently been taken to task by critics such as Theodore Roszak as responsible for many present ills. I find myself agreeing with many of these ideas, but I would reassure the critics that some of the real eagles of science today—people who see beyond the limitations, shortsightedness, and provincialism of which he accuses many of our scientific journeymen—are not guilty of the excesses generally cited. A whole generation of young people coming up now have begun to question and doubt what scientists offer. These young people have ripped off the protective cloak of high status that has permitted many questionable things to be done in the name of ''science.''

We may have done more harm than good to many students from kindergarten through graduate school by means of required science courses. Many young people come to view science as a fearsome, monolithic, impersonal, unresponsive enterprise. Many elementary teachers fear the requirement that they ''teach'' so many hours of science a week. They convey this fear to their students through the rigid ways they present science and through the non-verbal and verbal clues they give to children. The attitude, ''This is tough stuff, but we have to do it because it's good for us,'' sets up expectations that accompany many young people clear up to the time that they arrive in college. There, they say to me, ''I hate science because it's so hard, and I've always done badly, but they always make me take more.''

There can be no open and honest inquiry in an environment of fear, dislike, and complusion. If, by it's very nature, science must foster open and honest inquiry—pulling out all of the stops, and trying anything to get at answers and to expand our knowing, then something is wrong in an environment that produces unpleasant experiences.

A particularly telling example of cause-effect is in the story I recently read of a small town in New Jersey in which physics was excluded from a town's school curriculum. The president of the board, a woman, mentioned in her arguments to the board her own negative experiences in physics when she was a student.

There may be no need for doomsday pronouncements. Recent reports in **Science** indicate that science enrollments in schools are generally holding steady and may even be increasing. I wonder what would happen to these enrollments if all science requirements in schools were abolished. There are already strong shifts within the sciences away from some of the more abstract sciences and toward the more applied, natural, and social sciences. Some of the triumphs of space research, the adventurous explorations of the sea bottom and other such feats may make up for some of the ill that may be done in required science courses. In these ways, the public media—newspapers, television, magazines, books, and films—may be doing a good deal more to convey the real spirit of how people in science go about their business and how this business can be related to people than are the schools.

DO I WANT TO "DO" SCIENCE?

Research is private curiosity satisfied at public expense.
—attributed to a noted member
of the Soviet Academy of Science.

Here I am in a science department. I get paid for "teaching" science. Yet I reject the idea of "teaching" because I don't really believe that anyone can "teach" (make someone to know) anything. I can be a part of a learning environment. I decline to take credit for the fact that someone learned something, because things I have planned can rarely be demonstrated to have caused learning. Learning is an intrinsic, personal affair within the person.

All of a sudden I ask myself, after 17 years of intense activity in science, "Do I really even want to **do** science anymore?" I have rejected "teaching" it. What is really to be my role in the learning environment?

I have gotten interested primarily in the "people" side of things in the learning environment, and in that way I guess I'm a counsellor now. I like to be a counsellor if that means trying to be a real person with other people—**really** being myself, knowing that this may help others really to be themselves, too, so that we can share our mutual richness.

I find myself spending much time arranging parts of the learning environment within the physical plant we call a science department. I spend a lot of time ordering apparatus, organizing it into more or less "programmed" learning packages that **might** stimulate the process of learning. In a sense this becomes almost like being a museum curator at, say, the Franklin Institute in Philadelphia, or the Exploratorium in San Francisco, where most of the displays are packaged experiments, displays, and "hands-on" exhibits that demand your involvement as you walk by them.

I find myself liking to do what is almost public relations work for earth science. I like to prepare field guides and programmed field excursions that can be used by anyone who wants to explore an area. My interest in this comes from my own frustration in the lack of serious aids for people who want to look carefully at, say, the geology of a certain trail or road in Yellowstone Park, or the geologic history of The Grand Canyon. There is a huge gap between low-level, dull, text-booky "This is a rock and see the pretty minerals" books and advanced technical liturature that is detailed, deadly dull, and full of jargon. How do we establish a whole range of intermediate literature—not textbooks which keep on copying the same old things out of previous textbooks—but real "literature" that can help people maintain their excitement and explore more efficiently? I like to prepare these kinds of things—although the time-demands and lack of technical assistance in this area are terribly frustrating.

But if I want to be a really effective facilitator of learning shouldn't I be an active scientist in the sense of gaining fundamental new knowledge as well as merely translating technical stuff "down" into guidebooks or becoming a commercial "curriculum-unit" producer?

People who want to teach in college go through intensive research-oriented programs where emphasis is primarily on production of new information and extension, embellishment, or even creation of ideas and concepts rather than on working with learners. I went through the several years of this exercise, even though my goal all along was to work in the people-oriented area of learning facilitation. After finishing my research thesis I was pleased to have created a product that was considered by peers and professors as at least "acceptable." I was now a real scientist, I thought.

Then I got into further research, mainly during the summers. More and more I had the feeling that people involved in the teaching of science—even in elementary and secondary schools—**ought** to have the kind of curiosity that made them want to be directly involved in making original studies of their own. The "publish-or-perish" controversy of colleges seemed nonsensical to me because I couldn't really understand how someone who called himself any kind of a scientist or science teacher could **not** produce some serious work.

Doing research part-time and during off-hours and vacation times seemed not to be very effective or very satisfying, however. It started to seem burdensome and tremendously energy-consuming. Then I started to look at the nature of my "research" activity. Much of it was routine and seemed to be almost like re-inventing the wheel. Applying the same old techniques to somewhat new questions, sometimes even introducing a new technique, writing it up, arguing with an editor, and finally seeing it come out in print, began to lead me to feel "so what?"

Besides, I soon learned that many discoveries and inventions of new conceptual models seem to have a time that is ripe for their appearance. Just as I published the results of a study on some rocks from northern Norway, Jacques Martignole, in Canada, who had been working thousands of miles away from me published an article that suggested an almost identical set of ideas about the origin of a similar set of rocks there. Thus, if I hadn't been around, the world wouldn't have been any the poorer, for the idea would have been put forth elsewhere. Similarly, if Jacques had not been around, my version would have been. The time was right for the idea to be proposed. Einstein put it this way, "...in science...the work of the individual is so bound up with that of his scientific predecessors and contemporaries that it appears almost as an impersonal product of his generation." Kuhn emphasizes this phenomenon as an aspect of the growth of science in the following comment, "The very fact that a significant scientific anomaly so often emerges simultaneously from several laboratories is an index both to the strongly traditional nature of normal science and to the completeness with which that traditional pursuit prepares the way for its own change." Why all of that tedious work on my part if the discovery of the relationship or invention of the concept is to be inevitable anyway? Why enter into a competitive rat-race of trying to publish an idea **first**, so I would have "priority," if my "priority" is to be largely a function of the times rather than some truly unique and significant contribution that is **mine** alone. What ego trips the competitiveness, the priority, and taking-credit business must lead to!

In 1967-68 I took 15 months to devote exclusively to "hard" research, partially to see if "doing" science was what I wanted after all. I produced a mass of data and a lot of published material from this experience. I also found myself very lonely many times hunched over a microscope, or punching buttons on an x-ray machine or a computer card-punch machine for hours on end. There were, of course, stimulating times of working with other people on things that we were mutually excited about, and these were perhaps the best times.

As I talked to non-professionals about my work, and especially to younger learners in school situations I kept getting the question, "So what?" from them. "Who really cares about those obscure things you're working on? What does it all lead to?"

Morris Holland, a psychologist from UCLA decribed why he finally got out of relatively obscure basic research cn the human eye-blink. He said, "...I decided that I wasn't going to do any further research that I couldn't describe to my mother with a straight face."

Often I feel that way, too. As an example, I was working on an outcrop of rocks near Indian Lake in New York State's Adirondack Mountains one day when a state trooper stopped, curious about why my car was parked in what he thought was not an altogether proper place. In answer to his query about what I was doing, I gave a brief explanation of my purpose. He watched me, looking up at me silently and reflectively where I was perched several feet above him in the steep roadcut. Then he just shook his head from side to side and muttered, in dumb disbelief, "Are you for real?!"

I always feel a bit strange when I gather field information along roads or where there are people around, because people almost invariably stop and stare. Then I feel stupid, as if I am some kind of nut. And yet, when the curiosity of these people is strong enough to lead to interaction and a personal relationship, as it has for me many times, then maybe I am the best kind of learning facilitator possible. I have had young people follow me around in the field before who have later become intensely interested in science. Maybe the spontaneous relationship between us has been a part of the opening of another person's interest. By example of the work I do, nutty as it may seem, I may be at one of my most effective moments as a facilitator. Still, I have the feelings of strangeness and embarrassment ("Why don't those people go away?") when people watch me perform at something that I don't think of as a performance.

"Why do you want to know that?" has been asked of me so many times that I begin to wonder "Why, indeed?" I think there is, perhaps, such a thing as the **pleasure of knowing**, without any need for analysis or justification. This may be akin to the pleasure of solving a cross-word puzzle or reaching the top of a mountain, or standing for hours fishing. In each case there is a product at the end of the thing, and the product (finishing something, learning the piece of music by heart, seeing the puzzle with all of the squares filled in correctly, looking down from the top of the mountain, holding the fish) can be very solid or very ephemeral. The process of getting to it has been tedious-joyful, sad-happy, frustrating-rewarding, quiet-loud. Experiencing may be its own reward.

Another kind of self-gratification motive may get involved, too. Sometimes I find myself glancing at a technical paper on a subject I have worked on and furtively looking first to see if the author has referred to my work. I try not to "get caught" doing this for fear people will think me vain. Have I been recognized for my contribution? If I find my name then I feel gratified and important. If the author neglects to mention me then I feel, "Gee, I must do inconsequential work if no one even takes notice of me. I wish my work were cited more often." I have begun to realize that I can free myself from such insecure feelings. When I concentrate my energy on evaluation of past products I have less time left to deal with today. As I increase my ability to think about here and now, apprehensions about the outside evaluation of my past work become smaller factors in my life.

One thing I begin to understand about basic studies is that no one ever knows when a piece of knowledge gained and reported may be important. This applies to any field of endeavor. This is where again, the pleasure of knowing becomes perhaps the most important factor of "doing" science. If I do not find pleasure in it, then I do not **need** to keep doing it!

My own "doing" of science has also involved research activity in science education. How do people learn science? In what ways can we increase the rate and quality of their learning? What effect does improved science education ultimately have on science itself? Some of my early work involved comparison of approaches. If you give two different, matched groups different "treatments" which group learns the most? As my approaches to learning situations have evolved away from the "treatment" concept and more to the matter of "relationship" as a primary factor, I have moved increasingly into the area of so-called human-case-history terms. The complexity of learning and of the interactions between learner, environment, learned, and facilitator no longer lends itself to the oversimplifications used by people interested only in the vague notion of "cognitive" growth (as defined by responses on multiple-choice tests.) My particular form of data gathering now is a kind of chroniciling where my whole organism takes in a series of impressions of a situation, and communications of some kind, reporting and synthesizing my observations flow from my pen. Sometimes I feel guilty because I have not reduced my information to numbers, punched them onto computer cards, and gotten a numerical average complete with standard deviations, correlation coefficients, and other statistical indices. But as I think about it this whole process is going on in the computer of my brain, which is a much more complex and capable instrument than any electronic computer has yet become. I'm just beginning to feel that I want to and can trust my intuition and my own integrated systems of information gathering, processing, and retrieval.

From 1969 to 1972, my activies centered around learning theory, the psychology of learning, the effects of curriculum materials in the learning process, approaches in helping people learn science, and similar topics. We also did some "hard" research in attempting to quantify changes in attitudes as well as increase in "knowledge" that went along with various models of learning environments and management. During that 3 year period I fiddled around with my rocks to some extent. I read a lot, finished writing up data that remained on hand from previous field and lab work, and even gathered some new data, not in a very systematic way and not particularly with the intent of working it up for publication. But I got to feeling a little bit "out of it" as far as being an "active research scientist" was concerned (even though I steadily increased my involvement as an active person in the behavioral sciences.) Funny, that I should equate my own "activity" as a scientist so much with the hard geology. I guess that may date from the time I started out as a "real" scientist and the physicists, chemists, biologists, mathematicians, and geologists told me that the social scientists were not really quite "scientists." An idea like that dies hard, and I find it hard to break out of it and accept that I may just be more social scientist now that physical scientist. Or maybe what I'm doing is rejecting these limiting categories altogether. I see no reason to fit myself into someone else's categories (even though it may be more and more difficult for them to classify me).

Returning to full-time university work in 1972, I began to feel that I "ought" to get back into more "serious" hard-science activity. One myth I had to get around was the old wives' tale that if you get out of your field for 2 or 3 years you'll never catch up again. The idea behind this myth is that information, ideas, and concepts are increasing at such a tremendous rate that you just can't fall behind. I know now that the obverse is true: it is increasing at such a rate that there is no way **anyone** can keep up. As a matter of fact if you **try** to keep up you are doomed to be a literary drudge and can't possibly have time to do any work of your own.

In geomorphology alone, (a sub-field of geology devoted to the study of land forms) the number of published abstracts of work done in 1970, included 60,000 items! And in this small field, the rate of increase of new literature produced is actually lower than for scientific literature as a whole.

So I have now realized that, as in all other parts of life, the best thing for me to do is not to worry about what I haven't done in the past or how far behind I am, but simply to dive in, blissfully ignorant of the problems, and deal with new things as they arrive. What happens is that I can jump right over all of the trivial things that have happened and been published and jump right into a new set of problems, perhaps even a quantum jump or two ahead of where I might have been if I had "stayed current." Being "out of it" for a couple of years also makes it easier for me to jump to a whole new area of interest with fewer feelings of leaving an "old friend" behind, the old friend having already mainly slipped from memory.

I do not know yet for sure whether I shall want to start big new data-gathering efforts with respect to rocks. I am fairly sure that in the near future I may want to work more in team style to maximize the personal-relationship aspects of science that I am coming to value more and more. This will go along with my desire for an active working relationship with younger learners at secondary and college levels—and perhaps even with much younger children involved too. I hypothesize that the kind of learning environment where people may be happiest and learn most may be related to the extent that science areas in schools of all levels can become functioning laboratories where the acquisition of new knowledge and the generation of ideas can become a main way of operating as opposed to classrooms in which the primary activities are the chewing over of old notions, and memorizing of old information.

On a recent visit I made to a western university a young professor of biology and of science education expressed eagerness to introduce inter-disciplinary and student-centered programs. Yet for every suggestion that arose in the discussion he countered that he couldn't possibly do that without having to give up his research in ecology, which was very important to him. I finally said to him that I accepted his feeling, but that he must not really want to change his mode of operation with students and that he really obviously didn't mean it when he said he wanted to change. He might as well admit this to himself. We talked again later and I don't know whether or not I was successful in conveying to him the concept of a research laboratory as a learning environment where both functions are transcended and melded to the benefit of both rather than to the detriment of either.

I begin to realize another thing about my own "research" activity. I can define "science" in many different ways. In my case I am in a department called "geology and geography." Without even stretching the point I can undertake a whole new range of people-oriented research in the social sciences. "Geography" became my opening here just as "science education" was before. (Do I still feel that I must have an "opening" in order to switch out of my old physical science category?)

I can define my approach to science in my own way. From this approach in the long-run come some of the best new cross-disciplinary and transdisciplinary ideas. There are so many examples of this, and yet the "system" still resists the idea of each person making his own operating definition of "science," "humanities," "social sciences," and "art." In schools we generally impose restricted territorial definitions of each area and discourage learners from moving very far across lines. This old academic territorialism of discipline-oriented and discipline-related methods is what I still feel as an uncomfortable restraint even though I reject it intellectually. It is still there as a functioning part of most school environments although my awareness of its existence makes it easier and easier to discard.

When I think of people who have preceeded me across discipline boundaries I am encouraged. Roger Revelle, formerly a research oceanographer with the Scripps Institution in San Diego, went through a stage of administering a college and has since become a professor of population studies at Harvard. George Cressey, a geologist, went on to become a geographer and China specialist. Harrison Brown of Cal Tech moved from geochemistry into geopolitics. Linus Pauling, criticized though he may have been, has moved through a range of hard science and social science activites, including the winning of Nobel Prizes in both areas. He has continued to be successful, at least in the minds of his friends, in both areas. Perhaps because of his outrageous success in both areas he has enemies as well. H.G. Wells is a typical example of the scientist-philosopher-novelist-historian, as is C.P. Snow. Arthur Koestler became the journalist-traveler-psychologist-scientist. We all think of Leonardo da Vinci as the prototype renaissance man. It may still just be possible for wide-ranging renaissance-type people to develop, who are not bound by trivial societal, disciplinary rules.

If I can "do" science my own way, defining it and redefining it in my own way as I go, then I guess the answer to my question is, I do want to "do" science!

> He might have been a scientist if he had not been so versatile.
> —Georgio Vasari, describing his
> contemporary, Leonardo da Vinci.

OBJECTIVITY

> ...There is no objectively existing situation, as was supposed in classical physics.
>
> —Max Born

> Objective knowing is alienated knowing; and alienated knowing is, sooner or later, ecologically disastrous knowing.
>
> —Theodore Roszak

One of the attitudes that Roszak protests against most violently in science is what he calls the "myth of the objective consciousness." This is a prevalent notion that many people have about science. The idea is that it is possible to look at everything objectively, that everything can somehow or other be neatly simplified and quantitifed. Many scientists and science educators do indeed have this view. It is then conveyed in elementary schools, secondary schools, and in colleges. However, some of our finest and most creative scientists have been the very ones to confirm, even in tightly controlled and simplified experiments that the object of the observation is actually changed by the very frame of reference and perception of the observer. As long as a person is involved in any experimentation (and it is impossible that a person not be involved, even in a totally automatic system, in at least the design) there will be subjective bias involved. As I've heard it said about objectivity, "The only time you get real objectivity is when no one is talkin' to nobody about nothin.'" One of the phrases I most dislike is, "Now let's be objective about this!" Werner Heisenberg, one of the eagles of physics, has expressed it well in the following words, "we have to remember that what we observe is not nature in itself, but nature exposed to our method of questioning." Heisenberg's uncertainty principle, a major operating principle of science today, states that, at least at subatomic levels, the mere act of observation affects what we are observing. This is clearly true of social and educational observations, and I suspect that it may apply to many macroscopic areas of the physical and biological spheres of interest as well as to the psychological and social ones.

There is no such thing as really objective consciousness, and I want to help convey this idea in any interaction I have with other people. I also want to remember this in my own work lest I get overly confident about the significance of my ideas.

OBSERVATION, PERCEPTION, AND THE EXPANSION OF AWARENESS

> In the sense of unaware and as yet unlearned, our ignorance and our recognition of that ignorance may be the best motivation both for problem-solving and for creative activity.
>
> —Norman Hackerman

There is always a great deal more there than I can ever see. Put several people together and let each observe independently and each will see some slightly different things than the others. A group as a whole may add other things to the list as well. A blind or deaf person may add whole new dimensions of observations through touch, sound, or other kinds of perception that we "normal" people have let get rusty or have somehow never developed and refined. Perceptions and a very refined sense of awareness of my own process of observation are exceedingly important aspects of learning and creative activity that too often receive short shrift from both research scientists, scholars in other other areas, and from teachers working with students. Observation is often made out to be a cut and dried process. This is the one thing it absolutely is not. How do you "tune your eye" to see certain things or to measure with great precision?

How well do we use our senses in general? Probably only partially and very poorly at that. People (like Charles Tart) involved in the study of perception and workers who have recently experimented with so-called expanded states of consciousness and within the area of so-called extra-sensory perception suggest that we have a whole range of observational powers that we do not use. I am eagerly beginning to explore these potentialities within myself. How to pursue them effectively, I don't know yet. That's part of the problem-centered approach I want to use.

Bruner and Postman describe a study in which observers were shown a series of playing cards and asked to identify them after only momentary exposure. In the deck were a red six of spades and a black five of hearts. It took many exposures before any of the observers noticed that something was wrong. Their expectations and prior training (see spades as blacks and hearts as red) affected their observations strongly. Some observers never did spot that there was an anomaly of some kind in the deck. Familiarity with "normal" decks of cards structured perception and actually blocked observational capability.

In another study of perception, Simon and Chase compared the behavior of grandmasters in chess to that of experts and ordinary players. Using 25 pieces placed in real chess contexts on the board, they asked the players to try to reproduce the positions of the 25 pieces after short viewing time (a few seconds). The grandmasters showed 93 percent retrieval capabilities in 2 to 10 seconds of exposure time. Experts showed 72 percent retrieval, class A players 50 percent and novices only 33 percent. However, when the 25 pieces were **randomly** placed rather than being placed in reasonable chess positions, all players, from novice to grandmaster could recall the positions of only 3 or 4 pieces, on the average (12-16 percent)! We are thus not dealing with photographic memory as a pre-requisite for becoming a grandmaster. Practice and experience in knowing the **context** of chess apparently is most important. Perceptions and observational "powers" again are strongly conditioned by experience and by what the grandmasters **expect** to see on the board but which the novices don't yet know to expect there. Experience helps or hinders depending on what you're trying to do. It may hinder discovery of the unusual, but it facilitates operating under "normal" conditions and in improving or embellishing an existing context. New contexts may be overlooked if they are too incongruent.

Jonathan feels that we limit students who work with us so that they see the same things we do. We teach them to observe the same things we observe. We train them to see through **our** own eyes. (In extreme cases they even get graded down for not seeing the things we have seen and they get no "extra credit" for seeing more than we have.) Even if I'm not involved in "training" them, I know that I unconsciously, through lack of fuller awareness of the relationship between learners and myself, invite them to see as I see or fail to help them become aware of a dependency or an imitative approach that we allow to grow.

If we teach others to see through our eyes we set up a static and basically fruitless approach in which we retain more and more information about the same old things (which, it is true, may gradually be firmed up and modified as a result). For myself, I prefer to extend my own organism and to seek ways of facilitating great increases in observational and perceptual powers of people who choose to work and learn with me. I want for them to develop their own eyes and to bring to bear the unique resources of their own organisms.

As I have been writing most of this manuscript I have puzzled over the relationship of awareness, my total experience of myself and the world and "science."

> *As I wrote the last sentence, I started out with, "As I have worked on...." Then I crossed out the "worked on" because I became aware that the writing has not really been "working on." Things flow into me and the words flow off the end of the pen. I am pleased that my awareness led me to change that phrase. If it's really "work" do I want to do it? Work is usually something one does for someone else. If I reject this notion, then my whole attitude toward what I do during so-called "work-time" changes. My life flows in an unaccustomed way.*

I keep wondering as I look at rocks and more or less automatically attach names to them, "What in the world do I care if this is called a mica schist and that is called a rhomb porphyry?" As Lucretia wonders about the name of this flower or that, I think to myself "Who cares?"

As I walked around downtown Trondheim last week I found a big construction site where people were busy. Only they weren't building a new office building. They were delicately scraping away the dirt from old remains dating back to well before 1000 A. D. Old house floors and foundations lay unearthed. Part of a human leg bone was sticking out of a bank, still unexcavated. A 1000-year-old skull lay there with its excavator's cap jauntily perched atop it. Each piece was being catalogued, mapped as to vertical and horizontal location. Hours, weeks, years of analysis would go into these things. So what?

One day we took a boat out to the bird rocks on the west side of the island of Runde, near Ålesund. Literally millions of birds — gulls, terns, puffins, gannets, razorbills — filled the sky, layer after layer, flying about, diving, zooming. They looked like a cloud of gnats from our position in the motor launch. On the cliffs sat other birds squawking, beeping, chirping. Red numbers painted below many of the nests indicated that someone was keeping track of something or the other related to the nest occupants. Can you imagine a life of fighting your way through all of those nasty-tempered sea birds to seek more information about how they live?

Then I think of the bird watchers who spend hours and hours identifying birds, checking them off on lists, differentiating among them. Who cares?

> "I don't rejoice in insects at all," Alice explained, "because I'm rather afraid of them — at least the large kinds. But I can tell you the names of some of them."
> "Of course they answer to their names?" the gnat remarked carelessly.
> "I never knew them to do it."
> "What's the use of their having names," the gnat said, "if they won't answer to them?"
> "No use to **them**," said Alice, "but it's useful to the people that name them, I suppose. If not, why do things have names at all.
> —Lewis Carrol

And back to geology, think of the people who do that same thing with minerals — always differentiating, arguing about whether this one is indeed like that one or whether they are actually different.

And how about the chemist who discovers a new reaction and has it named after him? Months, years of laboratory work, dumping one chemical into a bunch of others and recording what happens. Or the physicist hanging weights on springs or shooting neutrons through an accelerator to see what effect is produced on some material or other, what "new particles," are interpreted from the tracks in a cloud chamber?

As I pore over my geological map of Norway, I wonder why in the world waste time thinking about whether the map says I am travelling over Devonian rocks or Precambrian and whether or not the axial surfaces of the folds are horizontal or vertical. Don't I reduce my awareness of what is around me and limit it by my preoccupation with detail? Theodore Roszak points out that the value of a map is forfeited for the person who forgets that the map is not the landscape itself. If we get lost in the detail of maps, we end up with inexperienced and shallow knowledge. Wise explorers know how important it is to have, in addition to the map, a native guide who knows the hidden resources and danger spots of the country and how we can best live there.

When I first decided that a "scholarly life" interested me I looked around for a field that might be worth pursuing. I finally rejected romance languages because, for one reason, I conjured up a mental image of myself sitting in a dingy library cubicle counting commas in the work of some obscure French poet. I finally decided upon science, and geology more specifically because I associated the idea of an outdoor life with that image. I was a little concerned because I also saw the geologist in my mind's eye as a person who always traveled with his eyes to the ground. I wasn't sure that I wanted to keep my eyes and awareness down at that level. I wanted to have them open to as many things as possible. Sure enough, I found out that I can turn geology into just counting quartz grains, the same as I could have turned French into just counting commas. In the long run, the "field" didn't really seem to matter much. I can do **anything** with my eyes to the ground or my attention limited to the number of quartz grains, commas, brush strokes on a painting, beats to the measure, batting averages of baseball players, or whatever else.

But I suddenly realized the other day that I can **use** even the so-called limiting aspects of "scientific observation" as a way of expanding my awareness rather than of limiting it.

> *I can limit my awareness or let it be expanded. I can concentrate completely on my writing at this moment, or I can be aware of the chuff-chuff of a diesel engine, of pretty, scantily clad Norwegian girls on their way to the beach via the path below, of the big, A-shaped porch on which I am sitting and writing this morning, of the way the shadows move as I wait until the sun comes around onto me later this morning, of the pines, woods, rocks, and rocky bay below. Perhaps my writing flows better as I include these awarenesses and use them rather than closing them out as I "concentrate on my writing."*

Take the way the shadows are moving around the house below me right now. Awareness of the whole astronomical aspect of that movement somehow makes me feel richer.

The bird island: At first, there was just a cloud of birds and bird shadows. They all looked alike. Then suddenly, a birdlover aboard the boat started to exclaim. And I was aware of not one kind of bird, but of many kinds. My awareness expanded from "bird" to lots of different kinds of birds. Each bird is just as unique as each human being. There are probably no two exactly alike and yet certain groups of individuals do live together, mate, have similar instincts, and behaviors. Diversity, uniqueness, and yet integration and togetherness. I know more, feel more, enjoy more about the whole through appreciating the uniqueness of the individuals and the common properties of the groups.

I can find joy in my awareness of a single pine needle, blade of grass, rock sample, salmon swimming in the river, wave in the bay, star, whatever I want to perceive.

In order to **name** things (objective consciousness??) I must first **see**. In seeing, I perceive and become more aware. Classifications, dull as I can make them be if I choose to, suddenly help me to expand my consciousness and to look deeper. Who cares what the name of that flower is? Caring helps me to see more.

Of course I can also choose to see just a speckled green and gold mat on the ground below my balcony, too. I can choose to see any tree only as a tree. And that's all right, too, as long as **I** choose to do it that way. I'm beginning to think though that I **can** be aware of both generality and detail at the same time and that the two somehow enhance each other and increase my overall joy and pleasure.

Perhaps I can learn to transcend the need for classifications and scientific reductions as aids to my awareness. Maybe I can eventually get myself "tuned in" so that I become fully aware of both uniqueness and generality in some kind of tacit way where words, verbalizations and mental "processing" are not necessary. But if I don't take my "scientificness" too seriously, I can accept as worthwhile for me verbalizations, descriptions, and "objectivity."

Maps are something I find myself poring over a good deal. Sometimes I catch myself riding along in a car, or sitting in the middle of an incredible new area and looking at maps of the area rather than the area itself spread out all around me. Am I limiting myself? The map is an abstraction of the reality around me. But the other day I realized again that maps also expand my whole concept of that reality. They limit me and at the same time allow me to expand my perception. I look for new aspects of both detail and generality. The map becomes a guide to a deepening and more acute awareness. Here I am, a fly speck on an enormous world in an infinite universe and yet maps, diagrams, "scientific interpretations" help me to stand back and obtain at least a spark of a whole new level of awareness about me, you, and "out there."

I guess "scientific observation" and the use of science as such is neither good nor bad in itself. It isn't something that I either "should" or "should not" engage in. What is important is my attitude toward it and how I integrate it into my whole life, how I allow it either to limit me or to expand myself more than I could have done otherwise. The choice of how I approach it and use it is mine.

AUTHORITY

> The authority of the teachers is generally prejudicial to those who desire to learn.
>
> --Cicero
>
> Our pedantic eagerness to instruct is always leading us to teach children what they can learn better for themselves...
>
> —W. Boyd, discussing Jean Jacques Rousseau

Frequently, scholarship appears to be very much authority-based. Almost any scholarly article contains a long reference list that ties the investigation back to earlier ideas and work. A great many things are taken for granted on the basis of earlier workers' statements. To a degree, this is necessary, for if I were to challenge every observation that every other person had ever made I would always have to start back at ground zero and there would be little cumulative growth of knowledge. We would have no "shoulders of giants" to step upon. Generally I come to trust certain kinds of measurements and observations that other people have made and am willing to build further on the data and ideas they have produced. Polanyi has emphasized how the growth of knowledge is dependent on acceptance of other people's work. Yet learners must learn to evaluate other people's authoritative statements and not accept them completely uncritically, either.

If I check out some of another person's data and find a discrepancy between his and mine, I may seek the reason for the discrepancy. Did the other person measure "incorrectly?" Is my measurement faulty? Or is there some other, and potentially more exciting reason for the difference that may tell me more about either the world "out there," about our measuring techniques, or about us as human observers? Thus I want always to maintain a healthy and active scepticism of what anyone else says about the world out there. But I want to use other people's ideas to best advantage in taking short cuts to increasing my own knowledge, too. There is some kind of balance between acceptance and rejection of what other people tell me and I will swing back and forth over this balance point. Sometimes I will be "taken in" by being too accepting. At other times I will waste time verifying older work, that I cannot improve on. I am not worried about not always being "dead-center" because that is not the nature of my organism. I want always to become more and more aware of when I am accepting an authority-based statement and when I am prepared to reject it.

Textbooks are generally terrible perpetrators of the authority problem. Few textbooks (and many technical books and articles as well) emphasize that even the most positive statements they make are only approximations. I am convinced that there is no such thing as a complete and absolute answer to any problem about the total world I live in. There are only weak and incomplete but successive approximations to "truth."

I prefer to see more stress on what we don't know, which exceeds by an unknown but probably infinite amount what we do know. About a year and a half after I first began lecturing on geology Bill Merrill expressed interest in seeing some of my lecture notes. He later mentioned to me some concerns about my emphasis on how little we know and how far we had to go. So much emphasis on the uncertainties might discourage beginning students who might prefer something more definite and secure to begin with. I never have found this to be so. In general I find learners far more intrigued by what things can be done and by uncertainty and opportunity for new explorations and experiences in new directions than by emphasis on a museum full of old ideas. I find so many learners ready and eager to participate in the real processes of original investigation rather than spending their time reading over what the authorities have to say about "how it is."

This feeling of dealing only with approximations makes it impossible for me to condone the multiple-choice tests that accompany so many science experiences in schools. I laugh when I recall a Regents'-Examination question on the "correct" explanation for the retreat of Niagara Falls. A study of the falls in the late sixties showed that the correct Regent's-exam answer was indeed no longer "correct." Yet students continued to be marked right on the discredited answer for at least 2 or 3 years after that. The idea that any explanation can really be called "right" or "wrong" is not acceptable to me any more. Even the most elementary "fact" is subject to the limitations of the measurer or observer and his frame of reference and technique. When you start getting into the area of hypotheses and ideas then there really can be only discussion. It is not even possible to ask someone to respond to the question, "What was Romey's explanation for +++?" My explanation would have been subject to the limitations of my ability to communicate. Of course, I suppose you could ask a student to "reproduce the diagram from p. 23 of your textbook" or "quote Romey's third sentence from p. 76" and then assign a right-or-wrong index.

Barry Stevens, referring to quoting authority, points out that such practice can tie her to the other person's thinking. In truth, she writes, what she does with someone else's thinking becomes her own. By claiming it as her own through her use of it, she takes full responsibility for this use. She feels that by referring to authority she could be looked at as avoiding responsibility for the idea later.

I accept full responsibility for use of your idea, Barry Stevens, even though I give you credit as an authority here! Your writing helps me clarify my own ideas, and I look at this as a way of saying, "I like what you say; I like it so much that I want to take it up myself and send it out again as mine when I write to others." Do we somehow fuse with other people when we allow a part of them to come into us in this way? This procreative notion fascinates me: I am inseminated by your paragraph, which enters me as I write this, and I produce a paragraph to which both of us have added genetic material. I have felt other people fuse with me when we have shared a feeling or an insight. This is knowing in an almost biblical sense.

IMITATION

As we were driving along yesterday, Cricket said to William, "Please put down your window."

As soon as it was down, Lucretia said, "Please put the window back up; I'm cold."

Gretchen said, "Why don't you leave it half way," as William closed it completely.

He said "I like to have it either all the way up or down so I don't have to look through a line in the middle of my window."

"You always have to imitate Dad!" said Cricket, referring to the way I had made exactly the same statement previously.

Imitation!

I have mixed-up feelings about it.

Right after I have seen some really first-class tennis players in action and watched them closely, my own tennis game picks up for awhile as I try to do what I have seen them do.

I imitate other people both consciously and unconsciously. Now that I am working to be more aware of my own processes I want for this to be less and less unconsciously. If I do it, I want to know it so I can decide for myself whether or not I really want to keep it in my own personal repertory of behaviors.

As I have written parts of this book, I have been reading things by Barry Stevens, Carl Rogers, John Stevens, and other writers interested in problems of awareness. Sometimes I have gotten an uncomfortable feeling that as I describe my own immediate awarenesses I might appear to be imitating their styles of writing. I am describing my own unique awareness, but how much is even the way I look at myself and talk about myself influenced by the way they say they have gone about their search for greater awareness? I think of talks I have given, things I have written, even some expressions that I like to use sometimes that I know I "picked up" from Bob Samples.

"Whom did you pick that up from?"

Cricket picks things up from people so readily. She copies pronunciations, ways of walking, phrases and sentences, silly talk of various kinds.

In summer camp, years ago, several of us developed our own special accent—"The Haccent"—and always used it in talking to each other (often to the distress of parents and other adults with us in public places). We still use it when we meet. We imitated each other a good deal.

When I was a little boy I recall going to vocal concerts with my father. He used to say, "One of the main reasons I want to go is to see how he breathes when he sings this one." My father, seriously interested in singing, used these professionals as models to help him improve his own singing capability.

When a child learns language, it's entirely by a process of imitation. Because of my own special interest in language, I consciously repeat things after people. When I hear a sound or a phrase done "just right" so that I really **know** how it was made, I want to repeat it, to roll it over on my tongue right away. Sometimes I want to get away from a person I am talking with so that I can repeat and practice the phrase I've just heard that person say. I like to go over those language records you listen to and repeat, listen and repeat, listen and repeat.

A couple of days ago as we strolled down a street in Alesund, talking English together, a couple of young Norwegians were following us at close range. Soon they passed us, repeating in English, in an exaggerated way, some of the English words we were using. My first feeling was annoyance, as if they were making fun of us. Then as I listented to them, I realized that they were just mouthing and practicing our English words in the same way I do Norwegian words when I follow Norwegians in the same way, trying to hear them and learn how to say their words.

Sometimes I find myself "practicing" a word or phrase I have just heard (even some words or a phrase I've just heard in English). Many times someone I know has come up on me by surprise and asked me why I'm making a face or has said, "Hm! Talking to yourself again, eh?"

I like to repeat things after people in various parts of the English-speaking world to see if I can copy accents in English. Last night I was at a get-together where our hosts and their friends were imitating various Norwegian dialects just the way I do with English ones. When I hear German spoken, my mouth automatically purses into an umlaut position.

I'm always struck by the way you can identify the students of some teachers. They dress like their teachers, wear the same kinds of clothes, adopt the same way of speaking. A good game in larger, college-level field-trip groups involves guessing which people are whose students.

Do people who work with me imitate me in the same way?

How much of my behavior is really "derivative" behavior that I have "picked up" by imitation?

I value uniqueness, being an individual, being free. And yet how much of my own learning and being is conditioned by what I see others do.

Look at **Sesame Street**. Learning by imitative play. **Strictly.**

One of the things I object to about television is the way it spreads verbal expressions and certain facial expressions and body language all over the U.S. in a matter of seconds. All of a sudden 200,000,000 people seem to be saying, "Sock-it-to-me!", "Sorry about that!", or "Would you believe...?" at once.

I think "Can't you think of anything original to say?" And yet, to me the phrase was "cute" and repeatable at first, too. But the commercials and programs continue to beat it in, Sesame-Street style, week after week. A phrase becomes faddish, moves in, is incorporated into wider behavior patterns, and its origin is forgotten. We become unaware of it as it is assimilated into our own language.

And yet, do I have the time and capacity to remain aware of where I picked up every word I use? I like to be aware of the origin of expressions I use. They can produce a momentary flashback or glow that recalls to me good feelings associated with a person or situation I especially associate with the phrase. Maybe there **is** room in me for an incredible awareness of the words and phrases I use, just like a rich warp upon which to loom today's weft. I am the sum of my experience, including my associations with other people, and I may become richer as I become increasingly aware of "where I got it from" and what I did with it in connection with my own processes.

Bill Bromery is interested in helping the education of black students in the geological sciences. Being one of a handful of black, PhD-level geologists in the U.S. he is conscious of his position as a role model—a man who has been successful. If he can do it, they can, is what they may be able to feel.

Jonathan told how one of his colleagues tried to imitate him in organizing a science class. It failed and the colleague blamed "the method." He could not **be** Jonathan. You can never be me, but maybe some of the things I do or talk about can be incorporated into your style.

"Incorporated!" That's a good word. "Put into the body of." Really assimilated and made a real part of me. At that point it's not imitation anymore. Then it's really part of me. If it's in-corporated then it can't fail to bear unique marks of me rather than you.

I talk a lot about apprenticeship-type learning. If I use "good" lab procedures and people work with me, they'll pick up good lab procedures. I won't even have to force it. No exams or coercion necessary; they'll do it without even knowing it. Trouble is, that also leads to their picking up my bad or inefficient habits to.

As I go out to make observations of natural systems, learners go with me and become aware of the way in which I take notes and observe. Whether I want them or not, they can (and do) begin to see things through my eyes. This is good to a point, because I may see much more than they do at first. Carlos Castaneda, as Don Juan's apprentice, only learns to "see" with help from Don Juan, although Don Juan never really "shows" Carlos how. Carlos has to learn and even to find out what "seeing" is by himself. Don Juan supports him in this quest and instructs him in the methods of sorcerers. But Carlos must learn to **see** all by himself. Perhaps the methods help. Perhaps the awareness of people who spend time with me expands if they **begin** by imitating me. My awareness can be likewise expanded by imitating the ways in which others use their processes.

William Wiley had the following to say about imitation when asked how he felt about having people imitate his art:

> If I imitated other people's work I don't see why they shouldn't imitate mine. It is like whether you are going to share your food or not. To think that you aren't influenced by everyone and everything you come in contact with is a great fallacy.

Imitation has always been one of the fundamental processes in learning, and it will continue to be so. I accept that I imitate and that others imitate me. But there is an important point of balance involved. It lies in how aware I am of when I am imitating. I want to be able to be aware that I am imitating and this may then help my functioning.

To the extent that I am aware, I can be free. To the extent that I imitate without awareness of my own processes I am not unique and am probably not developing my own potential as a human being, learner, facilitator, producer, or creator. I want to be aware of when others close to me imitate me, so we can deal with their awareness of this. They may grow faster and in more appropriate directions for them if they are aware enough of their own processes.

REDUCTIONISM VERSUS HOLISIM

Keep your eye upon the donut
And not upon the hole!

— Donut Shop Doggerel

Much scientific and scholarly activity is reductionist in nature. Experimenters make models of natural systems by reducing the number of variables they deal with. In so doing they make it possible to test the relationships between one variable and one or two or three others. Natural systems don't work that way, however. In natural systems, large numbers of components interact under conditions that may be constantly fluctuating. Nature knows nothing about standard temperature and pressure.

In studies of the chemistry of the earth, some experimenters study simplified systems and get precise (and if lucky, even reproducible!) results about systems that do not exist in nature. Then they look at descriptions provided by field geologists. Looking at the two kinds of evidence together they try to infer how certain kinds of rocks and ultimately how the earth's crust evolved, how it is like it is, and how its various components are distributed.

Other experimenters take plain, old, garden-variety rocks and use these for laboratory experimentation. They get various effects and results, but they can give no precise explanations of what interacted with what to produce what. So many components exist in natural rocks that little can be said about the details of chemical reaction that must have occurred under experimentation. Again, they must appeal to the descriptive evidence of field geologists about the distribution of rock types in nature in an attempt to zero in on what is **reasonable.** Always we return to the subjective judgement of the investigator to make any conclusions.

Physicists have had to reduce variables to an enormous extent in their attempts to arrive at general "laws" for the operation of the universe. When I think about how much they have simplified things and I look at the real complexity of natural systems I keep wondering if the general case of the laws simply doesn't mean much, so much is each natural situation unique and special.

I reduce things when I do geological work of my own. I go out into the field and find a rock outcrop. In order to analyze it I measure the orientation in space of certain planes and lines that I observe in the rock as it confronts me. My measurements represent only a tiny sample of all of the possible measurements I could make. In some places the larger mass of rock is very complex and then the question arises: "Are my measurements representative?" I reduce complexity to the relative simplicity of "what is representative." To do this I use my subjective judgement with all of the intuition and the summation of my total experience that it involves. I may collect a rock sample. A sample is a reduction. Is it really representative? I can make a whole study on the representativeness of my sample. I could invest months of work in that alone. I would come out with a range of sample types, and the range would perhaps show me one that statistically is more common than the extremes of difference. Different types may grade into each other or they may be sharply different. When I take the sample to the lab I may crush it up—more reduction. I may separate out the various types of minerals, I may take a sample of the mineral separate and then I may analyze that—several more stages of reduction represented in that experience! I may analyze the powder of the whole rock. To do this I keep reducing and separating the amount until gradually a few grains of dust are assumed to be representative of a hand sample that represents a tiny (but representative?) sample of an outcrop that is a tiny (but representative??) sample of a mountainside, which is a tiny (but representative???) sample of a range of mountains. I may get interested in individual mineral grains. New instruments now make it possible to focus down with an electron microprobe to a spot with a diameter of only one micron—one millionth of a meter across!—and to determine the chemical composition of the material at that spot.

In studies of lunar rocks, every new rock sample received and studied at first led to a revised explanation of the origin of the moon, the earth, and the universe. The lunar samples are carved up and, after each prospective investigator submits a detailed proposal about what he is going to do with the sample, he receives a tiny slice or hunk of rock or even just a vial of dust. No chance even to look at the larger hunks. They are mainly observed within huge, closed observation centers where they are touched only by remote control before being sawed up and sent out. Data from the very first tiny piece of lunar material that was studied here on earth provided the basis for a whole bunch of general statements about the history and origin of the moon. Even the first remote-controlled partial analysis sent back by the Surveyor satellites provided lunar scientists with an opportunitiy to spend thousands upon thousands of man-hours of human energy making hypotheses and general statements based upon what had to be assumed as representative and accurate data.

Nuclear physicists continue to find new elementary particles that are so tiny and short-lived that they never have been seen. Only their traces are found.

Biologists keep reducing their field of vision to smaller and smaller levels so that details of movement of elements at cell walls, the structure of cell nuclei and incredible aspects of microchemistry are studied. More and more powerful electron microscopes allow them to look deeper and deeper. Molecular biology is at a high point. Some people now specialize in biology and become professionals without even looking at live animals or plants.

How does the old saying go: As scientists grow older they learn more and more about less and less until finally they know everything about nothing at all?

To a considerable extent there is pressure to avoid the super-reductionist trap these days. Problems of the environment compel us to look at the world as a whole and the interactions of its living and non-living components on a large scale. We have to look at populations of animals and plants and how the whole population is doing. Here again, though, the notion of a population is a reduction-a simplication, for each member of every population of living things is a distinct and unique individual. Systems approaches are reductions, too.

In the earth sciences the recently expanding views of continental drift and plate tectonics are leading earth scientists to look for larger interactions instead of always down at the smaller and smaller ones. Views of small things sometimes provide triggers that help in the understanding of larger ones.

The increase in our understanding of atomic nuclei and of the smallest elementary particles can lead to greater understanding of the universe as a whole and of life itself. That is, if you believe in the atom! The atom is still—remember—just a reductionist concept. No one has yet seen an atom. We only infer its existence from a number of lines of descriptive evidence and theoretical considerations.

Leo Laporte said that he had woken up one morning at the age of 37 and realized that he had passed the crest of what he called "the actuarial parabola"—halfway through life. And where was he? He began to have a strong feeling of shortcomings in the reductionist approach he had taken; he expressed a feeling of traveling down a long tunnel that got narrower and narrower until he could hardly see any light at all from the small end. He started becoming interested again at looking at things as wholes.

Separating ourselves into "disciplines" called biology, physics, chemistry, psychology, sociology, geology, math, anthropology, art, literature and so forth may be one of the key ways that we limit our horizons and narrow ourselves. In Leonardo da Vinci's work, suggests Robert Hughes, it is not even possible to draw a line between art and science. His painting becomes a method for studying the earth's structure. It is, "the empiricism of sight itself." Leonardo's drawings of purely scientific and descriptive intent still have incredible aesthetic power. I think many people in the various disciplines simply are not really aware of the way they have allowed themselves to narrow their views to fit into narrow compartments. "Oh, we can't work on that here. This is biology class. You'll have to wait until chemistry for that, and chemistry is always offered in eleventh grade." Or, "Oh, you can't deal with that problem now, not until you've had two years of calculus, three physics courses, and chemistry through physical chemistry."

More and more I find myself wanting to look at my world as a whole. I realize that in a holistic approach I may need to make certain reductions—perhaps often. But I write here more of an attitude than anything else. As long as I continue to be truly aware of the limitations and risks of reducing things I can keep my eyes raised and be open to a larger view. I want more and more to treat my world and to be aware of it as the fullest world possible with the most fulfilled people possible in it. Generalization and reduction may help me to understand and to know, but I do not want to lose sight of the uniqueness of natural configurations and of individual people and animals. The specific becomes very much more important to me than the general, which may be only a reductionist invention. And yet, is there also some ultimate, transcendent unity into which we all fuse?

RANDOMNESS OR ORDER? CERTAINTY?

> I can, if the worst comes to the worst, still realize that the Good Lord may have created a world in which there are no natural laws. In short, a chaos. But that there should be statistical laws with definite solutions, i.e. laws which compel the Good Lord to throw the dice in each individual case, I find highly disagreeable.
>
> —A. Einstein

Albert Einstein assumed a great underlying order for the universe. In this particular he joins many other physicists, past, present, and future. If there is order, we ought to be able to write general laws to which there are no real exceptions and we ought to be able to predict what can and cannot happen, how it will happen, and perhaps even when. Einstein was upset by ideas such as Heisenberg's uncertainty principle and Bohr's complimentarity principle. These led to the view that there is a great deal of randomness in the universe, and that the only real generality may be a statistical one rather than one that applies to specific cases. It emphasizes the important role of specificity and uniqueness.

If I believe in substantial randomness in nature, my approach to knowing changes. Everything is more open to question. There become fewer pat, authority-established answers. Maybe none. The way I help people learn most certainly is set and governed from outside. I have to accept more fully my own responsibility for myself and my own actions once my uniqueness is more fully legitimized in a more largely random world.

Konrad Krauskopf, in an article entitled "A tale of 10 plutons," shows how different 10 different masses of granite are that he has had experience with during a lifetime of geological work. Rather than trying to lump them and generalize, he dwells on this uniqueness and poses the question of randomness in nature. F.J. Turner expresses dismay at the way the lunar geologists have tried to apply earth classifications to groups of rock materials which appear to have great differences from earth rocks. True, similarities suggest the operation of similar processes, but one can too easily overlook the differences by too-eager comparison and generalization.

An important concept contributed to science through geology is the notion of uniformitarianism. This suggests that the past can only be understood in terms of our understanding of present-day processes. I like this emphasis on process and flow. If we really understand todays processes, we may also be able to predict future **kinds** of happenings and developments, too. However, the actual ways in which processes occur may change, too, as well as the more superficial changes that any part of a process by itself can cause. In earlier periods of the earth's development some different environmental conditions and processes must have existed in order to permit the creation of earth features and rock types which do not seem to be forming today. In these cases we can't use present-day processes to explain such occurrences, because the processes that formed them have ceased to occur, due to significant changes in the overall environment of the earth. These features and processes which might have created them are often referred to as "preactualistic." If I accept this idea, it reinforces further my infatuation with the idea of uniqueness in the physical world as well as among humans.

PROBLEM-CENTERING VERSUS METHOD-CENTERING

Abraham Maslow devoted much attention to the differences between what he termed problem-centered versus method-centered approaches to science and other areas of knowing. To me this becomes a key distinction that affects my concept of how I want to be involved in both helping people learn and how I want to seek further knowledge of my own.

In method-centering, an investigator or a learner begins by developing his competence in a method or methods of approach to a problem. He learns the skills associated with a certain kind of microbiology, field ecology, ornithology, history, or political science. Then he seeks problems of interest that allow him to use his skills. This leads a nuclear physicist to choose problems in nuclear physics, a steroid chemist to choose problems in steroid chemistry, a nuclear-magnetic-resonance man to choose problems involving the use of his apparatus, the electron microprobe specialist to search out samples and materials suitable for studies with his instrument and the professional educator to study what he knows he can measure in a "clean," acceptable way. It is at the heart of the disciplinary approach to knowledge and is related to what T.S. Kuhn calls "normal science." Geologists deal with rocks, mammalogists with mammals, organic chemists with organic compounds.

Method-centering leads into the approaches that presently predominate in education. In these the presumption of a hierarchical kind of learning is made: "You can't study that until you have first learned this." Generalized rules of method are established which assume that all people — unique as they are — will more or less fit into the prescribed order and scheme. At one time you couldn't work on physical chemistry until you had already been through descriptive general chemistry, qualitative analysis, and quantitative analysis first. Now, because someone decided to try it, physical chemistry has become a part of most introductions to chemistry. Is that even "good?" My view would be, for some people, yes, for other people, no.

Method-centering restricts the field of operation in both research and in education. It sets up conditions under which people tend to confine their efforts to problems for which methods of approach already exist. This leads to more and more studies of the same kinds. True, it may lead to greater refinement, but it may not necessarily, in fact it probably will not lead to a real broadening of our potential knowledge.

Problem-centering, on the other hand, begins with a question I am interested in solving. "I wonder what would happen if...?; I wonder what causes...?; I wonder how....?" How to approach the question, consideration of method, does not enter into the initial posing of the problem. Once the problem of interest is posed, there are lots of ways of following up on it:

> Has someone else already tried to get some answers that may satisfy me?
>
> Does my past experience equip me to handle the question easily? If not, am I willing to seek new experiences that will equip me?
>
> Can I find other people to work with who, as a team, can bring to bear on this problem the kind of power we may need?
>
> Are there existing methods that might be applied to the problem? If not, is the problem important enough to go ahead and plunge in, inventing approaches as we need them?

In problem-centering, boundaries between disciplines blur and even disappear. If there are linguistic aspects of the problem, then some attempt will have to be made to deal with them whether I am trained in linguistics or not. (For linguistics, in the above sentence, substitute the names of other disciplines you want and keep reciting the sentence over and over until you tire of the exercise).

Problem-centering allows me to ask any questions. The only "unaskable" questions are those we think we don't have a way of answering. If we center on the problem itself we may find a way of answering a question that didn't exist earlier, all because we have taken a positive ("I want to know") approach rather than a negative approach ("No one has ever been able to do this before").

In problem-centering I may get into messy stuff. Because I am really exploring rather than treading on a well-trodden path. I may have to try unconventional things. People may say "That's not scientific!" By this statement they acknowledge a narrow view of what science is. Maslow suggests, "What needs doing, is worth doing even though not very well." On the other hand, "What isn't worth doing, isn't worth doing well." The first approaches to any problems—the most exciting ones—must of necessity be tentative and full of errors to be corrected and guesses to be refined. If the gathering of knowledge is indeed a series of successive approximations and if, as I believe, it is impossible ever to know everything about anything, then you have to start somewhere with any problem. However "bad" the first attempt may later seem, it was a start. This is one of the reasons I am so much inclined to defer judgements of "good" and "bad" with respect to the gaining of knowledge, either by young learners in schools or by senior researchers in their labs. Knowledge shown later to be inadequate or unsatisfying for some reason may then be replaced by more adequate and more satisfying knowledge. No need for judgements of bad and good. Only a need to allow things to keep flowing and for the approximations to get better all the time. Somewhere I saw a statement, "Failure is bad. Experimentation often results in failure. It therefore obtains that nothing should ever be done for the first time."

The effect of problem-centering in education is to open up the classroom. It destroys distinctions between chemistry, physics, biology, earth science, math, integrated science, music, art, language arts, industrial arts, and physical education. It demands abandonment of the process of going through textbooks chapter by chapter. It says to the learner: "What is an important problem you want to work on?" And it gives permission for the learners then to pursue that problem.

Barry Stevens suggests that it might not even be necessary to start with a problem! Problems will emerge on their own without any need to seek them out. Then, all we need do is let our lives flow and respond to exciting and compelling situations as they appear before us.

FORMALITY VERSUS INFORMALITY

In many ways scientific inquiry and scholarship in other areas comprise formal procedures. "Science" and "scholarship" convey to many people a note of stiffness, conservatism, methodicalness, and organizedness. The scholar and scientist appear as otherworldly eccentrics. Representation of "the scientist" in popular literature, in advertisements and elsewhere in the popular media frequently show "the scientist" in white lab coat. Professional meetings confirm the same image of academic formality. Rows of scholars sit stiffly listening to colleagues reading seemingly interminable papers where ideas are couched in what seem to be an obscure, mystical, and incomprehensible language. We joke about this image, but it is real in the eyes of many people, including some scholars and scientists and many teachers as well. Something in our educational system and the way scholars represent themselves perptuates this image.

Scientists and scholars in other areas are as unique, unpredictable, and different as any other group of people with some vaguely common interests and modes of operating. Bill Fyfe, a fine geochemist who has been honored with numerous international medals, operated in just about the most informal way you could imagine. He seemed prepared to take all sorts of risks, to jump into any sort of problem he was interested in, and to try it. His lab was always a beehive of activity, with debris everywhere. Somehow out of that hodge-podge emerged sophisticated, intuitive, solidly based studies of great significance. Sharing many of the same facilities in the same department was Adolf Pabst, an orderly and meticulous person for whom everything had a place and everything was in its place. If you worked with him, you observed strict rules of carefully formalized procedures and care of equipment. Pabst also is a highly respected, internationally known mineralogist who has behind him a long lifetime of significant and prolific contributions. Both are warm human beings. Fyfe in the same informal way that is reflected in his working style, Pabst in the more formal way expressed in the organization of his laboratory.

For me, I prefer the informality and more immediate warmth and excitement of the intuitively organized, problem-centered group. I accept that others thrive better in the more formal, method-centered context. There is room for both and I feel it important to emphasize and enhance these differences. In general, science is too-much identified with a formal approach and schools tend to ignore largely or completely that a high degree of informality is necessary and useful for many learners and professionals.

A recent annual report from the Carnegie Institution in Washington, one of the world's leading research laboratories, describes an attempt at deformalization at one of their conferences in the following way:

> The format of the conference was unstructured and informal; there were few prearranged talks. Discussion proceeded spontaneously for most of the conference, and considerable effort was made to stimulate interaction and facilitate participation. For each session only a chairman was named and a topic outlined. Chairmen initiated the sessions with an overview or review of the topic at hand, and discussion — either as volunteered or solicited short talks, or free-form—proceeded spontaneously.
>
> The looser, more congenial atmosphere of the conference, combined with the pleasant country surroundings of Airlie House, encouraged the interaction desired by the organizers. There was both a confrontation of diverse views and a focusing of diverse expertise on the central subject of plate tectonics. The generation of excitement and the sharing of knowledge were immediate results. The outcome of the conference is expected to significantly affect the direction of research on the application of the tectonics model to earlier data.

Similarly at a recent lunar science conference an informal approach is reported to have led to a much higher level of communication than is common in scientific meetings.

Belver Griffith and Nicholas Mullins write of what they call "Invisible Colleges." These are groupings of scientists who discover a common interest in a given problem. They form an informal communicative group with intense interaction centered around their common interest. Examples include Bohr's quantum mechanics group, Delbruck's phage group, Skinner's operant conditioning group, and others. Gradually, as the interests of various members of the Invisible College change, the group begins to fade, even as its members find other affinity groups with which they may affiliate for further activity.

I want to help in the formation of such informal **affinity groupings** within any learning and working environment I am associated with. Rigid and formalized groupings that have fixed beginning and ending times (classes, courses, single-purpose research and development groups?) inhibit the freedom of migration that I feel is necessary to professional activity, work-life of all sorts and learning.

SERIOUSNESS VERSUS JOY AND FRIVOLITY

> You can think too much about life, and that interferes with the living of it....Life is the minute-to-minute living of it.
>
> —L. N. Tolstoy

Learning is supposed to be serious business. That's what usually kills it. Dan was scandalized when they used the lobby of his new building for flying paper airplanes. Loren waited until late one night to go racing around the corridors of our science building on his ten-speed bike. If I never allow myself to feel frivolous and to act frivolous in the place where I seek knowledge and **while** I'm doing it, I'll probably never try out any **really** playful ideas. Much personal growth and many important ideas result from playfulness and frivolity. These are important qualities that each of us has within himself or herself either close to the surface or, for some people, hidden down in the depths.

If a pleasing result gives me joy, then let me leap up in the air and shout it out.

Sometimes joy is in me without any special cause. It's just there. One winter's day I came whistling across a snow bank and Mary Jane came whistling across another from the other direction. We just ran up to each other, threw ourselves in each others arms, hugged and hugged, and spun around together laughing with glee! Then we skipped off, each in our own direction. We learn a lot together too!

I can't force joy or frivolity, but I want to accept and express them when I feel them. I want to accept them and their expression in others even when I don't feel them and don't want to participate.

A sense of the ridiculous may be important in seeking knowledge.

WHERE DO WE START?

One popular myth about the work of scientists is that their "method" involves starting with data and observations, making empirical generalizations, and then arriving at hypotheses to explain their observations. Most of us journeymen do indeed proceed in this way. However many of the big leaps in science happen the other way around. Ernst Mach, the physicist, considered that all knowledge derives from sensations. Einstein early accepted the notion that men delude themselves into enunciating as "laws of nature" what are actually summaries provided by their own senses, fallible as these are. Einstein wrote in an early journal, "colors, space, tones, etc. These are the only realities. Others do not exist." Later, Einstein departed more and more from this idea. In working out his theories of general and special relativity, Einstein started with **a priori** ideas about relativity because it seemed, intuitively, that the relationships he proposed must hold. He didn't particularly want to be confused with information and data at first and even proposed the idea that if the data didn't fit his theories then it must be the data that were wrong rather than the theory. Subsequent tests often confirmed his faith in his intuitive sense of what ought to be going on. Einstein trusted the functioning of his whole organism working in some unknown but integrated way. Many major new ideas have occurred in this way. Sometimes **a priori** generalizations turn out to be poor approximations of reality in the set of successive approximations that are called the search for truth.

Probably an Einstein could never make the kinds of intuitive leaps he did without access to a great deal of information and to a large matrix of ideas that started from observation and empiricism. But these two extreme approaches and everything in between them plus any other possible approaches all ultimately complement each other. Attempts to force a single, consensus approach are bound to be limiting. Fortunately there have always been brave renegades, controversial figures like Einstein who are confident enough of their unique powers that they pay little attention to the angry imprecations of the journeymen. I want to see environments developed that encourage and foster the kinds of new, obscure, outlandish, intuitive, "wrong" approaches of the eagles of science.

MODELS, FANTASY, AND MULTIPLE WORKING HYPOTHESES

When I examine myself and my methods of thought I come to the conclusion that the gift of fantasy has meant more to me than my talent for absorbing positive knowledge.

—A. Einstein

Cricket and I just went for a long walk over the mountain from Sykkylvsfjord toward Langenesvannet, a little mountain finger-lake. I purposely left my geology pick, camera, data book, surveying transit, and collecting bag behind. I wanted just to be aware of the mist hanging over the mountain, of the jig-saw puzzle of lichens on the rocks, the sheep-bells and cow-bells ringing around us, the transition from farm meadows through mountain-side forest into the alpine tundra on top, the blueberry plants we've been watching carefully to see the first signs of purple on the still-green berries, the bird calls, the stilling of the roar from one set of waterfalls as we went over the pass out of Sykkylvsfjord and the sounds of new ones as we descended on the other side, the purple, bell-shaped foxgloves we had not seen before, and many other things that over-attentiveness to the rocks might somehow have reduced in my awareness. It was Cricket who started to notice some beautiful slabs of colorful rock that lay broken along the trail. She asked how they formed and what they were called.

As I listened to myself explain, I was aware of the incredible number of assumptions included in every phrase I uttered and the gross oversimplification that even a more carefully detailed story would involve. It struck me how preposterous it is to pretend to know any part of the true story of those rocks that may have formed hundreds of millions of years ago. And yet the tale seems perfectly reasonable to me on the basis of my professional experience.

The best story I can make up is only a model of reality, whatever reality is. My story would change at least in its minor details and perhaps even in its basic form as I gathered or received new information on it.

My model, my knowledge, represents a fantasy trip of sorts as does any explanation I come up with. Virtually all such explanations share this quality of being only models of reality. The danger is that sometimes we ourselves come to believe our own stories and we convey to others with less technical knowledge that what we say is close to truth.

I was around recently when two professors from another university visited our learning community. When they happened upon a senior who was working busily on a problem and showed interest he began a long and much simplified explanation. He said things that someone might tell an entirely uninformed person. Our visitors suddenly realized that they had been cast in the roles of laymen and that they themselves regularly make similar explanations, turning what is already a model into an even more simplified model in order to make a point quickly. We alter our models in the details depending on the people we are addressing.

Sometimes I wonder why I care about these models, and then I realize that it is simply for the pleasure of knowing and playing in much the same way that I might play chess with William. The game enhances my awareness and pleasure in what I observe. I have been interested to see how sculptors and painters, Lucretia among them, have been attracted by some of the same shapes and configurations that have importance to me in my model-building. For them the attraction is entirely an aesthetic one to begin with and yet when we share aesthetic and scientific viewpoints we both feel richer and more aware not only from our increased depth of observation and awareness but also from the interaction and relationship we share.

One of the aspects of model-building we use a lot in the earth sciences is what have been called multiple working hypotheses. We are faced with spread-out information in field work and what we observe or look for is much affected by what we are looking for and the ideas we begin with. Thus, the more different ideas I have as I start to record a set of observations, the more likely I am to be aware of more aspects of what lies right before my eyes. Then I let my fantasy wander as far as it can, spinning out potential models (working hypotheses.) Each piece of new data is hung out in front of all of those hypotheses to see which one or ones it fits along with. Gradually the weight of the evidence may lead me to prefer one hypothesis to another. This way of working helps to sharpen up the story and make it more pleasing and acceptable in the most economical way possible. I hope to get the most out of a visit to a field locality in this way, ideally. I would like to become aware of everything there to avoid the necessity of many return visits. Because of the impossibility of ever seeing all (in that no matter how observant we are, the models themselves are continually changing and really significant relationships do need to be checked) I often find it necessary to return. Furthermore, when I find something **really** exciting I want to return again and again as to any favorite place where I feel excitement.

Straumgjerde.

GOALS

> Il faut chercher pour trouver, mais pas pour trouver ce que l'on cherche.
>
> —ancient French proverb

> If I don't have a goal, how can I make a mistake?
>
> —Barry Stevens

> "Cheshire - Puss," she began, rather timidly,... "Would you tell me, please, which way I ought to go from here?"
>
> "That depends a good deal on where you want to get to," said the cat.
>
> "I don't much care where—" said Alice.
>
> "Then it doesn't matter which way you go," said the cat.
>
> "—So long as I get **somewhere.**" Alice added as an explanation.
>
> "Oh, you're sure to do that," said the cat," if you only walk long enough."
>
> —Lewis Carroll.

I used to think that **my** goals were pretty important for learners in my classroom. I still do have goals for myself and what I want to do in a learning environment, but I have mainly gotten away from the business of having specific goals that I think other people should meet. My own life flows along more easily when I get away from goal-directedness for myself, too. When I get deeply involved in my own goals I become unresponsive to other things around me that may be far more exciting and worthwhile if I were just willing to shift goals. Having strong goals and moving firmly toward them in spite of everything going on around me becomes a kind of future-think in which I can well lose the potential of the present moment.

I have stuck myself into goal directedness right now as I "forge ahead" (a typical expression of goal-directedness) to finish this book. And yet, when it is finished, I will probably look back on it, as I have done on other such things in the past, and see it as some kind of record of what was, that may have little real reference to my life of tomorrow. Today, I don't feel any particular things pulling me away from my writing, though, and so I feel a natural flow that is all right. Yesterday it was one of those brilliant, sunny days where you can see forever, and I decided I would probably not write my quota for the day or spend my "time on the book."

Gretchen and I went out to run a few kilometers together when we first got up, absorbing sounds, colors, and the good feeling of our own hearts strongly beating and blood coursing through our veins. Later, we drove out to photograph some mountain and glacier scenes that I had been waiting for two weeks to capture in the right light. (Another piece of goal-directedness surfaces.) Afterward we went to the river and tape-recorded sounds of the water. (That's a new goal, something I started to do on Saturday when I realized that the sounds of this place will be important, too, as I prepare learning packages based on experiences in this area.) Afterward, everyone wanted to soak up the warm sun, which we had not seen for several days, so our immediate goal collectively shifted to taking the sun. I ended up writing after all while basking. The nature of the creative process fascinates me right now. I abandoned this to go later to a high, mountain lake up in the tundra. A new goal emerged from my goal-bag: just trying to be aware of what was around me -- an incredible mountain range at the south end of the lake; snow and glaciers; gulls nesting on an island out in the lake; tiny alpine plants, caribou moss, and ledges forming a prickly cushion for me to sit on; waterfalls and cascades tumbling down the hillsides. I tried various awareness "exercises" until William got tired of sitting. We noticed large numbers of flat pebbles ("Fjordane layered gneiss," said the analytical me), and the invitation to skip stones was too strong to resist. In a way, we managed to let things flow yesterday. And yet I would be fibbing to myself if I pretended that many of the choices I made were not controlled by my old goal-directedness.

I guess I don't really think that goals are bad. They seem, at this point in time at least, to be a strong part of my life. As long as I am aware that they are affecting me I at least have a better chance of accepting them or rejecting them for the moment. I can choose among them better, when several opportunities present themselves at once, if I am aware of my goal directedness, of the immediate options I find attractive, of my mood of the moment, and of the fact that I am in control of my own life. I can become unhappy, unpleasant, and what is most ironical about it, unproductive in working towards a goal when I let the goal "take over." Singleness of purpose becomes self-defeating except in cases where I am so involved and am so much enjoying a process that I let my life flow for a time in one main direction. Responsiveness to new potentialities in my total extrinsic and intrinsic environments improves my chances of learning and experiencing more things that can help me to grow.

Much science and other study at their best, especially basic research, flow along in the same manner: when we are not obsessed by excessive goal-directedness. Some of the most important creative acts (discoveries) come about when researchers depart from the problem they are supposedly working on and follow a new line of interest that suddenly presents itself, saying, "Here, look at me and see how much more exciting I am than what you set out to do over there!" Barry Stevens mentions the doctor in New Jersey who was furious when he learned that Alexander Fleming had just discovered penicillin by working with the same molds that the other doctor had been throwing out and cursing because they were spoiling his other cultures. Fleming allowed himself to depart from a prior research design to follow-up a new factor that presented itself. The other man did not. George Pappas tells how George Cotzias, working on the role of trace metals in body metabolism, observed the development of symptoms similar to Parkinson's disease in workers from manganese mines in Chile. The flow of his work, unhindered by excessive goal directedness toward body metabolism, led him into further work on neurological disorders. He ultimately developed L-dopa, which now is used to relieve symptoms experienced in Parkinson's disease.

A research proposal or plan ends up as a set of goals. A teacher's lesson plans do too. The worst thing that can happen to my research or teaching, however, is for me to feel bound to those specific goals or to the methods I have spelled out in the proposal. In order to leave themselves freedom to alter goals and approaches, some scientists go so far as to write proposals for work that is largely already completed. Then they use the new funds to explore new avenues. To satisfy the accountability people they publish their past research which shows the results promised in the original proposal. In this way, they stay one jump ahead, always "proposing" to do what they have just completed and then using their new resources to move ahead into the unknown area of new, as yet unarticulated goals and approaches.

> *Lucretia, Cricket, Gretchen, and William just left. The alternative they offer to my morning's goal of writing does not interest me. I choose to remain here; beside that, I'm enjoying the process of writing today.*

Sometimes I get very busy in my office. I may not even be enjoying what I am doing very much and my productivity may be low. Yet sometimes when someone pokes his head in the door or comes in and plunks down on the floor or in a chair I feel annoyed at the interruption. I am beginning to realize that these interruptions may offer me alternatives to help me depart from my still obsessive goal-directedness. When I let myself go and am willing to respond to the person who has come to see me and be with me I often discover a new and more useful and profitable track for the time being. And the other work always gets done eventually ... if it really was important after all!

In Boulder, I used to look up at the mountains early on some winter mornings. Seeing the sun on the snow, high up, sometimes led me to decide to go skiing for the morning instead of going to the office. When I finally went to the office in the early afternoon, I easily got the equivalent of a full day's work done in 4 or 5 hours or less. I don't do that often enough. Will I be ready this fall to leave the office or lab on the spur of the moment and go out for a bike ride with Marg, a walk with Mary Jane, a field trip with Russ and Peter, or a morning skiing with Val, or a beer with Dodge?

This past spring I announced that I would be going out on field trips on Wednesday, Thursday, and Friday afternoon. This became a somewhat goal-directed business, and sometimes we forced ourselves to go out even though the weather was miserable and the rocks too wet to tell us what we had really gone to find out. At other times the days were just right. As we left campus we often stopped the van and invited people we saw along the way to join us. Every now and then someone would spontaneously jump in with us and have a splendid afternoon with us as opposed to some other activity that was being looked forward to as dull and uninteresting.

Don was enjoying his participation in a conference we held in South Carolina. Suddenly he got up and said, looking apprehensively at his watch, "I have to go now." Lepper said to him, "Only if you **choose** to go." After a little thought, Don took responsibility for his own selection of goals and stayed on for several hours. I can place my goals in any order I choose. I can abandon goals any time I wish. I can spontaneously adopt any new goal I wish to. If I let other people's goals for me or even if I allow my own goals to control me, I may miss not only the joy, but also the potential for experiencing, growth, and possibly whole new dimensions of productivity and creativity that spontaneity offers to me.

If I plan for what learners **should do** and try to impose my goals upon them I can help set them up for a life of dependency and unresponsiveness. I can help them build facades to escape from reality rather than facilitating their unique growth and willingness to live as spontaneously as possible. If I decline to set up goals for learners who work with me they can learn better to take responsibility for coming to grips in their own way with their own lives and ways of working, producing, being.

I do still have a goal for learners who work with me, after all. It is the same one I have for myself. This goal is for us all to become more responsible, more self-directed, better able to set personal goals and deal with these, more likely to respond spontaneously to new situations, and better able to let our lives flow. Coincidentally, from a cognitive point of view, I think we will all learn subject matter better and more easily and advance both knowledge and ourselves more if we can implement through action the values expressed above. If learners, who work in this way go on into careers in science, knowledge and science will advance more rapidly. I think that attitudes of the general public toward the acquisition of knowledge will improve and that research, scholarship, and education will receive better public support if more people have a chance to work in this way. I think that there will be greater scientific literacy and appreciation of scholarship in other areas among the general public, and that people will follow the explosive growth of knowledge with more interest and in a more informal way. When I force people toward limited cognitive goals in education I think that I can in the long run do more harm to them, to me, and to the various cognitive areas than I might do good. When I open the environment and allow each person to take responsibility for his own goals, I have confidence that great things will happen in both people and in all areas of learning. But, of course, I cannot predict what these things will be. Thus I can live in the present and work with what possibilities I see in it today rather than losing energy through preoccupation with tomorrow and with narrowly conceived and pursued goals and expectations.

THE PLATEAU EFFECT

I reach plateaus in my own learning experiences. The "plateau" effect is especially well-known to me in the field of languages, where a lot of my early experience was concentrated. I find that I can rapidly develop enough of a vocabulary and knowledge of grammar in a foreign language to communicate in a rough way about my basic needs. "Hotel-Swedish" or "Hotel-Finnish," I call it. It's the kind of stuff you can get from those "Learn-Spanish-in-20-easy-lessons" records. You get a little fancier version of it at about 100 times the price from a full-blown individualized Berlitz course. At the end of this kind of rapid acquisition of skill I always have a heady feeling about how much I know. But beyond this stage of simple, rudimentary communication comes a long and arduous period during which it seems that I make no progress at all. Perhaps a fit analogy would be the melting of ice or any such phase change, where you keep on putting in more and more heat and yet the temperature of the system remains the same. The latent heat of melting hasn't been added yet. Learning seems to take place in the same way. Skills are learned in spurts instead of in an orderly, progressive fashion in equally satisfying increments of learning.

I was on the "rudimentary-Russian plateau" for what seemed like an endless time, and then - pow! All of a sudden it seemed as if I could read everything and understand everything and say everything at once. The same thing has happened in other languages. I suspect that functional use of various skills in higher mathematics — which is really a language more than anything else — may develop in abrupt steps separated by what may seem to the learner long, tedious periods of drill, stumbling, and little progress.

I always have done all right with respect to the language plateaus, because as frustrating as they may be, I know that I can expect them. I realize that when I am on a learning plateau I'll just have to keep plugging for a long time with little apparent gain. I even know that I can't predict just how long it'll take before the next rewarding progress occurs. But I've come to enjoy even the process of working hard while on that plateau, because it feels so good once I hit the next riser, where the slightest little bit of effort seems to produce fantastic results.

I had forgotten how true this is of the theater when I took a small role in a local production of **Richard III** last Spring. It seemed to take me forever to get my lines down, and I wondered at first if maybe it was the onset of old age or something. Then I thought back to previous experiences and remembered all of the frustration I felt on each plateau at that time, too. Fortunately, this time again those last few rehearsals seemed to produce the spurt of progress needed to weld the production together.

I have felt the same thing in University chorus, too. We do a pretty good job of reading a piece through and get to think of ourselves as a tremendous ensemble. Then stagnation seems to set in and we detect no improvement. We haven't quite got the rhythm and we keep missing that damned B-flat in the middle of the 43rd measure. Suddenly one night the number falls together.

Plateaus are common in research activity. I gather just a few data and a great idea comes to mind to tie things together. Then I work and work and work and everything seems to fail. Nothing fits together. Suddenly, as if by magic something that holds together arises as a reasonable first approximation. This applies to specific laboratory skills in my experiences, too.

Many creative artists and scientists describe experiences during which they seem to be out in the middle of a wide, endless plateau, making no progress at all. They experience sporadic rises up to new levels of skill, production, or creative power.

How often do we recognize the plateau effect in learning environments? Usually we expect people to perform on **our** schedules. Points of evaluation come when we are ready to give tests rather than when learners wish to use them to show their power. When I studied integral calculus during a summer session at Berkeley we always had the test 3 days before the concept had dropped in place for me. I lived in mortal terror and came within an inch of dropping out of graduate school, "What, a 27-year-old graduate student and you can't even manage the second semester of freshman calculus?" I know now that there was nothing wrong with me. But I certainly didn't know it while I was in that course! I think that mineral, rock, and plant identification skills, any taxonomy for that matter, are among those where people feel the plateau effect strongly in the sciences. I have seen learners work for months and become discouraged because they just don't seem to be getting anywhere. Then, all of a sudden, they become functional and confident.

Some people may not meet plateaus in the same areas I do. They may make more slow, steady progress than I do. They may then meet plateaus where I didn't. It's always tempting for me to say, "Oh you shouldn't have any trouble with **that; I** didn't." And yet the same person, in another area of interest could easily say the same thing to me.

My plateaus come in different places than yours. I do not expect you to perform on my schedule anymore. Furthermore, I decline to accept your schedules as a basis for my progress. I will not allow your schedule and your progress to affect my feelings about my own worth. And I do not want your feelings about you to be affected by the rate at which I happen to progress. All of a sudden one day you'll be on an up slope ahead of me. Another time I'll get there first. Often we may be on the same plateau together. At other times we'll be on plateaus at different levels, but that does not make one of us any more or any less than the other.

I want to be more aware of the existence of potential plateaus and where and when to expect them. Then I can be more patient and understanding as I work with other people. Even though I might not correctly predict where a plateau might appear, I can be prepared to receive empathically another person's feeling when he does enter a period of apparent difficulty and low productivity.

I could make a contour map for each person that would show the terrains of the learning experience - separate maps for effort expended, satisfaction obtained, and general progress. And the maps could only be drawn **after** the learning had taken place.

Recognition and acceptance (awareness) of learning plateaus will both help me to learn and also help me facilitate learning and improve the learning and producing environment for others.

INTELLECTUALISM AND ANTI-INTELLECTUALISM

> The most beautiful thing we can experience is the mysterious. It is the source of all true art and science
>
> —A. Einstein.

Ever since I started listening to the arguments of educators I have been aware of endless discussion about intellectualism versus anti-intellectualism. People who propose change in a direction of introducing new elements of knowledge and experience into education are almost invariably accused of "anti-intellectualism" by defenders of the status quo and by people who would move back in a direction of their own educations. The ideas of Rousseau, Thoreau, and other long-dead radicals who believed in natural, experience-centered education have now been included within the realm of acceptable study by self-styled "intellectuals." A recent British television series based on **Tom Brown's Schooldays** showed the Rugby headmaster, Dr. Arnold, trying to introduce, into the British public schools of the 19th century, geography, political science, and other disciplines that are now widely accepted. Others around him considered him to be anti-intellectual because of his departure from "rigorous" Latin and Greek.

With the inception of big federally-sponsored curriculum projects came a torrent of protest from numerous quarters. It has taken some sectors of the geological profession a full ten years to accept that the Earth Science Curriculum Project provided useful materials for secondary school earth science. Many earth scientists and earth science teachers still reject its "hands-on" approaches to education in this area as anti-intellectual.

When you get into the area of open schools or their immediate ancestor, the Deweyian progressive schools, many parents, teachers, and students begin talking about "playtime" or "advanced kindergarten".

In 1970 a small group of us tried to implement an open-model science program at the University of Colorado. We had to devote incredible energy to mere survival in a hostile environment. Back-door gossip and head-on confrontation did everything possible to inhibit the success of our efforts and to divert time and effort that we had reserved for developing our learning environment and interacting with learners. Statements such as, "It's all right, I suppose, but it's not **science**" or "I suppose you can do that if you want, but we think that rigorous, intellectual activity is more important than play." Two thirds of the 20 students involved elected to join our "anti-intellectual" group and engaged in work which would have been difficult to categorize as trivial or non-intellectual if evaluated by a sympathetic, cross-disciplinary group. More important, several students who elected the more open environment told us that their attitudes toward science in general had greatly improved through their experiences. Nonetheless, this experiment was aborted at the end of the year, by administrative edict, because that system could not tolerate this alternative mode of learning.

I am always interested to look back at the eight-year study of Deweyian progressive schools. This extensive study, which is, unfortunately, little publicized, showed clearly that the intellectual development of students educated in the 30's in "progressive" schools was every bit as "intellectual," even by traditional standards, as that of students in traditional schools.

A senior official of the National Science Foundation accused a project I formerly worked with (ESTPP) of being "anti-intellectual" because our primary focus was on human values in teaching-learning situations. There seems to be a common attitude that failure to stress traditional science content means a rejection of content in favor of emotion and intuition. On the contrary, working to free the intuition, to integrate and use emotional factors in learning environments, to seek new ways of perceiving and conceiving, and to expand consciousness seem to me to represent the highest kinds of intellectual and scientific behaviors and values.

The meaning of "intellectual activity" becomes a major issue upon which there is little agreement. A large element of snobbery appears in those who restrict their definitions. In my present institution, students technically have permission to cross-register in courses available at a local 2-year agricultural and technical institution. Yet when students seek to learn auto-mechanics, welding, or to pursue other "vocational" interests, they are frequently denied the possibility of credit because, "these are not intellectual pursuits, have little to with liberal education, and are not suitable for students of the quality of ours." Effectively, we put on our collective high hat, and turn up our collective nose. I reject restrictive definitions of this type.

In education at all levels, I seek a broadening of the definition of "intellectual activity." The need for an intellectually literate population is extreme. Intellectual and scientific snobbery can only damage and limit opportunities for a creative, knowledgeable society. Any kind of activity in any context is, in my opinion, valid, viable, and worth support as long as it helps learners (in their **own** opinions) expand their concept of the world and of themselves. Just 3 days ago I attended a meeting held by the National Science Foundation in Washington. At that meeting it was announced that existing educational programs of NSF were disbanded as of that time, and the Foundation was completely reorganizing its efforts. One of the key new efforts was to be specifically in the area of increasing scientific literacy and working with attempts to improve career opportunities in science. Both of these directions, if any real heed is paid to societal needs, will require a shift away from any snobbish designation of new and unusual programs as "anti-intellectual" merely because they are different in their goals and approaches. (Nearly two years have passed since I originally wrote the last few sentences, and I regret to report little change at NSF!)Kuhn has pointed out that scientists and educators who adhere to any one educational, social, or scientific paradigm may be unable or unwilling to comprehend the nature of a different paradigm and of the consequences of adopting it. If you operate on the basis of a completely different paradigm or set of premises than I do, and you expect me to produce results that would devolve from your paradigm, then I cannot satisfy you. You call me anti-intellectual (= "bad") rather than accepting the **differences** that I represent as a result of my adherence to a different paradigm. Charles Reich refers to differing states of consciousness and points out that people who are members of his "Consciousness-III group" in many instances simply **cannot** be accepted or understood by people who have not yet reached that state of consciousness.

Being interested in open education I operate according to a different paradigm than do people who are not operating in this arena. I can dismiss research and ideas produced by a "traditionalist" as senseless and mindless just as he can reject mine as anti-intellectual. Awareness of this problem may help both of us to accept each other or at least to listen rather than rejecting outright what each other are doing.

I used to accept a different paradigm than I do now. I accepted that teachers should control behavior of students, should operate mainly in the cognitive domain, and should **cause** students to learn certain things in certain orders. I accepted that the key role of the teacher was to be a selector, purveyor, and conveyor of content. As a follower of Jerome Bruner's early idea that there is an intellectually honest way of teaching anything to a child of virtually any age, I found that I could "force feed" some very sophisticated concepts and behaviors. John Merrill and I showed that ninth-graders could easily deal with supposedly "college-level" concepts. I subsequently convinced myself that high-level graduate-school materials are within the grasp of many people in their early teens.

I used to read the **Journal of Research In Science Teaching** with great interest. Now, suddenly, I find much I read in it "trivial" (to me) and I reject it. Why? Because I have rejected one paradigm and accepted another. In a similar vein, many journals end up rejecting contributors' articles because the authors operate according to a paradigm that the editors do not understand or accept. A common reason for rejection is that an article is "unscientific" or "anti-intellectual." I accept that there may be "good" articles and "bad" articles, but criteria for rejection or acceptance frequently include unconscious acceptance or rejection of certain paradigms which lead to a lack of communciation between editorial board and authors.

My level of consciousness has changed and I now find irrelevant to me things that I previously considered to be relevant. Yet I propose acceptance of alternatives, too. If I really mean that, then I will not reject in an out-of-hand manner what a "behaviorist" or someone who follows yet another paradigm suggests. Instead I will try to find useful elements in their work by seeking to understand the paradigm under which they operate as one way of looking at a situation.

I recently reviewed for a publisher several chapters of a manuscript dealing almost entirely with systems approaches in education. I took it immediately to be basically anti-humanistic (in the same way that others may consider some of what I do anti-intellectual?) and rejected it. Yet there are good ideas in it if you understand the authors' paradigm: that the teacher's function is to prepare people for a system by using a carefully structured model of the system to educate them.

Perhaps it is important for learners to have access to people operating according to many different paradigms, if we hope ultimately to help them expand their consciousness. This means that we need alternatives.

One thing is certain, the application of labels such as "anti-intellectual" or "anti-humanist" only obscure the real issues and create blocks that inhibit the construction of effective learning environments.

QUALITY FAIR: A NOBEL DRAMA

Scene: The Swedish Academy's conference room in Stockholm. The Nobel Prize committee is meeting to nominate its winners. Large, sumptuous room with big leather chairs surrounding a highly polished antique-wood table, crystal chandelier hangs from the ceiling. A group of old men are sitting around the table. Files and papers are stacked everywhere. A clerk scampers to and fro retrieving documents for the committee members.

Gustavson: There are so many people we might give the prize to that I think we must look all their records over carefully. We want to make sure we choose the scientists of the very highest quality. Therefore we have had our staff calculate some quality points to help us in our selection. We have two people whom we should compare now - both of them Germans. One of them, Einstein, is well-known to all of you because of the uproar and newspaper publicity over his Theories of Special and General Relativity. I don't really understand it myself. It's too theoretical and I like to see lab work, myself. The other one is Zweifelsen, who has also been recommended by our correspondents on the continent. His work is nice and easy to understand.

Olavson: Well, let's look over these records and see what we can make of them.

Petersson: Hey, look at Einstein's SAT scores!

Anderson: Oh, those are for his "Scholarly Aptitude Test" aren't they?

Gustavson: Yes, that's a new test we've had constructed for people who want the Nobel Prize.

Petersson: Look how low they are. The guy missed all of the questions on Newton and on Gravitation.

Helgeson: Maybe he just misread the instructions and put his black marks between the wrong dotted lines. A lot of his papers talk a lot about Newton.

Gustavson: No, I think we must trust the results of the SAT. It has been standardized in tests involving thousands of scientists, and it is true that Einstein only came out in the fortieth percentile. Whereas if you look at Zweifelsen's SAT's, you'll see that he's in the 99th percentile. He got almost every question right.

Ingerson: I don't think we can make a good decision on the basis of this one index. I see that there are other tests in the battery. Let's check those out, too.

Gustavson: Yes, I agree with you. Let's look at their PRE scores.

Anderson: Isn't that the new "Professional Record Examination"?

Gustavson: Yes.

Petersson: Wow, this is terrible. Look at Einstein: He worked for years as a patent office clerk. Couldn't get a job in **any** university - not even as a research assistant. He came out in the twentieth percentile.

Olavson: Yeah, and Zweifelsen went right into a plush assistant professorship at Tubingen and moved right up the ladder. He's in the 99th percentile here, too.

Gustavson: It's beginning to look pretty slim for Einstein.

Helgeson: But what about his RPA?

Anderson: You mean his "Research Point Average"?

Gustavson: Yes.

Petersson: Well, the way ETS (the Erudite Testing Service) set this exam up, lab research is a very important factor. Old Zweifelsen really has got the years in the lab behind him to back up the quality of his work. Look at that average: He visited his lab 350 days out of last year alone - and it's certified by the Lab Visitation Board, too!

Olavson: And Einstein doesn't even **have** a lab. What's more he couldn't even test his own theory. Had to wait for a bunch of Englishmen to watch several eclipses before anybody could even be sure he was on the right track.

Ingerson: But the RPA score also includes a factor based on number of publications, doesn't it? And I see that Einstein has a lot of papers out in the **Annalen der Physik,** which is a pretty well-known journal.

Gustavson: Yes, he has some long theoretical papers out. But he never provides any data. The guy seems to just work out of his head. What is this he has written in the margin of the test? ..."all I need is a pencil and a pad of paper."

Petersson: Aha, but look, Zweifelsen has twice as many papers out. They may be short ones, but look at that list of titles.

Helgeson: But was there any attempt to note the quality of the journals with respect to each other? I've never heard of any of the journals that Zweifelsen published in. He seems to be the editor of the one where most of his stuff appears.

Gustavson: Come, come, my dear colleagues. We mustn't quibble over such trivial matters. I really think we must trust the judgement of the ETS test markers. After all, they're high quality professionals when it comes to writing tests that do the job.

Petersson: I see they have another score in here, too, the TPA.

Anderson: Let's see, that's the "Teaching Point Average," isn't it?

Ingerson: Yes, but I don't see what it really has to do with the Nobel Prize.

Gustavson: We feel that our winners should have shown the ability to communicate their results and to teach others about the new things they've done.

Petersson: Yes, and look, Einstein has done everything he could to get out of lecturing at the University.

Helgeson: He **has** been a professor at some pretty prestigious places, though. Let's see, where is he now? In Berlin at the Kaiser Wilhelm Institute isn't he? - Full Professor, too?

Olavson: Yes, but, one of his conditions for going there was that he never have any **regular** lecturing duties. He wanted to lecture only when **he** wanted too.

Helgeson: But there **are** other ways of teaching and communicating than just by lecturing aren't there? And he has written several "popular" articles to help people understand his ideas.

Ingerson: Not only that, but I've seen some feedback from the days when he was at the University in Zurich. He spent a lot of time sitting around the cafes with students, taking walks in the woods with them and that sort of thing. As a matter of fact I've heard that you usually couldn't even tell Einstein from his students in those days.

Gustavson: Colleagues, I must remind you that we can't keep bringing up these extraneous factors. The exam results show quite clearly that Einstein hasn't met classes regularly for years. He hasn't been doing a proper job of teaching as we define it.

Helgeson: But the man lectures to huge crowds wherever he goes and he is able to use simple analogies to describe very coherently what his theories mean.

Anderson: Those things are not part of "teaching" as defined by ETS, so I think we should not waste time on them. The purpose of the ETS score is to give us a nice numerical index so we can simplify our selection process. We can't re-examine every question or we'll miss the smörgasbord tonight. And Einstein again is below the 40th percentile.

Michelson: Zweifelsen, on the other hand, is shown by his TPA tests to have been giving his same set of physics lectures every Monday, Wednesday, and Friday at 8:00 A.M. for the past several years. It's nice to have a good predictable teacher like that, isn't it? He really communicates the fundamentals. Runs labs for his students twice a week, too. Even wrote his own lab manual. Lots of good fill-in questions.

Ingerson: I don't think we can base everything on the SAT, PRE, RPA, and TPA, however. After all, these are just index numbers and we know that the correlation between these scores and real scientific quality is not all that strong.

Gustavson: I agree, colleagues. We must look for another criteria, too. Let's go back and look at these men's high school and college transcripts.

Helgeson: Agreed!

Ingerson: Let's see, Zweifelsen was first in both his high school and college classes and carried right through to a high honors Ph.-D.

Petersson: Good Lord - Do you see this? Einstein was actually kicked out of Luitpold High School! It says here on the transcript, "your presence in the class is disruptive and affects the other students".

Ingerson: Looks like he also had problems finishing his Ph.D. at Zurich and had a lot of trouble getting into school there, too.

General murmuring from all in the room.

Gustavson: Well, colleagues, I guess we are agreed that we simply can't consider Einstein any further.

------------Curtain------------

DEALING WITH INSTITUTIONAL INHIBITORS TO CONSCIOUSNESS, CREATIVITY AND KNOWING

THE EFFECTS OF SCHOOLS

> The coercion had such a deterring effect (upon me) that, after I had passed the final examination, I found the consideration of any scientific problems distasteful to me for an entire year.
>
> —A. Einstein

When I think "school" I think of a special and somewhat unnatural place — an institution. Schools everywhere look pretty much alike. In the little Norwegian village where I am writing this the school building and its facilities look almost exactly like the ones my children use in Canton, New York, and have previously used in California, Colorado, Syracuse, New York and Oslo. They look like the ones in Australia, the ones in Nain, Labrador at the eskimo boarding school run by the Canadian government, and in Novosibirsk at the special science and math school. Chairs or desks in rows, teacher's desk in front (sometimes in back in the more "progressive" schools), with black-board all along the front of the room. The rooms are full of people about 6 hours a day and empty and locked up 16 to 18 hours a day. Classrooms are open only 180 days of the year and closed the other 185. (Summer sessions and special uses may involve some of the rooms for a few of those 185 "non-school" days.) Yet we complain about inadequate physcial plants! Too small, we say. Few schools anywhere in the world have done much about inventing new use patterns. Instead we continue to tolerate increasing school taxes and costs of fancier plants. I don't understand how my university can continue to operate as I walk about the campus in summer and over the long holidays and see endless rows of closed, deserted dormitory windows and classrooms. Increase the tuition again! Build another building! Hold the size of the student body and faculty **down** to the status-quo figure. Must preserve the institutional character! Above all else, **avoid** change.

Perhaps the most serious problem of all lies in the way educational facilities are locked up within the schools, mainly unavailable for learners who might enter as "free" learners. Schools constitute a well-financed monopoly of fundamental learning resources.

Art rooms, industrial-arts areas, and science rooms are more often thought of as work-rooms. In some schools these may be occupied during most of the hours when the building itself is open. The pattern of use in these rooms tends to be less formal too. Perhaps they can becomes key spaces in helping to transform the school.

I don't know, though. In several open schools I have visited recently, the science areas seem to be among the dullest. They have a sterility and a lack of people exploring that makes me feel sad. Perhaps this reflects the attitude towards science that the people in charge of these areas have. In some public, open-space schools the science area has actually been removed from the main open area of the school in which most activities take place and has been stuck off in a separate room. At open-space elementary schools I have visited in Colorado and Texas, the science room is even kept locked except at set times when teachers teach children in it. Totally closed with respect to open and informal exploration by the children.

Another characteristic of schools is the way they sort children out by ages. Parents mainly accept that our 6 year olds should always be with 6 year olds, and our 14 year-olds should always be with 14 year-olds. And then, later, we worry about there being a generation gap! We've built one right into our schools and assured its continuing existence.

School is generally hierarchial in nature and authority-based. Students have few rights with respect to teachers; teachers have few rights with respect to administrators. In the school system in my town an art teacher requested permission to accompany her husband to a professional meeting in the west so she could visit art museums and build her own competence. Her request was denied. She paid for a substitute out of her pocket and went anyway. She didn't play the game of "calling in sick," which would have kept her out of trouble, but she went west anyway and did not hide the reason. She returned to find herself suspended and later dismissed for insubordination even though she was tenured. A number of parents protested and she was finally reinstated. A second teacher, untenured, was asked to resign because of "unacceptable behavior." He happens to have been one of a handful of teachers whom students felt free to seek out for informal counseling. And he was the only one who was prepared to offer serious help and counselling to students with drug problems as opposed to a one-way ride to juvenile court. He also ran an open curriculum classroom and wasn't afraid to let the good results of the students be known. Some of the essays Gretchen wrote for his group were the most sensitive and free things I've yet seen her put down on paper.

I do not describe here any single school that is a bad example. There are few public schools in the country from which you can't pull similar anecdotes illustrating use of hierarchial power to the detriment of teachers, students, and the school itself. The institution called school becomes a powerful filter to remove things that are different and unusual from the learning environment we provide for young people. It attempts to filter out uniqueness and to create "normative" adults. O. J. Harvey's studies have demonstrated that authority-oriented people **almost exclusively** occupy administrative posts in public schools.

Change seems to be slow in the institution called school. This goes back to the notion that the job of the school is to train children to fit society, to conform. But society itself is changing rapidly and many young people do not accept being shaped for this purpose. I would like to see the schools help prepare young people to **mold** society rather then to fit in.

Students are not generally encouraged to be revolutionaries either with respect to the discipline they study or the societies they are to live in. Einstein was a student at a time when a revolution in physics was about to begin. Yet school tried to stamp those movements out rather than encouraging them as healthy for both students and science. Fortunately, Einstein, a quiet dissenter, simply did his formal work as required and went on to get his **real** education elsewhere, on his own.

All this would not necessarily be bad except that school attendance is mandatory and educational resources are looked up in the school buildings. Even private schools are supposed to be approved and certified and generally tend towards the same operating pattern as public schools. Young people who go to "unapproved" private schools may be legally declared truants.

During the past 3 months we have been busy setting up a summer workshop, under support of the National Science Foundation, to develop local leadership teams to implement open educational environments of the type fostered by ES. We have required a substantial commitment from local school districts in both financial and moral support for our teams of teacher-leaders before we will expend our monies in support of the district teams. Our approach is toward an integration of subject-matter areas and the starting of small, core-type alternative programs in which at least selected students and hopefully a cross-section of students, are given substantial responsibility for their own learning. We seek to foster the growth of creativity and human potential. When we contacted the science supervisory group for the Boston public schools we were immediately closed out right at the top of the pyramid. A single man was able to deny use of the program for a major metropolitan school system! We tried to come up again from the bottom, through lower levels of the schools and found that approval still needed to be obtained through the same man. Actually we have since found other access routes and we know that individual principals and teachers, on their own initiative, but sometimes at considerable personal risk, can introduce both the material and approaches we are fostering in our workshop. Nonetheless, single people in positions of relative power can be in a position to screen out the new and exciting and to perpetuate the old. Multiple approaches are not commonly favored in the upper echelons of the system. "To hard to control, you know."

Paul Goodman, Ivan Illich, and John Holt have become spokesmen for the deschooling of society, the abandonment of any compulsory system of public education. They favor the idea, generally, of using society itself as a school. Marshall McLuhan has called attention to the way in which the media now provide such a rich learning environment that the very matrix we live in will provide the same order of learning that schools can in their present form. In a film entitled "The Medium is The Massage" McLuhan proposes that before 1900 children could learn more inside school than they could outside. Since then, however, and especially now, he says, **school actually interrupts the learning of children.** I find myself increasingly in agreement with the "deschoolers." My ideal becomes a series of publically supported and free learning-resource centers, regularly staffed by competent scholars, scientists, artists, skilled laborers, musicians, and others and kept open as nearly as possible 24 hours per day and 12 months per year. The cost of public education would, I think, be much reduced and the effectiveness in fostering uniqueness, creativity, and educational development much increased. Experiments on using the community itself as the school were part of a now-postponed plan for the "Minnesota Experimental City." The Parkway School in Philadelphia has been successfully using the community as its "school" for several years. Probably such experiments will have to take place in entirely new, planned communities rather than in older communities with existing systems. In those, the vested interests of the ruling bureaucrats at all levels may simply be too strongly organized to change modes of operation so drastically. Bureaucracies are probably the most entrenched and stable elements of society. They have lived through the French Revolution and the Russian Revolution without even missing a beat. Emphasis may have changed, but the bureaucracies continued to function.

The so-called open-school movement has begun to introduce flexibility into a few schools and systems that have allowed open schools to exist as alternatives. Many of the suggestions in this book can work best in an open-access environment, whether it be a section of a conventional school, an open school, or a free learning-resources center.

ON REQUIREMENTS

> Just as eating against one's will is injurious to health, so study without liking, for it spoils the memory, and it retains nothing it takes in.
>
> —Leonardo da Vinci

Requirements start from the first day of the first grade. In the early grades of all but the more open schools, every activity is required. All the children do virtually all things as a group, and no real options exist for other things. Generally, grade schoolers don't think of having required and optional subjects. They accept whatever comes along as what they are supposed to be doing. In elementary schools, the people who are aware of a feeling of "requirements" are the grade school **teachers.** In many places gradeschoolers still stay with a single teacher all day long and that teacher is supposed to be able to help the children learn effectively in all areas. Programs for the training of elementary teachers are usually a hodgepodge of required survey-type courses. Many elementary teachers have learned to think of science, an area of special interest to me, as different, special, and too difficult for them to handle. It has been rare for me to meet an elementary teacher who, upon learning that I am a "scientist," doesn't begin to apologize for a lack of ability to deal with science. Science becomes a burden for many elementary teachers. Their lack of good feelings and confidence is transmitted, as a feeling and a root attitude, to many young children. They come to feel that, "Anything Miss Jones thinks is hard must be really tough. I'll never be able to do it if she can't."

A TRUE-LIFE PARABLE OF THE ELEMENTARY SCHOOL TEACHER WHO WOULDN'T TEACH SCIENCE

Carole signed up for Helen's seminar in science. Helen told the class she wanted them to be an informal group discussing science papers. They read papers and discussed them. They wrote papers. Carole didn't talk a whole lot in the seminars and didn't see much of Helen outside of the seminar. At the end of the term Helen gave each student an hour-long oral examination. It was supposed to have been a "chat." Carole summarized her work of the term by telling what things she had been through during the term. Carole said, "I want to ask you some things about relativity now, because I finally know some things I want to ask." Helen said, "it's too late - relativity was the subject of discussion during the first week of the term, you know, and therefore it's too late to learn about it now!" Then Helen said, "You're not a deep thinker; you are a very shallow thinker. At first I thought I might give you a B, but now I've decided on a C or D. Oops, your hour is up now." Carole went away, her head low. She thought to herself, "I guess I can never teach science to my elementary students very well. I'm a shallow thinker and scientists are supposed to be deep thinkers.'' Helen had expectations she didn't make clear to Carole. Helen thinks she is an ''open,'' ''humane'' teacher. Carole could have played Helen's game if Helen had admitted that she had a game. Carole thinks of herself now as ''shallow.'' She probably won't teach much science.

A TRUE-LIFE PARABLE OF THE ELEMENTARY TEACHER WHO MIGHT TEACH SCIENCE AFTER ALL.

Carole later entered an ''open'' class where there was no hidden game. She would decide what she wanted to do herself, and she could grade herself. She decided to plan some activities for children. She set up some experiments and played with them. Later she found a group of eight elementary-school children who lived near her house. One day a week she would play with them. They played with the science experiments Carole had designed. They had a good time and learned some things. Carole learned that some of her activities for the children were good ones and that others didn't work very well. At the end of the term she sat down with her instructor and told about her results. She said she felt good about her work. She told how badly she felt about her dealings with Helen during an earlier term. Then she gave herself an A for her work with children. She said she might teach science after all, even though Helen had said she was ''a shallow thinker.''

One of William's grade school teachers had the whole kit of SAPA science materials in her classroom. Yet in her parents' night spiel she carefully avoided any mention of anything other than the subject areas in science her syllabus ''required'' her to cover. I later asked her about the SAPA materials which, although they are rather inflexible, at least provide a chance for some rather structured ''science play.'' She told me about how bad she was in science first and how she couldn't really handle the SAPA materials comfortably. But she hastened to add that she did use them once in awhile. Later, I happened to open some of the drawers in the lab to look over the stuff myself. None of it had even been unwrapped! I do not fault the teacher for this. I fault the concept of requiring her and others like her to deal with areas in which they have such bad feelings about their own lack of competence. This is inhumane to both the teacher and his or her students and ultimately can raise further blocks to the children's later learning by setting up a phoney notion of difficulty.

By the time junior high school rolls around, you have a little more ''choice'' in what you may study and what you are allowed to avoid. But you still have to take certain required things. American History is one that I seemed to have to take over and over and over and over until I was almost nauseated by it. I still find it uninteresting for the most part. Science is another. Many of the people who didn't gain a strong dislike and fear of it through their teachers' tacit but subtley expressed antipathy develop it here. In spite of all the new NSF-sponsored science curricula for junior-high school, science courses remain dominately fact and memory-centered. Science becomes a language full of hard, obscure new words to be learned, and it also may involve a lot of calculations which have become more advanced than ever since the research scientists got their hands on the curricula.

This continues through high school where further science requirements join requirements in other areas. So-called electives (of which there is never what you'd call a feast anyway) occupy a small number of the total courses recorded for any student.

College raises new science requirements. In a few colleges abandonment of science requirements has led to immediate and drastic drops in enrollment. At Berkeley, within two weeks after one general science requirement was dropped nearly 90 percent of the students had dropped the main course used to satisfy the requirement. At Case Western Reserve the geology department prepared for the drop expected after removal of the science requirement by gearing up to offer the most exciting new program possible. They sent out special advance literature to all new students coming in and were rewarded by only a slight drop in enrollment instead of the usual catastrophic one. Since then their enrollment has risen again because they are now responding to the needs of the students. What ever happened to the free market in education? Somehow students, especially in the compulsory public schools, are not considered to be full citizens in a so-called democratic society.

I issue this as a challenge: Work toward the removal of requirements at whatever level you are involved, as student, teacher, administrator, or parent. If enrollment drops then work to help create more attractive options. Captive audiences are poor places in which to encourage the growth of creative powers and the increase of knowledge.

CONTENT

Bill Elberty had just expressed his approval of a student project that involved a study of diseases in a certain part of the country. The project was to receive credit under the title "geography." The chairman of a powerful faculty committee called Bill and questioned both his assignment of credit as "geography" and his expertise in being able to help the student. I wonder what he'd say if he knew I allowed geology credit to several people who wrote plays - one about the problems of a frigid woman? I would justify it to him on the basis of its "earthiness," I suppose. And how about Callie's geology credit for flute lessons?

I can limit my content area as tightly as I wish to. If I feel constrained by these limits the problem is not in the "content." It's strictly within me.

Usually when I find people who claim to hate a subject, what they really hate is the narrowly defined area they have been told is geology, biology, physics, math., English, art, or sociology.

When we began our new "geology and geography" program as a student-centered learning community, we told people they could select any point or points of their interest and move into studies of the earth and it's people as they chose. During the first term we were stuck with a bunch of old course titles (a problem of administrative paralysis). So we told people that the titles had only the significance they chose to attribute to them. People were signed up for things called "petrology," "mineralogy," "stratigraphy," "structural geology," and so forth. I said, "If it says petrology on the record and you'd rather learn about the distribution of mercury in fish livers than about rock classification, then go with the fish livers." I also said, "If you'd rather write poems - do that, and they don't have to be about rocks either." Many people couldn't handle that at all. As the term progressed I talked to some people who were signed up under the petrology designation to see how they felt about their activities. Some said, "I'm tired of working on rocks; I'm really not interested in them much." In answer to my query, "Why not do something else?" They replied, "But I'm signed up for petrology. That means I have to do rocks." They refused to believe that they were free from the titles they registered for. Since then, we have a new arrangement by which people can sign for "projects." This leaves them free to move about as their interests change. Even so, people have gone ahead on their own and have put up compartment walls so that a group still chooses to go off and do petrology and, if you question them, some will still answer "I have to do that for petrology even though I don't want to." No matter how explicitly you state the permission to be free from courses and titles students and faculty build new boxes just like the old ones. We even worked it out so that students could have project titles of their own choice listed on their transcripts to describe what they had actually done as opposed to listing the name of an "approved" course. Most of the learners in our group now choose titles like "petrology," "mineralogy," "stratigraphy," and "structural geology"! Same old boxes!

They elect to continue being method-centered in approach rather than problem-centered. That's the way we've been brought up. It gets scary outside of the boxes. It's easier to follow along and go though the textbook the way "everybody else" did it. This makes a complex world seem simple.

In our experiences with new learners we have "courses" entitled Introductory Geography Projects and Introductory Geology Projects. In these Bill Elberty and I have tried to be as explicit as possible about the essentially infinite range of activities that we consider as acceptable. **No** constraints of mine or his construction. And yet we still have people saying, "I just can't get interested in rocks!" Me: "Then change and work on something else." Learner: "I can't; this is supposed to be geology!" Even the hardest-nosed of professional geologists doesn't limit geology to **rocks** these days, but somehow the myth persists that the geology box is confined to stones.

Things are beginning to get better now. Somehow the word is beginning to get around that we really mean it. That we don't limit people. There was an incredibly fine amount of diversity this last spring in a group of 60 new people I worked with. Bill is feeling it strongly in his groups, too.

I suppose I still show some hazy outline of the old content area. I prefer to call them possible foci. These are the foci of my own active interests. The materials we have in the labs suggest activities, and these channel people's exploration toward areas of our special competencies. Seeing us work hard setting up programmed lab materials and ideas, some people use these because they think they **ought** to. (Might hurt our feelings if they don't!) Others use them because they want to find out more about our interests. That's a reason that I like for exploration: an excuse for us to get to know each other in areas of special interests.

Others approach them to find out about a new line of subject matter and then feel free to leave them when interest dwindles. Or they feel free to commit themselves to further pursuit when they become absorbed or decide that, even though dull, the material is of value to them in a growth direction they are pursuing.

To me, the important thing about content is that it is everywhere present. People I know have criticized open classrooms because they say there is "no content." When we put in our proposals to NSF for the ES materials we had them sent back to us with comments that said, "Where is the **content?**" To me, there is no such thing as "no content" — maybe just a content different than the one you expected. So maybe these people are really saying, "I don't see **my** content in it." When people talk about a content-centered approach — really strong on content — that sounds like foolishness to me. All that means is that the teacher or the curriculum-maker has set up limits and is trying to impose limited subject matter on someone else. The total environment that surrounds me is the content for my investigations. If I limit myself to the content you choose, neither of us may grow very much. If you pursue your chosen content and I pursue mine and we find a common point of interest, then we enhance each others' growth.

COVERAGE

One of the problems we faced in developing materials for ESCP was the problem of coverage. We were trying to bring together material and ideas from all of the earth sciences. All 70 of us on the writing team had strong vested interests and wanted to see our areas well-treated. First-draft manuscripts we produced were twice as long as the final version that we published. In shortening them, we did not appreciably reduce the number of concepts included. Rather, we reduced the number of examples we used to illustrate concepts and we tightened the writing up. This had the effect of making the material harder to read and less interesting. Still, we felt that we had to retain everything in order to cover our areas adequately. The thing ended up like an outline version of the elementary, college-level textbooks for all of our areas combined.

For the Biological Sciences Curriculum Study (BSCS), the problem of vested interests was resolved in a unique way. They could not agree on a single approach and so they wrote 3 separate versions, the Green, Yellow, and Blue versions. These are all separately published. They contain some overlapping materials, and their pedagogial approaches are similar, but the organization and presentation of subject matter is different in both approach and in sequence. In ESCP, we kept re-making a single version to produce some kind of consensus compromise. At first I was proud of us for not being so mixed up about what was important to cover and how. Now I see wisdom in a multiple-version approach. Consensus weakens. Alternatives strengthen and allow multiple approaches. The only trouble with the BSCS things is that once you're on a track, you stay there even though one of the others, or a combination of the 3 might be better. Also, it is not the learner who selects the version. In most places it is the teacher or the district administrator's staff who make the decision.

During the first year of testing of ESCP we expected our eighth and ninth grade customers to "cover" all of that material during the course of a single school year. Teachers and students alike raced along, dropping interesting sections long before they wanted to. Frequently, in order to cover concepts, they eliminated some of the lab investigations. Yet doing the labs was the main object of the whole program, so we had said. The program reverted to just another textbook-oriented course where you rush through a book just for the sake of covering it.

The result of emphasis on coverage was that people rushed through the book for the sake of finishing it rather than for the sake of knowing, exploring, and developing their creative faculties and awareness of the earth. It is a little like taking one of these whirlwind tours of Europe: 15 countries in 15 days, and then you're supposed to know all about the place! In the very superficiality of the "tour" most of the flavor is lost. Or it's like cramming your food down without chewing it. I like to savor my food, to delight in it. The same with travel; I like to settle into a place, just as we are spending several weeks in one small Norwegian village this summer to really know the place and its people and ways. I like time and an unpressured environment where I can read paragraphs of a book over and over again, where I can look up outside references that support my other reading, where I can put down one book for a few days and pick up another, leaving the ideas of the first to gestate for awhile before I resume reading it. This is the way I assimilate things. This is not to say that browsing rapidly through a set of materials or traveling rapidly through an area is bad by way of introduction. But I want to choose my own speed and depth at any given time and so do most other learners I encounter. To be "required" to cover certain ground just because that's what's in the textbook, without any disgressions, is antithetical to pleasurable, functional learning. In my own schooling it often annoyed me and turned me off towards subjects. Learners face this same problem of coverage in every subject they study. I can't begin to count the number of times I've heard teachers say, "Oh, we'd love to do that, but we simply don't have time with all the material we have to cover." For me that statement sounds the death knoll for an effective, intrinsic, inquiry-oriented learning environment that fosters growth in awareness, perceptiveness, and knowledge.

At the other extreme from the people interested in coverage are teachers who choose to make sure every student "really understands" every concept along the way and "really demonstrates acquisition" of every behavior suggested in the set of objectives that may be suggested. In those classes the group often bogs down and gets horribly stuck. Cricket took an ESCP course in eighth grade. By the end of eight months, they had only gotten to Chapter 7 or 8 (of 26). They had gone over and over and over and over and over each point so many times that none of the students had any even remote interest in the course. Sitting as I was at the time as director of the ESCP group I felt terrible about the way our curriculum, the one we had such a grand time creating was involved in turning my own daughter off to earth science!

If we are ultimately interested in how to gain knowledge, how to stimulate growth and motivation, how to leave learners with a good concept of their own capabilities and a taste for learning, if we are interested in learning as an on-going, life-long process, then the material "covered" and which curriculum is used are virtually irrelevant. What is important is the way in which learning is encouraged to proceed.

LINEARITY

> ...the road to a scientific discovery is seldom direct, and...it does not necessarily require great expertise. In fact, I am convinced that often a newcomer to a field has a great advantage because he is ignorant and does not know all the complicated reasons why a particular experiment should not be attempted.
>
> — Ivar Giaever

If we were to follow the ideas of Jean Piaget very strictly, we would probably have to adopt a rather linear attitude toward learning. There would be definite major stages to pass through in a set order. This view has been carried forward in science education by people such as Robert Gagné and is reflected in most of the materials produced for the NSF-sponsored curriculum projects of 1957 to the present. I find the mathematicians and physical scientists — physicists and chemists especially — more restricted by linear approaches than any other groups in my experience. In the early days of the Intermediate Physical Science (IPS) program, so the story goes, you couldn't get permission to use the materials at all unless you agreed to use them in exactly the order that was prescribed and unless you had been through an approved IPS workshop. This rigid and linear approach has appeared in other physics-related materials, too.

The ESCP staff fell into that trap too, in our earlier days. We set out a definite schedule that teachers **ought** to follow. The project staff at first felt that you **had** to cover the whole program and that you couldn't possibly cope with chapter 6 until you had mastered chapter 5. The idea of beginning with chapter 15 and skipping around or of using the materials as occasional, special activities was frowned upon. Several of us in the writing conferences fought against this idea and felt that people ought to be able to start anywhere, anytime, skip anything, add anything. The idea of flexible use later came to be accepted and publicized when the group of us that shared a common mistrust of linearity gained control of the project staff. Our printed materials, however, continued to project a strongly linear approach. As a project staff we later went so far as to create what we hoped would be an ultimate in non-linearity. We printed our new ideas on colorful cards which were packaged in random order so that **no** linearity as intended by us, as the materials producers, could be found at all.

The idea of linearity is to many people an attractive one. It would seem at first to simplify the instructional process and would allow all people always to be working on the same things at the same times. This should, it would seem, lead to more group support and more efficiency in helping people. Or, if we allowed different rates to different people, it would at least allow the teacher to know that each student would have been exposed to a common background by the time he reached any given stage of progress along the specified line.

The fly in the ointment is that people don't develop that way. Each learner receives so many stimuli from outside of his school environment, and the learnings from these are so diverse that each individual is bound to have a different background of preparation and interest from each other one.

Each learner discovers relationships in a different way, through the integration of new ideas with what he already knows. We don't begin to understand yet just how discovery (=learning) occurs in people or how we can program it. In effect we can't really program it at all and we can't predict when it **should** happen. When it does happen it is a surprise. Surprise is implicit in the notion of discovery. All we can do as facilitators is try to set up conditions in which the greatest possible number of avenues for discovery are present. Linear approaches imply that there is **a** way or a limited number of ways.

Even reading through a same chapter in a single book and doing a given set of laboratory exercises, individual learners will come out with different learnings, depending on their interests, no matter how focused the chapters and exercises and no matter how specific the questions asked. Discovery and learning require a certain degree of attention from the learner and attention **cannot** be required. It is an intrinsic possession of the individual. A teacher who orders "Pay attention," is really making a plea for a student to change the direction of his or her attention. I am always paying attention to something, but it may not be what you want me to attend to. The most effective learning environments legitimize the attention of the learner toward whatever its direction may be. I **can** force my attention, but I am likely to keep wandering away from it. If I capitalize on my attention (and awareness) as they occur in me, I will learn most rapidly. I assume here that attention in **any** direction can and will increase my learning. If a teacher or curriculum order me to pay attention to a pre-set line that has nothing to do with my awareness and intrinsic attention of the moment then I am unlikely to be an effective learner.

Sometimes "attention" is being paid even though a person may be doing something that makes him appear totally absorbed in another activity. I recall one instance of a ninth-grade boy apparently totally absorbed in playing with a small ball he had on his desk. A class discussion was in progress. The teacher was making a point and was at the same time feeling but not expressing irritation at the boy's "inattention." Suddenly, out of the blue, the teacher was aware that the boy was talking, calling attention to an error in calculation that the teacher had just made. The teacher's attention was actually split all the while, partly involved in irritation over the boy's inattention and partly involved in talking. The boy's apparent inattention concealed the fact that his mind was actually open, like a trap, ready to "catch" a point worth attending to!

> *Sometimes when I seem totally absorbed I am very much aware of other things around me. As I write this I hear what Lucretia says to me from time to time, and I often respond. At other times, in deeper concentration, I may be totally unaware of her presence. I just was aware of a chill. Scarcely breaking stride in my writing, I pulled on a T-shirt. Some cute Norwegian teen-aged girls just passed our yard, chattering. I am aware of their conversation, of the breeze, of gulls squawking, of a chickadee.*

No matter how deep my apparent concentration, all sorts of things are being received, and I may at any moment shift the focus of my attention. It is only when I am annoyed by "interruptions" that I realize my attention has actually wandered spontaneously to something else. For me, the moment of irritation at an interruption is often the best moment consciously to accept the flow of my attention and to change what I am doing. Sometimes as I am writing, the family will be scuttering about all around me and I may seem oblivious to them even though I may be hearing and understanding much that they say and do. At other times a much lower level of activity on their part may annoy me. At those times I realize that I may be tired of writing, that I have dried up, and that it's time to have some coffee, to sit and stare out the window, to read, to wrestle, or otherwise to give myself up to some other activity.

Linear requirements inhibit me greatly. That is why I decline to impose linear schedules on others. They simply don't work!

CLOSURE

I used to think that each lesson had to have a beginning and an ending. In ESCP we programmed all of the labs so that there was a carefully organized post-lab "discussion" to make sure the main points of the exercise were brought out and reviewed. Take a look at almost any textbook. There's always a section of review questions. Or a chapter summary. Or something like that. As a matter of fact the review materials may make up a significant proportion of the text. This goes back to the old style: "First you tell 'em what you're going to tell 'em; then you tell 'em; then you ask them to tell you what you told 'em; then **you** tell 'em what you told 'em; then you test 'em on what you told 'em."

Closure leads to emphasis on the factual material and on formulated concepts. I am interested in the processes — including the feelings — by which the concepts are formulated and the so-called "factual" information obtained. The compulsion to finish things off, to get to the end of a chapter, to go over and summarize and move on to the next thing to finish is restrictive. It keeps me looking ahead to finishings rather than delighting in the happenings of the moment. When I got into J. R. R. Tolkien's trilogy, **The Lord Of The Rings**, I found myself so absorbed with individual happenings of each page that I did not want to look ahead. I did not want a chapter to end. I wanted to savor each moment of the reading. I gradually lost track of what went before, and I was unpreoccupied with what was yet to come. I found excitement in each page and the unfolding process it represented. I was surprised when all of a sudden one day I discovered I had finished the three volumes.

Textbooks and methods books all want the moment of **closure**, where you zero in on the real thing, where everything comes together just the way it should. More and more I want experiences to be beginnings of things that will go on and on. If we really end up with closure, then the involvement may not have been worthwhile.

That is one of the things I don't like about final exams and why I have stopped giving them.

> Did you ever think of the odd way we talk about "giving" exams. As if they were some kind of gift. It's better to give than to receive. Thus teachers are more virtuous than students. How about "taking" exams. How can you refuse? And where do you take them? Can you leave them there?

To me, final exams signify the termination of an experience or an involvement. I'd rather just let my experiences hang there, unfinished, so I can have a feeling of continuation.

Sure, I finish things and I like to do that, too. I want very much to finish this book, for example. I have a lot of things I want to say. Once this comes out in print I know that it will help a lot of people out there know something about **me**, and from past experience I know that some of them, perhaps you, who never even heard of me before, may seek me out because you read this. If you do, it'll be because you see that we match up somehow and might be-together - work-together - feel-together to mutual benefit and joy. As people I work regularly together with read what I put down here, this provides a short-cut through which we can avoid some of the chicken shit-bullshit-elephantshit (as Fritz Perls calls them) we accept from each other, no matter how hard we try to avoid it, when we try to get a feeling for each other.

Peter Fenner has a label for ability to bring about closure. He calls it "terminal facility". That means a person can work through a project, communicate about it in some public way, and then call that one stage "finished." When I publish this manuscript, this book is closed, so to speak, and I can move on to the list of other projects I want to do. In a sense, the project is done from a writing point of view, **but it has just begun from a communicating point of view.**

Maybe that's one reason I'm sometimes disappointed when I see that someone working on a research study or set of ideas related to things I have studied has not referred to my work in the area. This becomes a failure of communication on my part at that point. That study of mine is really **closed** when no one needs it any more. So was it even worthwhile spending all the time to put it together?

I guess so, because my life becomes a continuing effort to communicate what I know, what I feel, who I am to other people. I can never know what efforts of mine will succeed and which will fail. It makes me feel good to speak out to people and to come together with them. Likewise it makes me feel good to receive their communication too when they write or otherwise get in touch. That's why I always find myself encouraging other people to communicate, too. I have gotten to meet a lot of good people I would not otherwise have gotten to know because they have read things I have written or become somehow aware of things I have done. So maybe that's one reason for writing or doing them. Maybe that's a reason for finishing "projects", for bringing about at least a limited form of closure. I find myself more comfortable thinking about each completed communication as a progress report rather than any kind of definitive statement. Each thing I write becomes a moment of stock-taking, the recording of some points in a process, but, I hope, without any real conclusion or terminus.

When we did **Richard The Third**, the last performance was a moment of closure. But in a sense it wasn't, because it was only a pause in communication between me and Gretchen, Pam, Pat, Ken, Steve, Jon, all of whom I saw last month in **Miss Reardon Drinks a Little.** And it was good to see them afterward and, in a sense, share in their moment of pleasure in that experience.

Endings are bitter-sweet feelings to me and I like to savor them.

Are the moments of closure in your affairs bitter-sweet moments when you regret the ending of the experience? When I used to do "post-lab" discussions and give tests I recall lots of bitter and very little sweet. I remember when I used to take or teach regular courses finishing with relief the taking of tests, grading tests, ending the course. ("The course is now over! Whew!!") Last year, when we didn't have closure in these forms I had the good feelings of just appreciating whole dimensions of themselves that people seemed willing to share. Things that went way beyond geology — and yet that was there too. It was good with many people just to sit together for a while and say "See you!" at the end instead of "Whew! It's over".

I don't want the end of an experience with learning to be a moment of death. I want it to be a moment of insemination, birth, continuation, resurrection.

I finish things but I don't want to think of them as really terminating. My attitude towards "finishing" is one of the big things involved here.

Closure is not a concept I want to focus on in the environment I occupy and share with others. Points of communications can occur when an individual brings together what he wishes to share with me, but I reject closure for any group of the whole. Closure in the sense of a moment of recorded communication is a personal thing which I want to occur when it is intrinsically ready to happen. If I force it, I am convinced that I inhibit the development of consciousness.

BLAMING

I see myself ready to blame other people for all sorts of things. At ES we occupied a branch office and reported in to a head office in Washington. Much of our correspondence was "blame-oriented." Often, the blame had nothing to do with a particular situational problem that needed to be solved. Instead, it frequently referred to an accumulation of past peccadillos. "This is just like what you people did two years ago;" "Please tell us who exactly is responsible for this error." This is what Eric Berne and others in transactional analysis call a parent-child transaction. We were treated as bad children, and guilt feelings produced by the transaction detracted from our creative productivity of the moment.

Gretchen came home from school today without a favorite necklace. During a girls' varsity basketball game she had given her necklace to a friend who passed it, together with other jewelry, to the team manager. After the game, the manager did not return the necklace. No one would take responsibility for its loss. Blame! Let's find out who is to blame.

Then I remember a time in my seventh grade "shop" course. In a teasing way, I poked a comrade in the rear with a thumb tack one day while we were all doing an exercise in drafting. The teacher descended upon me with fury and turned me into an example of a "low-lying snake in the grass" in front of my peers. Blame and punishment! Only recently have I begun to think of that particular situation without entertaining fantasies of retribution against that teacher. I still harbor a feeling of blame towards him. In **Tom Brown's Schooldays**, the good Dr. Arnold takes young Tom before the whole school for a caning based on blame for poaching quail. Tom had been framed by Gerald Flashman, an older boy. Gerald's father had ordered Gerald to get even with Tom for incidents in which Tom had thwarted amorous and other plans of the senior Flashman.

I attended a geological society meeting in which we maintained a hospitality suite for alumni and friends. Some visitors took it upon themselves to smoke marijuana in our suite. Several students blamed us for allowing this to happen as also did some colleagues. "Bad children!" We had not behaved as they thought proper, yet none of them had taken responsibility to do anything about the situation, knowing during the affair that they disapproved of our "tolerance," except to place blame **after** the fact.

The threat of a possible anonymous note to our college administrators arose, but rather than accepting this possibility and being prepared to deal with it, we wasted days' worth of energy dealing with blame.

In a science curriculum project a few years ago the business manager was caught red-handed in a multi-thousand-dollar embezzlement affair. The lawyers and senior administrators seemed more interested in establishing blame than anything else. Thus, they dealt ineffectively with the problem of documenting a reasonable loss, submitting an insurance claim, improving their regular audit procedures, and rearranging internal financial responsibility patterns in order to avoid recurrences of such situations. They haven't gotten any money back yet to my knowledge and are dealing with a time lapse that makes a stale claim for them. All because blame was so important to them. The project lost thousands of man hours of staff time devoted to placing of blame. Good hours that could better have been spent on production activities. The real loss was probably doubled by preoccupation with blaming.

Once blame is introduced, the person being blamed begins to defend himself and justify his behavior. This often is followed by cross-blaming. The person blamed seeks a cause for blaming his blamers for other things they have done. You blame me for something and then I dredge up an old resentment I have against you and hurl it in your face to deflect, in the eyes of a real or imaginary audience, the blame from me. Most blaming situations deteriorate into unpleasant, energy-consuming games instead of providing for a healthy release of feelings of resentment and transition to a position of positive activity and improvement.

Blaming gets very repetitive. In a blaming session, the blamers keep coming back to the position, "Ah, I told you he was to blame." In serious cases this can go around and around for hours, weeks, or more of intermittent blaming.

Blaming comes from preoccupation with the past rather than concentration on the present with a healthy amount of planning for the future. I feel that we cannot, as people, really avoid blaming people and circumstances when things go counter to our expectations, but the problem is to become aware of when our blaming becomes an end in itself that is unrelated to future growth and to general progress. Because it is human and inevitable that we do (and will continue to) establish blame I want to be ready to deal with this in people. I want to translate my blaming into an open admission of general resentment. Then I can allow the resentment to be accepted as a feeling which requires no extensive justification but simply needs to be expressed, and gotten into the open. Then I want others to accept my feeling and leave it behind as a basis for growth and planning. What is important is to recognize the inevitability of blaming, to help others become aware of their own "blaming behavior," and to encourage the translation of this into open expressions of resentment requiring no cross-blaming, cross-justification, or defense. Then we can move directly to positive action aimed at growth, progress, and learning.

This mode of operation becomes critical in the operation of environments designed to foster creative behavior. I hear blaming going on among people for a number of things. Here are a couple of examples.

Blaming	Translation
George never comes to group meetings and several people say he wrecks the possibility of group interaction. The group that does get together ends up spending much of its time blaming George and others who are not even present. Perhaps after several sessions of blaming someone goes to George and lays blame on him. He becomes defensive, cross-blames the rest of the group for behavior that gives him a reason not to come, and he either retreats completely from the group or else begins to come against his will and sits and sulks as bits of blame are periodically hurled his way.	The group accepts George as a free agent. In an open environment his permission not to come is real. Group members start to blame George then translate this into personal statements of resentment. ("I resent that you are absent from our group.") These are transmitted immediately and directly to George but with no expectation that he will defend. If he tries to defend himself, the group pushes him to translate his defense into a direct expression of any resentment he feels. Any repetition of blaming and cross-blaming statements is rejected in favor of positive discussion.
The lab is left in a mess. A group comes in the next day to use it and has to spend time cleaning up before they can even begin. They then spend half the morning looking around to find out who didn't clean up the lab.	The group accepts the dirty lab as a real problem, cleans it up, and goes to work. People feel resentment and express this openly via several signs they hang up. They do not seek a culprit, but rather publicize their resentment openly.
We had crushed up some rock samples of large size to do some analytical work on them. One night we found that someone had dumped a beaker full of plaster of paris into our rock powder and had broken the beaker as well, leaving ragged shards of glass in the powder. We spent time worrying about whom we should blame and how to trap the culprit.	We accept the contamination of the sample as the fact that it was. Because we feel great resentment we express this through the communication channels of the lab group. We do not seek to place blame. We also recognize a need to find a place where our samples can be kept out of the general traffic flow pattern and we encourage a reduction of traffic flow through that area.

LABELS AND PEOPLE-CLASSIFICATIONS

Labeling is the perennial substitute for thinking.
—Susan Sontag

He's a C student.
George is a trouble maker.
Old Smith is a terrible lecturer.
Labs are a drag.
Science is hard.
His I.Q. is only 93.
Jones is a genius.
Long-haired hippy freak!
2.0 grade-point average.

Labels follow people everywhere. They work contrary to creative expression. "Once a good student — always a good student," becomes true because our expectation of good studentness is transmitted in such a way to the student himself that he **does** perform well. This is good for the peole with the "good" labels attached to them, although even their development may be channeled in unnatural ways by other people's opinions and judgements which may or may not reinforce a direction of really maximum potential and ultimate happiness and productivity. For people with the label "substandard," in whatever form it takes, self-image may be doomed to assault after unjustified assault.

As they say, a police record follows you around forever. So does a school transcript. So do lots of other insidious labels.

In one drawer we put all the "inner-city kids." In another drawer we put all the "pot smokers." In a third drawer are the kids on the "honor roll."

"Humanistic Education" is a label I've had problems with recently. It expresses a lot of things that are important to me just in its inclusion of the word "human." I used the word "humane" in the title of **Risk-Trust-Love: Learning In A Humane Environment**. Right away a whole group of people started to come at me antagonistically. "That means you're the good guys and we're the bad ones, huh? What you do is humane and what we do is inhumane." The labels "humanists" versus "traditionalists" now are almost weekly fare in our campus newspaper. I fail to find much similarity with what I believe in and write these days and the idea that a lot of people are carrying around with them about so-called "humanistic education." As an associate editor of the Journal of College Science Teaching I used to receive most of the manuscripts with the words "humanistic" in their titles. We got enough of them so that it must have been a bandwagon label. What I call "humanistic education" bears little resemblance to what I read in about three quarters of those manuscripts. To me, it means "centered around the person" as a whole human being. To them it meant everything from programmed instruction to a new way of giving a favorite lecture. But it got you on the bandwagon. That's one reason I purposely left the word "humanistic" out of the title and chapter heads of this book. I'm my kind of "humanistic educator" not one that fits in any category with that label on it.

"Open School" is a problem label, together with "open education." When we tried to start an open school in Boulder, Colorado, we were immediately taken as meaning open-space schools. We fought and fought to correct that impression, but even as we were voted down by the school board, the reason that came out had little to do with what we were talking about — just about our misunderstood and incorrectly defined label.

"Encounter group" is a label that causes problems. Immediately that means to some people that we're all going to strip off our clothes and make phoney true-life confessions. If you read Carl Rogers you get a different picture, but only the people who care bother to do that. We get a lot of fearful people into our groups just because of a misunderstood label. I've tried recently to avoid the word "encounter" and try to use words such as "support," "Communication," or else no prefix at all. Better ignorance and freshness than mistaken expectations and label-based fears that keep people away from potentially worthwhile experiences.

The label "scientist" bugs me lots of times. That makes me some kind of kook in a white coat who does strange things in the lab, and that people look at as different. "Geologist" does the same thing. "Dr." does the same thing — putting me in a category of miscellaneous doctors rather than letting me be taken as me. It sets up barriers I want to break down.

Here in Norway, or whenever I travel abroad, I don't like to be labeled "American." That immediately limits the interaction people are prepared to have with me. It sets us up for trivial conversation on things I may care little about. The trivia labeled

"America The Beautiful" or "My Country - Your Country." This kind of stuff falls in the category of interaction Fritz Perls calls "chicken shit."

I don't want to see people's labels any more. I prefer to meet them as they are. Also, I decline to identify myself by labels. I'm trying to avoid labels like "geologist" or "college prof" or "science educator" or "white anglo-saxon protestant." These things structure my relationships in directions that can help to limit my interaction with others rather than leaving it open.

Personality classifications provide labels that require special discussion. I have said that I want to focus primarily on people and their creative potential in the educational process rather than on any limited area of subject matter. I want to accept people as they come to work with me or to seek assistance from me. I recognize each individual human as truly unique, and thus I want to be very careful about the human tendency — which I certainly am aware of in myself also — to generalize, lump together, and classify. Many psychologists have gotten into the business of classifying people according to their personalities just as I classify my rocks and minerals, a biologist classifies his frogs and liverworts, a chemist his ketones and alkenes, and a physicist his high-energy particles. These classifications make me uncomfortable because they tend to become simplistic labels that lead us to forget the real, multi-dimensional person being classified. It's a little like IQ and other measures of so-called "intelligence." Values are attached to the labels and it is better to have a "high" IQ than a low one. If you have a low IQ people may say you're a dummy, even though in some other dimension you may be the "smartest" of the lot. Highly creative people frequently show mediocre scores on standardized tests.

Nonetheless, each of us does this classifying to some extent. Sometimes we group people by geographic origin, sometimes by other affiliations they may have:

> Blondes have more fun.
> Southerners are prejudiced against blacks.
> Blacks are musical people.
> Swedes are slow, farm boys.
> Vermonters are taciturn.
> Englishmen always keep a stiff upper lip.
> Italians are so terribly effusive and loud.
> Puerto Ricans are sneaky and likely to stick a knife in your back.
> A Jew will take you for every cent you've got.
> Irishmen are good only to be cops.
> WASPS are supercilious, conceited snobs.

College people always look down on any kind of real physical work.
Plumbers are illiterate.
Working class people just don't appreciate the arts.
Democrats are radicals.
Sorority girls are snobs.
People on welfare are out to rob us of our tax money.
Rich people cheat on their taxes.
Young men are dangerous drivers.
Boys like science and math; girls hate these subjects.
Boys who take ballet lessons are sissies.
Girls who climb in trees are tomboys.

The list continues on and on. None of these statements can be applied to any large percentage of the group of people they purport to characterize, although the statement about Vermonters may apply to a few more Vermonters than to Italians, let's say. There **are** national characteristics. There **are** various conditioned behaviors that individuals in some groups tend to show as a result of their general conditioning. Italians do eat more squid than do farmers from Kansas. Statistically, more men than women do go into science.

A recent study involved the placing of a number of normal people into mental hospitals. Each member of the team, working out of Stanford University, got himself admitted to a mental hospital by describing symptoms of schizophrenia. Once he was admitted, each subject's task was to convince the hospital staff that he was "cured" or had improved sufficiently to be dismissed. It took one of the subjects nearly 3 months to obtain his release and others also took several weeks. During their stays in the hospital, the subjects described the attitude of staff toward them that resulted from their "labels" as schizophrenic. Virtually all of the treatment they received and the attitudes the staff held toward them were based on the labels that had been given rather than on responses to them as individual humans. After the study was published as a warning, it was much publicized in popular news magazines. Psychiatrists and psychologists associated with mental hospitals shouted "Foul!" But, as the director of the study pointed out, the main point of the study was not so much to "expose" mental institutions and poor diagnostic techniques, but rather to show how a label such as "schizophrenic," once conferred upon a patient, could follow him around and make it almost impossible for him to receive really personalized and humane treatment that **responded** to his real personal situation.

Similar studies have shown that young people classified as slow learners have received "special" treatment that reinforced their own opinions that they were slow. Human potential can be submerged and held back by such designations and classifications. Classification can stand in the way of unique responses of facilitators and employers to unique human beings.

I suppose it is part of our nature to try to classify each other, just as we try to classify all other things, in constant attempts to simplify a complicated world. But remember that **all** classifications are unreal intellectual constructs made for our convenience and are by their very nature, limited.

For a while I was enamored with classifications of personality because they helped me to see human interactions in a different light than I had seen them before. The first of these systems that I became acquainted with was a system developed by O. J. Harvey of the University of Colorado. Harvey's system includes the following personality types:

> **Type 1:** Authoritarian personalities. These people believe strongly in external fate control. Their beliefs are strongly centered around various notions of right and wrong and are often related to a strong religious control they accept over their lives.
>
> **Type 2:** Anti-Authoritarian personalities. These people oppose any authority at all. They are rebels who, in a sense, are a reverse image of type-1 personalities.
>
> **Type 3:** Dependency-based personalities. People in this category try either to become dependent on others or actually control others through their own dependency. They insinuate themselves by an excessive kind of servitude. One manifestation of this might be shown in the person that always insists on serving everyone else. With regard to the person who controls through depending, a good example would be a grandmother I know about who refused to learn to drive. Her need to get around became her way of controlling her children by turning them into her chauffeurs.
>
> **Type 4:** People in this category are very independent and free in their actions. In general they don't control others nor do they need to. They are acceptant of differences in other people — even extreme differences. They have few feelings about what other people should do. They represent an ideal of the free person.

Harvey and his colleagues have prepared a battery of paper-pencil tests that make it possible to classify people in this scheme. One, called the "This I believe" test includes questions such as: "This I believe about marriage:", "This I believe about my country." In responding, test takers are supposed to write down a few sentences expressing their beliefs on the topic presented. The test is then "graded" or classified on the basis of a complex value scale offered directly by Harvey and his colleagues or people directly trained by Harvey. This allows the somewhat subjective scale to be applied in a reproducible fashion. People taking the test are put under pressure of time and ordered to finish on time with some either vague or explicit threat hanging over their heads. The reason for pressure is Harvey's belief that people's **true** personality characteristics only come out when they are under stress. This is what might be called a **core** personality. From an intellectual point of view it is easy for me to say that category No. 4 is the ideal category and the one I would like to belong to. Then I can structure my answers in such a way that I can show myself to be what I might like to be rather than as I am. However, under stress I am more likely to come straight through as I am, because I don't have time to create a new me.

A second test that Harvey administers is called the Conceptual Systems Test, a multiple choice form. This test is graded in a mechanical way and is probably less discriminating and easier to "second-guess" in terms of allowing respondents a chance to show themselves more as they would like to be than as they are.

Harvey's tests have been applied in hundreds of studies performed by Harvey and his colleagues and students. Some results show a tendency for people who have been in the educational system for longer periods of time to be more and more in type 1 — the authoritarian mode. Administrators have shown up as strongly authoritarian in studies by Harvey's group. Teachers with longer service also concentrate in category number 1. Almost no teachers in category 2 are found among teachers and administrators who have been in the system for more than a couple of years. Very few category 4 people are found among upper level school administrators or teachers with long service.

One of two things must be happening in our present public educational system. The idealistic (category 4) and rebellious (category 2) personality types are being selected out of the system in their first 2 or 3 years of teaching, during which period a number of people in these categories **are** found within the system. Or, alternatively, people with personality characteristics of categories 2 & 4 are becoming conditioned by the system so that their original personality types have been submerged or changed in a direction of greater authoritarianism or greater dependency. The concentration of experienced teachers with category-1 and category-3 personality characteristics and the concentration of administrators with category-1 personality characteristics are alarming factors to me.

Charles Reich classifies people according to their levels of consciousness. People at the level of "Consciousness I" largely reflect the pioneer work ethic. Such people are energetic and hard working, but they work largely for themselves and not for society. Self is seen in narrow terms, and self repression is a strong factor. Consciousness I led to the development of America in a wilderness continent. Many people who hold this level of consciousness still live among us. Into the "Consciousness II" group fall the political and social liberals of the Franklin D. Roosevelt — John F. Kennedy ilk. From people of consciousness II has come the Corporate State. Organization predominates over the individual. Consciousness II arose as a result of the failure of Consciousness I in which excessive individualism led to gross irregularities, conspiracy, and destructive competition. But Consciousness II led to control of individuals by the Corporate State to an extent that individuals became lost from view. Consciousness II still dominates American Society and institutions, including the schools. Reich feels that a new consciousness that he calls "Consciousness III" has arisen among young people today. It is seen in its more extreme form in some of the communal living arrangements accompanied by strongly implemented feelings of personal freedom and independence seen in some of today's youth culture. Most of today's open school movement has probably grown among people in the Consciousness III group. Client-centered therapy among psychotherapists and student-centered learning environments in education reflect "Con 3" values. Harvey's category 4 personality falls within this general group.

Theodore Roszak also describes the new consciousness of youth and its current rejection of an overly rational and non-intuitive approach to life, knowledge, science, and technology. The Corporate State becomes an oppressive villain. Reich's Con III is founded upon liberation. As soon as the individual ceases to accept societally-imposed values and individuals begin to build their own life-styles, culture and philosophy, we are in the realm of Consciousness III.

Self and the absolute worth of every person are the beginning points for Con III. Comparative merit is rejected, as are general standards of "excellence." Each person is unique. A sense of spontaneous community becomes a keystone for human relations. The implications that growth of Consciousness III has for schools and society at large are obvious.

Armstrong has also discussed a 4-category personality classification. He makes the point that a person in one of the higher-numbered categories may be capable of accepting the views of a person in a lower numbered category, but that the reverse is not true. The freer, more independent person is able to accept the narrower attitudes of the more authoritarian or dependent people, but these people may be totally incapable of understanding or accepting him or his life style. Armstrong posits that many of today's students are relatively free people and many teachers are relatively authoritarian. This leads in many instances to an inability of teachers to provide effective assistance to their "free" students. Authoritarian teachers misinterpret the behavior of many free-personality types as rebellious. They feel that students are trying to disrupt and that they hold personal grudges against authority. This is often an inaccurate and destructive view.

All personality classifications are reductionist in their approach. They define and classify human behavior in too simple terms. Instead of recognizing an infinite variety of personality types, all differing from each other in significant ways, these classifications divide us all into 3, 4, or 6 pigeon holes and establish barriers that need not exist. They may encourage people not to try to communicate. "Oh, I'm a 4 and you're a 3. There is no possibility of our communicating." At ES we used to play guessing games — assigning people to categories on the basis of only superficial knowledge. This was usually supposed to be in jest, but I believe that there was more seriousness to this than we realized. I think we actually came to believe that some people's behavior could be predicted on the basis of the category we assigned them to. We structured our awareness in such a way that we may have overlooked new ways of understanding people and of being understood.

As an example, two teachers in a recent workshop we conducted were victims of this problem. George had always classified Hank on the basis of observed "teacher's room behavior" as a "jock," a person interested only in sports and with few other dimensions. Living together with Hank and being involved in encounter groups with him allowed George to see Hank as a sensitive, multidimensional person. Now, after years of standing apart from each other, they have begun to communicate and to share important leadership functions in their school.

On the other hand, by actually creating artificial types of personalities in my own mind, I become aware of times that I feel dependent or authoritarian characteristics in myself. If I do not like these aspects when I discover them, I can behave in different ways. I am especially struck by the importance of stress as a factor that effects my behavior, and I sometimes catch myself feeling, "Oh-oh! That was '1' behavior" when I am pressed on one point or another. I also now want to be more acceptant when someone I am working with in a learning situation, in scientific research situation, or in some other life situation is strongly stressed and shows a behavior that is uncharacteristic of him or her in less stressful times but may indeed show hidden or repressed personal characteristics that it later does us both much good to deal with specifically in our interaction.

Thus, I see personality classifications as useful awareness builders, as long as I keep reminding myself that they are only simplified models and do not represent real people. If I allow my interactions to be limited by a classification system, I will not function effectively as a facilitator of learning or as a member of a problem-solving team. My own life will be much the poorer for the lack of depth in my relationships with others.

One thing is certain, I do not want my interaction with any person to be affected by advance records or classification profiles that set up expectations within me. I do not wish to know your I.Q., what school you came from, the opinion your teachers had of you, your grade point average, whether or not you are on a scholarship, or how you rated on O. J. Harvey's **This I Believe** test or what your last employer thought of you. I want for our interaction to begin from as fresh a point as possible. If it is possible I would like for you to come to me without expectations of me as well. If we can meet, as nearly as possible, as two ordinary people, and begin our interaction from that point, we may then have the best possible chance of discovering each others' true interests, values, and personalities. A creatively based partnership has the best chance of forming under conditions of maximum freshness and lack of prior expectations.

CONSENSUS

> "The vote went 51-49. We won!"
>
> "Because a majority of you have voted for prohibition, there will be no more drinking in the United States."
>
> "The President has decided to continue his bombing of Cambodia because the polls show that thirty per-cent of the people back him. Only twenty-nine percent are opposed. The rest are undecided."
>
> "The mayor received an overwhelming mandate to continue his programs, capturing seventy-three per-cent of the vote. Voting was heavy for this area considering that this was a municipal election. A full forty per-cent of the registered voters turned out. The number of black voters eligible for registration who have actually registered is now up to thirty-five percent."

"Consensus" often leads us to compromises that really satisfy neither side. Very democratic! I guess I don't really believe in democracy if it amounts to tyranny of the majority.

As far as I'm concerned, I want each person to be free to follow his own trends, to lead his own unique life in the way he chooses as long as he does not enter into someone else's living space (taken in the broad, metaphorical sense). Whenever I infringe upon someone else's life, we need to confront each other and seek a solution between us. I do not have relationships with society or with government, with my family, or with a class. I only have relationships with individual people who are affected directly by what I do and who affect me directly by what they do.

Is this a simplistic notion for a simple society? It'll probably work fine as long as we all live on farms, forty miles apart. But are we now so dependent on what each other produce that we have to **be regulated?** Does the majority know "what's best" in terms of regulation?

There is an easy way around the demands of consensus, and it doesn't have to violate democratic traditions. It is called **alternatives.** People who don't or won't agree with each other simply leave each other alone and live in their own ways rather than hammering out a consensus, compromise viewpoint that is satisfactory to neither. There are undoubtedly limits as to how many alternatives are acceptable. But alternatives still provide a potential solution worth trying.

> Can we allow the power companies to pollute the air seriously over New Mexico, Colorado, Arizona, and Utah to benefit several tens of millions of people in California at the expense of just a couple of million in those states?
>
> Can the "hawks" go on and violate Southeast Asia or other areas of military and political conflict while the doves go off and live in their own corner?
>
> Can the mafia take all of its bad guys over in the corner and set up an armory?
>
> Can the American Nazi Party go ahead and shine up their rifles?
>
> Can those nutty nuclear physicists go ahead and explode their nuclear devices as long as they do it over **there**?

There certainly are some things that involve survival of mankind as a whole and that we may **have** to agree upon or die off.

But there are a lot fewer things in that category than we readily admit.

If we accept majority rule and "forced consensus" as the rule for all things that govern our lives we will live poor lives indeed.

If we accept a single set of rules (the majority set) for organizing **The Schools**, we can impoverish the learning environments. Schools are a place to deal with personal responsibility and values, not a place to avoid them as we now do. Schools are an excellent place to work toward alternatives. It's too late to start at the adult, war-making stage.

How can you deal with the roles of science, humanities, or arts in society unless alternatives can be explored by young learners? How can you deal with the learning of physics, literature, chemistry, languages, or environmental studies by setting up one or two or three permitted ways dictated by a majority. We know so little about how to facilitate learning and to foster the development of values that will lead to growth and positive evolution of the human race. I think we have no alternative **but** alternatives in education. Consensus in education is as dead as the dinosaurs.

I can work against consensus by legitimizing alternatives directly in the community I work within. I can legitimize alternatives simply in the way I am with people. I can accept their viewpoints and mine both as legitimate. I can reject any attempts by them to "persuade" me, and I can accept their ways without attempting to convert them to a consensus with me. **I do, however, need a consensus on the validity of alternatives!**

POLICY: WORKING TOWARD ADHOCRACY

He considered regulations the last refuge of mediocrity.
—Martin Duberman describing John Andrew Rice

As far as I'm concerned, the only policy is that every person is responsible for himself or herself. And yet I don't even fully implement **that**. Sometimes I worry about what others are learning, whether they're getting what they need and want, whether they're happy or not. Yet there is no way I can control all of that. Maybe personal responsibility isn't a policy after all; it's just a basic fact. It **is**, no matter what I do or don't do!

To me, policy is an attempt to rigidify and stabilize things so that we don't have to make decisions about individual cases. I put in a request to have an additional telephone placed in our x-ray lab where it would be open for emergency use at any time. The response: "Our policy is not to install extra telephones in departments." We requested a xerox machine at our end of a 1,000-acre campus for the thirty three percent of the faculty and students who work there. The response: "It's against our policy to have extra xerox machines." Incidentally, two machines coexisted in the administration building only one floor apart.

A question I am often asked as a department chairman is "What is the departmental policy about..." I reject policy in favor of working with individual situations. Some administrators, teachers, parents feel that they save time by having policies. I don't agree. People spend so much energy complaining about "the policy" that they would be better off and less frustrated seeking a positive solution for each issue.

Lucretia used to say to Cricket, "The rule is that you must be in by eleven. Cricket spent incredible energy trying to circumvent the "policy," often successfully, and there was friction over the **rule**, rather than dealing with individual cases.

Policy is a real way of trying to avoid responsibility. If I can say, "The policy is...," then I can avoid saying, "I get uptight when you...and I do not want you to do it." Using policy is a way of helping me keep from appearing like an unreasonable authoritarian. It is so much easier to say, "If you do this, the policy is that you will risk losing your position," rather than saying, "If you do that, I may fire you." The latter way of putting it requires me to take full responsibility for getting rid of you if I do initiate procedures to do so. I can't say anymore, "I'm a good guy and I really like you, but I have no alternative because **they** force me to do it." It also forces you to take responsibility. If it's really important enough to you, you'll go ahead and do it anyway, with full knowledge that you may lose your job. When you actually do it, if I reject "policy" notions and accept responsibility for me, we'll negotiate it. I may fire you; I may not; because **now** is not then any longer; it's **now.** (I can cop-out again by saying that "My policy is always to carry through on my word. I said I'd fire you and therefore I must!")

When I don't set policies and enforce them people can accuse me of being wishy-washy. As a matter of fact people usually do accuse of "softness" other people who choose to respond to situations rather than invoking policy. I **might** just lapse into favoritism and not really be fair to people. So what? If I do and we are operating honestly, we'll deal with any excesses of this type that either you or I fall into.

I remember courses I used to teach at Syracuse when I would come up with a whole new scheme at the beginning of the term. Then, as the term wore on and I saw certain things not working, I said to myself, "Gee, I'd like to change this, but it wouldn't be fair in the middle of the term. People will think I'm being inconsistent and capricious." And so I blundered along, knowing it was wrong and telling the students that it was too late to change by then. I was refusing to take responsibility and was copping out by blaming the problems on the system that I had created. That was somehow easier than just saying. "Oh, the hell with it! Let's sit down together and work this out so we can get the most out of the time we have left."

Recently, in statements of my feelings that I have been duplicating and sending around to the people in our learning community, I have been putting in at the bottom a place that says, "This policy is good for today, only. It may be changed by the time you receive this note. It represents my feeling and opinion at the time I write it."

It may be hard to get away from "policies." I've had forty-two years of conditioning to accept (and to make) policies. I still fall into the trap of unconsciously accepting other people's policies as a way out of having to act, myself. And I still fall into the trap of setting up policy as a way of trying to avoid responsibility and decision-making related to things that are important to me. But as I become aware of both explicit and hidden policies I'm actually having fun working around them. "Hidden" policy is most fun; becoming aware of hidden policy often leads to a most positive and delightful realization, "Oh, God! Have I really been doing that!" The delight comes from knowing that all I have to do is stop!

I see two extremes of organizational patterns. In one of these, a vertically-organized system, the person on top issues the rules and policy, and subordinates then enforce them down the line. So we get the concept of the administrator as enforcer. Garbling occurs down the line.

The second kind of organization is a horizontally-organized system. This can be interpreted as every person for himself, but, if it works, everyone is responsive to everyone else and accepts the value of diversity.

Robert Townsend implemented a flexible organization tending toward horizontal structure in the Avis Rent-A-Car system. He made some important breakthroughs in developing a successful operating model of a flexible and responsive business organization.

Saab and Volvo have recently moved toward systems of greater personal responsibility — horizontality — in their car assembly procedures. The John Deere company uses team assembly for its tractors, and many other U.S. firms have now begun to experiment along these lines. How to replace the old assembly-line concept? A Danish firm allowed some of its tractor-assembly groups to set up their own assembly lines "democratically" rather than having each line set up by a foreman, in the old style. The lines that were self-organized showed significantly higher and better productivity than the control group lines which continued to have their members assigned by a foreman to positions on the line. On the self-organized line, workers shifted positions often, so that each person fulfilled many different tasks at different times rather than becoming specialists in "left-rear-tire nut tightening." All of the members of the self-organized (horizontally organized) lines felt special pride in their product.

A television program I recently saw showed a group of anthropologists who had been air-dropped into an area of New Guinea populated by primitive people. They had never seen any of the trappings of modern civilization. The research team stayed with the natives for an extended period of time trying to find out their reactions to twentieth century gadgets and, coincidentally, observing the mode of life of the natives. At one time, the research team asked for help in building a helicopter landing pad in the jungle so that new equipment and supplies could be received more easily. They explained that a huge bird was coming in and needed a "nest".

The day came for building the pad. A bunch of the natives showed up and started to mill around in apparently aimless fashion. No one took a "leadership" role. Finally a native went out into the woods, and a chopping noise was heard. Soon chopping noises rang out all over the jungle. Logs began to appear in the clearing. Individual natives started to lay the logs out. Sometimes one worker would set a log out, apparently in place, and another would come up and remove that log, putting it in another place. It looked like absolute chaos, according to the research team. No one supervised. And yet, at the end of the day, the pad was complete and ready for the big bird. The research team members expressed the view that it would have taken a trained crew of European workers, using decent equipment, at least twice as long to do the same job.

I worked as an unskilled laborer on a power plant construction job in Colorado one summer. I was to do only what I was told to do. We ended up spending hours sitting around waiting for roofing material to be brought in to us. We were working as the roofing crew that week and there was no invitation for us to hunt out other kinds of work that might hasten the completion of the project. I didn't have to take responsibility. That was up to the Peter Kiewit Company and their vertically-organized system. I wonder how many extra man hours it took us to finish? Twice as many as needed?

Last spring after our university theater production of **Richard The Third**, we all stayed around after the last performance to tear down the set. It was an incredible construction: a whole building to be disassembled. Bets were taken about how long the take-down would require. Kathy, the stage director, said, "Under four hours." Ken bet Kathy a six-pack of beer that it would take over four hours. When I went up after removing my make-up I looked around for someone to tell me what to do. After all, I was just a dumb actor and knew nothing about how to take that particular set down. Soon, it became apparent that no one was going to tell me what to do. So I grabbed a hammer and set to. Everyone else seemed to be doing the same thing. Every now and then somebody up above on one of the upper platforms would shout down, "Hey, you nut, not that piece yet, I'm standing up here." Every now and then I'd shout a warning to someone, too. Whenever anyone started to fall, trip, or step into a danger area, someone would be there to caution or help him or her. We swarmed over the set like a bunch of ants. Absolutely **no** organization. Kathy (the set boss) and Tom (the director) were both fellow ants as far as I could see.

We had the set down and the whole stage and backstage area spick and span within two hours. All of the usable lumber had been neatly stacked for the next show, nails pulled out and all. Food and drink even materialized. No organization? Horizontal organization! Just a bunch of people with a common interest and goal and a great deal of caring about each other.

When six of us went out to Oregon to work on some problems involving volcanic rocks we tried to let the organization be horizontal. In order to do this Bill and I, technically the "faculty leaders" and the people who "had charge" of the grant monies financing the trip declined to make decisions for the group. When one person did try to make a decision for the group, any one of us could simply decline to operate on the basis of that decision. Compromise was required often, mainly because we only had two cars for the six of us and thus could not easily split unless we were willing to move off to separate modes of transportation — which still would have been possible had we not been able to compromise. When we stopped at night, somehow camp got set up and meals were produced. All of us participated in various ways. We did not set up any "duty rosters" or organization charts. If I wanted something done, I did it. Others did the same. No one asked, "Can I help you do this...?" or, "Would you like me to..." Basically people would simply say, "I am going to..." No one needed to ask anyone for permission. If one of us didn't like what another member of the group "was going to...," we could either express our disagreement or we could accept his decision and live with its consequences. Rarely did I hear the phrases, "You should..." or "You shouldn't..." I did hear, "I like the way you..." and "I felt uncomfortable when you..."

When we had an ES curriculum materials workshop at the A2Z Ranch we had a cook to take care of the main food preparation, but we took care of the dish-washing, snacks, and clean-up. Here, too, we seemed able to avoid rosters whereby we became **committed** to be a certain place or do a certain thing at a certain time; where a schedule became a constraint.

The same thing happened at an encounter group Gunner and Fritz invited me to attend. At our organizational meeting, Gunner announced that the group would have to set up its own arrangements for food, sleeping spaces, and so forth. He would not make those decisions for us. All he wanted was for all to commit themselves to several hours of work sessions per day. Food got bought, meals got cooked, dishes got washed, messes got cleaned up. Everyone seemed involved. I at least was not aware of anyone "gold bricking" in any significant way. If they were, I'm sure they would have been confronted with that perception. At certain times, Gunner would move around and say, "O.K., time to get to work now." And we would assemble as an overall group. Actually, we were "at work" all of the time anyway in the sense of encountering each other and working on our personal awareness. Further, when people wanted out of the big group, they left. If someone didn't show up when Gunner called for a work session, we noticed it and some people expressed concern. But Gunner always treated absence as any person's right. Decisions to be there or not to be there were treated as a matter of personal responsibility. "Charlie is not here yet" was treated as a piece of information and a statement of group awareness rather than as a statement meaning "Charlie should be here. Someone go get him."

Barry Stevens describes her disappointment at returning to the Gestalt Workshop Center in British Columbia and finding that kitchen-duty rosters had appeared on the walls and a vertical organization had begun to insinuate itself.

Class schedules are devices of vertical organization. Registration for courses lasting fifteen weeks (or five weeks or one week) are devices of vertical organization unless you can drop them at any time. I have always chuckled at school organizations that have a "last day to drop a class" or "last day to add a class." Such "last days" are attempts by the organization (**them**) to assume responsibility for students.

Jim decided right at the end of the "add-a-class" period to add a second credit in geology and drop one in another area. I "approved" it. Unfortunately, he waited a day to hand the slip in. His request was denied. So the Dean told him he'd have to run it through the academic policy committee. They turned it down again. We tried the Dean again and then back to the academic policy committee with a petition. Finally Jim's change of schedule was approved. What an incredible amount of energy and bad feeling just so that a learner can be allowed to determine for himself what his tuition money is to be paid for! Jim's time, my time, the Dean's time, plus the time of several faculty members and student representatives on the policy committee (two rounds for all parties concerned.) Imagine how much energy would be freed for learning, feeling, inquiring if we just would agree to let learners make these simple decisions for themselves and take the responsibility that life will demand of them anyway.

Schedules in a vertical organization tell me where I should be, regardless of whether I or anyone else feels like it.

Information sheets or blackboards or newsletters or a shout down the hall in a horizontally organized (disorganized?) group allow me to be where I am, when I want to be. In a horizontal organization a free flow of information and communication can replace a fixed schedule.

A horizontal organization does put demands on people. If they want access to what's going on, they have to take responsibility for keeping themselves informed. If they miss something then they're responsible.

I recognize the complexity of the communication problem in larger groups. It's easy to keep informal and to participate when six of us are on a field expedition involving two cars or when twenty-five of us are isolated at a Wyoming Ranch forty miles from the nearest town or in the Adirondacks at an isolated hunting lodge. I thus make some compromises. I commit myself to be at a certain place at a certain time next week, not knowing whether or not I'll feel like it or not. But at least **I** commit myself, and if I feel too far off I can call it off, too! I may want to "schedule" a field trip in order to get transportation and other details arranged. If the weather is terrible or I don't feel up to it though and still make myself go, then I must take responsibility for a bum trip from my point of view.

I don't accept vertical organizational or the schedule box anymore. The registrar can't schedule **me** anymore. He can print something, — whatever he chooses, but I'll then work with the learners **I have committed myself to** in order to find arrangements that suit us all. I don't commit myself to organizations and schedules any more. Only to people I agree to work with. And I can terminate an agreement with a person anytime we both choose to do so — or should I say whenever either one of us decides to.

I can work toward a more flexible mode of operation even in a rigidly organized, vertical society. All I have to do is **think horizontally**. The Dean's position "above" me only exists if I accept it as an above-below relationship. My position **above** a member of my department, faculty or student, only exists if I view it that way. If I view us all as being on a horizontal level and send out and receive communications with that attitude, then a functioning kind of equality begins to develop.

MAY I, MOTHER?

I was brought up to ask permission politely for all sorts of things.

> May I borrow your mineralogy book?
> May I check out a geology hammer?
> I'd like your permission to miss class today.
> I've got a chance for a ride home on Thursday; so would you mind if I didn't came to lab that day? Otherwise I'll lose two whole days of the holiday.
> May I take this test over again? I'm sure I can do better.
> May I sign up for your interterm course?
> Would you mind if I cooked dinner tonight?
> **CAN I HELP YOU?**

When I ask permission I subordinate myself to the other person. If the other person grants me permission then I allow him to take responsibility for me. "But you said it'd be all right if I....." Barry Stevens suggests converting requests for permission to positive statements:

> I'm borrowing your mineralogy book.
> I'm checking out a geology hammer.
> I'm taking the key to the darkroom.
> I won't be in class today.
> I'm going home on Thursday, so I won't be in lab that day.
> I'm taking this test over again.
> I'm signing up for your interterm course.
> I'm cooking dinner tonight.
> I'm helping you do this.

Listening to Gretchen recently, I've noticed that she is often saying things in this positive way. I like it. I feel her strength and positiveness when she tells me what she has decided to do rather than asking **if** she can.

I heard about one elementary school teacher who virtually made a rule that people would **say** that they were doing something rather than asking **if**. The whole tone of her group changed into one of positive regard, more open communication, and greater self-assurance on the part of her students.

When I was in graduate school I once just moved into a new and better office and told my advisor, "I've moved into that other office." He was outraged. But he didn't make me move! And I **did** get my degree! This same advisor used to advise us to **do** rather than to ask. He was ok! "If you ask, I might say no!" he said.

Many of the people in our open learning community are still asking permission to do a lot of things. I find myself responding "You can't do it if you have to ask permission." When they ask, they're asking me to share responsibility for their actions. Then I have to make policy or enforce policy. Policy has no place in an open community.

If they **state** what they are doing, then I can accept them for the positive, self-assured people that they are. I can state an equally positive reverse position. I rarely feel I have to do that. But when I do, that's ok, too.

> Student: "May I borrow your mineralogy book?"
>
> Me (Thinking): "I really don't like to let that book go out, but I want people to have access too" — moments of conflict and hesitation follow.
>
> Aloud: "Well, I guess so, but please don't keep it long.
>
> Student: (Thinking): "Gee, he's kind of hard to deal with on this. He doesn't really want me to have it. I can tell." — Goes out feeling hesitant and not very self-assured.
>
> **ALTERNATIVE SCENARIO**
>
> Student: "Bill, I'm taking your mineralogy book."
> Me: "Hey! I use it all the time."
> Student: "Don't worry, I'll bring it back in the morning."
> Me: "Ok!"
>
> It's not always that easy.
>
> Larry: "I'm going to start locking the darkroom next year.
> Me: "The hell you are."

After that we had a long discussion about openness in the learning environment and who can lock whom out of where. But it was an open and positive discussion and wasn't characterized by the "Mother, -May I?" quality.

Suppose Larry had just started locking the darkroom door on his own? That might have worked out fine, too, because a locked door needn't **necessarily** mean denied access. It just sets up another step in the access procedure. That might even be a good step.

> Thomas Edison was once asked, after he had finally found a successful filament for an electric light bulb, "You found a workable filament after five hundred tries. Wasn't this terribly frustrating? How did you feel on the 499th try?" To this, Edison responded something like the following, "I felt fine; I knew 499 ways that didn't work!"

My relationship with people during the past few years have convinced me that recorded judgements do more to inhibit functional learning, self-actualizing behavior and a comfortable and productive environment than any other single factor. Some people have had home and extra-curricular life that has promoted the formation of a highly positive self-image. For students who just happen to like school-type learning and who happen to be placed with good, person-oriented teachers, self-confidence and self-esteem grow without regard to the way the system as a whole operates. For others, who come to interact with me after years of being judged and being told over and over what work they should do and what their work is worth, we have a high barrier to get over before significant exploratory and creative behavior can emerge.

I decided several years ago to let people enter on their own terms the environment that I occupy. Let them share it with me as they wish to use it. As their interest in whatever they are doing (be it dancing, hair-combing, making love, painting pictures, telling jokes or, at the opposite "extremes" deriving equations, quantifying the relationship between stream velocity and bed load, or mastering the chemistry of complex proteins) enters the domain of scientific approaches, perception, and analysis **then** we start to work on it as more strictly defined "science."

Thus I accept that a learner in a so-called "science course" may do other things far outside the realm conventionally defined as science. The other things may be the very access routes that can later open up the world of science. Fortunately, "science" doesn't really exist as a separate entity. It is a sector of human enterprise that is totally integrated with other human activity. There is no way you can avoid involvement with science in our civilization any more than you can avoid eating. We are assailed from all sides by science. We observe our world. We make conclusions about it. Regardless of how formally we approach things, we all do science in some form or the other.

If I accept that a learner may come into the learing environment and do as he chooses, if I accept that any activity leads to learning of **something** and that "science" is often involved somehow or other in anything anyone learns, then I must decline making an evaluation in the form of a grade.

When Dwight Allen took over as Dean of the School of Education at the University of Massachusetts, he ran into a conservative faculty group opposed to change in the evaluation system. Here is how he says he handled it.

> ...you have to behave quite differently before you can change (institutions) simply...For example, we did away with grades. Again, we didn't set out deliberately to do this, but we took advantage of the situation that occurred. You see, in the first semester with the new faculty we got together in the School of Education we gave 77 percent A's. Now, this did not endear us to the hearts of our liberal arts colleagues because it played absolute havoc with their grade-point averages and their predictors. So we went to the faculty senate and said, 'Look, please help us to get out of your way. Let us go pass-fail so we're not fouling up your grade-point averages.' And with a big sigh of relief, they let us do it....

My approach for the time being is a similar one. If grades must appear and students "want" them, let them assign their own. In the meanwhile I also work within the system to change the rules. The problem is a deep one. As long as we have "academic credit," "merit systems," and such factors to deal with we leave people in positions of having to think about legitimacy and other people's expectations rather than the kind of open exploration which most favors increase in awareness, level of consciousness, and creative power.

If I test someone, I am not finding out **what** he has learned. I am evaluating whether or not he has learned what I want him to learn. If I no longer accept that I can tell a person what he **ought to know**, then I have no basis for making an extrinsic evaluation. I can make an evaluation such as "you can't tell the difference between quartz and feldspar." This statement does give a person information about himself. But I see no value in recording this. Let the learner do what he chooses with the information that he doesn't recognize the difference between quartz and feldspar. Who else needs to know that? (In the professional or preprofessional this example becomes nonsense because I assume an intrinsic motivation to learn the difference between quartz and feldspar in anyone who is trying to become a person educated in the specific areas of geology. I don't need to push it there.)

My attitude toward evaluation and toward the lack of boundaries between science and other areas of human activity has led me to deal with evaluation as follows:

I feel that any learning experience - perhaps I should just say any **experience,** because learning is an inherent part of experiencing, is multi-dimensional. There is no test I could apply, no set of questions I could ask, that could possibly indicate the real dimensions of any experience. The only way I could really know this would be for me to be actually in the other person's skin and for me to be **infinitely aware** of what was going on inside that skin and outside of it.

What I just wrote scares me a little. It implies that I cannot fully evaluate even the dimensions of my **own** experience. I cannot assess what I myself have learned from an experience until I come to exercise that learning later. This goes back to the notion of **tacit learning** I discussed earlier. Five years from now something that I am absorbing as I sit here writing this may emerge to combine with a set of other factors in the form of an idea or a broad understanding. If it does emerge in that way, people will say to me, "Where did you ever learn that?" This has often happened to me. I have seen it happen so much to other people, too, that I am confident that we learn and store an incredible amount of both information and skill that we only find out about much later if at all. I have no idea how much I really already know. I keep astonishing myself. I keep being astonished at the things Cricket, Gretchen, and William come out with and at the things the people I work with in the learning environment all of a sudden bring to bear on their work and play.

If I realize that I cannot assess even my own learning, this helps me to let things flow more easily. I can choose not to worry so much about whether I'm really learning what I **should.** What I should learn is what I am learning. Trying may actually inhibit learning. Excessive trying may be a block, an inhibitor, to perception. I know that when I force myself it seems to take forever to learn something. At other times, when I let things flow, I am astonished at the way I absorb things and make them functional for me. Concentration, in the sense of forcing, may inhibit. Awareness, in the sense of flowing, seems to facilitate my functioning.

But isn't some kind of evaluation useful after all? Don't other people's opinions help me? Yes it is, and they are...I think. As long as the evaluation is primarily for information rather than for a public record. Recording what a person **can** do well may be useful, but recording other things is probably not useful. I want to be direct with other people, and I want them to be direct with me. When someone asks my opinion I want to be able to say, "I don't like that piece of work" but not, "Your work is no good." That difference in phrasing is important to me. In the former, "I don't like that piece of work" I take responsibility for my own feelings about it. In the latter I express myself as if I have some kind of absolute knowledge of what **is** bad or good. I know that some things I do are positively valued by some people and negatively valued by others. Where is the "good" and the "bad?" Only in the mind of the evaluator. Even when "everybody" says, "It stinks," another person might some day come forth and mutter to himself (or aloud if he's really courageous), "But **I** like it."

I want other people to feel free to say to me, "I don't like your work," when I solicit this information. And I want to be free enough and confident enough to say, "Hey, you're right, I just realized that I don't either." or "Thanks for your opinion, but I still like it!"

I still find it hard to say "I don't like what you did that time." When I do, you might stop "liking" me. That always hurts my ego, because I like to be liked. But as long as I take responsibility for my feelings and don't try to express absolute judgements of your work, I stand a chance of providing useful information to you, and you to me in the reverse situation.

Direct contact and comment on each others' immediate work and processes are essential in the environment I want to work in. Recorded, long-term judgements have little place.

I also want to develop a greater sensitivity to when are the good times to **defer** any judgements at all, too. At certain stages of my own learning and exploration, I don't want inputs from **anyone.** My ideas or processes may be in such a delicate condition that any forced judgement from outside may be destructive. I'm bound to continue making mistakes and blundering in on people, shooting off my mouth when they least need it. And I accept that my friends will continue to do this to me, also. But we can all develop greater sensitivity to when we are intruding and to when our evaluative comments may support or inhibit. It all comes back to awareness of each other and of the environment we share and its limitations and advantages.

THE LESS - IS - MORE HYPOTHESIS

Mies Van der Rohe, the architect, demonstrated the attractiveness of simplicity. The less complicated a thing is, the less cluttered, the more attractive and useful it may be. The Japanese express this value strongly in many of their architectural and art forms.

> *The restfulness of a simple environment is important to me as I sit here in a rough Norwegian summer house. With its sparse Scandinavian furnishings, it fits in well on the hillside, and the magnificence of the natural surroundings is enhanced and itself enhances the restful and simple quality of this room.*

The principle of simplicity, often known as Occam's Razor, is a well-established means of selecting preferred hypotheses in science. Given a number of different multiple hypotheses, a general practice is to take as preferred the simplest hypothesis that goes along with the information available. We don't say that the hypothesis is true, but merely that we prefer simpler, more easily imaginable explanations to more difficult, less understandable ones. This may be a reductionist notion, but I still find it esthetically attractive. In the physical sciences, investigators seek the most simple and elegant formulations possible and are rewarded by their peers on these grounds.

Still, as in all other things, I do not necessarily always wish to seek the most simple approach or solution. Sometimes I enjoy clutter, a busy environment, and busy explanations too. Embroidery can add a great deal of beauty and spice to the more spare look of a sweater or tablecloth. Sometimes ginger-bready victorian environments please me. The baroque and the rococo attract me, too. I want a range of complex and simple configurations to choose among depending upon my moods, but I incline towards the simple most often.

What does this have to do with organizations and with creativity? I offer the hypothesis that reduction and simplification of bureaucracies in governments, corporations, and schools and concentration on humans within the system rather than on the system and its organization, can have the same good effects that simplicity has in architecture, art, science, literature, music, and elsewhere. The less complex the organization, the more it tends to respond spontaneously rather than in fixed, organized, and predictable ways. The fewer the rigidly defined channels, the more effectively, pleasurably, and naturally the processes of learning and producing may become.

Christopher Jencks suggests that real improvement in education and learning is probably not closely related to increases in school budgets and physical plants. Among the important factors that probably transcend the school in importance are things such as genetics, environment, family background, and even television. School budget, education policies, and teacher characteristics are minor factors, relatively. In this result I find another message in favor of getting away from ideas of conventional schools and in favor of turning centralized learning facilities into resource centers, rather than houses of detention.

Less-is-more may then come to mean, **the less we interfere with people and their unique ways of exploring within a rich environment encompassing all aspects of society, the more they may grow in ways consonant with their own potential.**

THE FIRST-YEAR HYPOTHESIS

When I work with groups of educators concerned with science education, with the development of creativity, and with other aspects of education at various levels, I always advocate the introduction of freer alternatives within the system. A common reason for rejecting the things I advocate is, "oh, you can't begin that in the 7th (9th, 13th, 17th) grade. We have to change the elementary school first. By the time people reach us they are so conditioned that there is little hope of changing them." On the other hand, the elementary teachers say, "Oh, our children are not mature enough for that approach. They couldn't really learn if we left them to themselves." Many students, by the time they reach junior high school feel that they are too conditioned to be able to learn on their own. If those of us interested in change through alternatives were to listen seriously to those statements, we would simply have to give up in despair and go off to start another private free school rather than trying to get public and larger, established, private institutions to accept alternatives.

I agree that primary school is the best place to begin to offer children substantial freedom and alternatives. The experience of the British infant schools and of the North Dakota public schools are sufficient to indicate how easy it is to introduce freedom, personal responsibility, and student decision-making at that level. But so far, my main area of operation has been with older students and I am unwilling to give any human being up for "lost" just because he has had no substantial amount of freedom in schools for his first 6 (9, 12, 16) years of school. I am prepared to start with any learner at any age and in any context, to provide him with an open learning environment. My experience is that he will learn to cope and will grow at a rate equal to or greater than he could in a more "closed" system. I have observed a phenomenon which may help, however, in determining the levels at which a highly changed learning environment may have a maximum chance of success on an institutional level. Figure 1 will provide a basis for discussion.

The diagram indicates high motivation, expectations, excitement and hope when children first enter school. Who has failed to notice the excitement of the first day of school when a 5 or 6 year old, feeling very important, first goes off to school, book in hand? Who has failed to notice later in the year, in many children, a falling off of interest, a disappointment. To some extent each

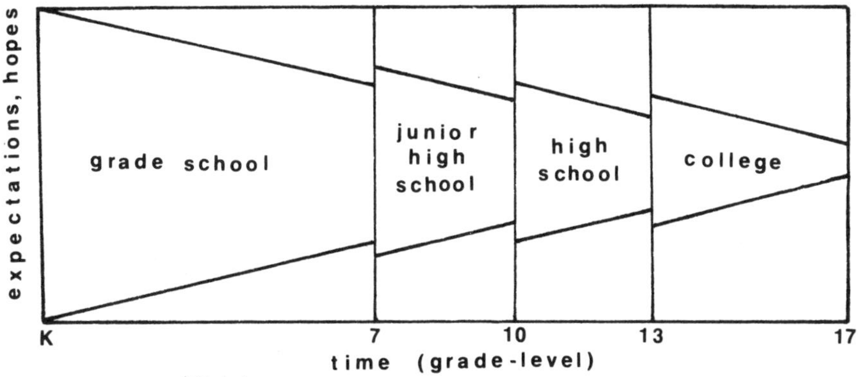

year brings with it hopes for a better, more pleasurable and profitable experience. I recall, especially in the earlier grades, my hopes that next year's teacher (or class or experience) would somehow be better. For the diagram to be more representative of reality it might be necessary to show spurts of increased hopes to accompany each such change. Somehow, it was usually the same, although occasionally a really good teacher or group or class would make a better than usual year. Usually, within a single school, we sort of knew what next year's teacher or teachers would be like, for the word always got around.

When we changed schools, however, at the transitions between leaving the grade-school environment and moving into the whole new environment called junior high school there was a **real** increase in my expectations and hopes for improvement. Going into junior high school felt again like the first day in school had felt. Entry into high-school produced the same increase in expectations and hopes.

I have shown that the expectations and hopes in each unit of involvement fall lower than in the previous one. That is because we always found out that, in spite of our initial hopes it was **still** the same old school, ruled in the same old way, with the same old tests, grades, homework, assignments and pressures. Basically there were the same formal relationships between us and our teachers, the same old, "Yes, Miss Jones, Yes Mr. Smith." The same never listening to us. As Holden Caulfield, in **Catcher In The Rye**, describes his interaction with old Mr. Spencer, "He wasn't even listening. He hardly ever listened to you when you said something."

The diagram represents in graphic form my idea that each time a learner enters a significantly new level of the educational system his expectations and hopes for a new and better situation increase. As the student proceeds through a given level of a system which is really the same in its basic distrust of the learner and in its paternalism, he is conditioned, his hopes fall, and he does what he is told. Nonetheless, regardless of how conditioned he may have become, every time he or she changes institutions or buildings (and even on a finer level every time he or she changes teachers or courses) there is a surge of expectation that "things may get better." This is, in my opinion, a basic human quality: The hope that things may get better. In any case, I propose that the beginning of grade school, the beginning of junior high school or middle school, the beginning of high school, of college, of graduate school, and of any new job may be the time for maximum expenditure of energy in creating changed and improved modes of education and for the introduction of significally different alternatives.

In a system which introduces free and open alternatives specifically designed to respond to the expressed needs of individual, unique people, it may be possible to reverse the diagram so that it looks like the one shown in Fig. 2.

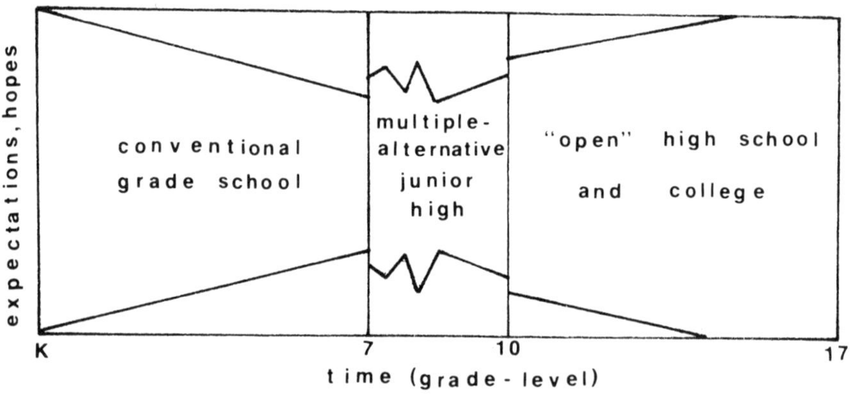

This diagram shows an ordinary grade school that conditions a student and reduces his hopes and expectations. In the succeeding multiple alternative junior high school the student has a period of coping to deal with, characterized by relative highs and lows. Once coping behavior is attained there is growth of hopes and expectation rather than reduction as in ordinary schools. There probably is still a positive jump in expectations upon movement to other institutions, and if they operate in the same open or multiple-alternatives way, growth of expectations will continue. A continuing "opening" process is likely. People in such situations are developing processes of self-actualization and self-realization that leads to maximum possibility for development of unique potential.

What about a mixed situation where some of the middle segments of an educational system are open while others are closed? Another diagram may help:

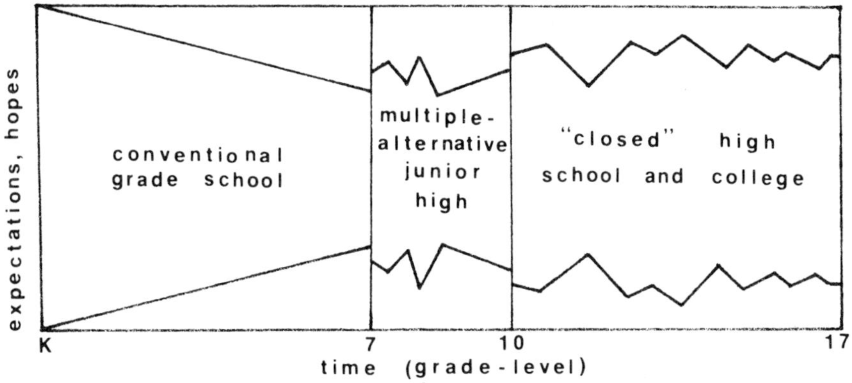

In this instance the student's open experiences may be followed by low periods and a new need to re-examine the system. The **overall** level of hopes may still be a good deal higher than it was during the totally "closing" progression shown in diagram 1. Probably, the rate of "decay" of hopes is also lower, because the learner now has a greater sense of the **possible.** He may, in fact, become an important change agent in his own right, but he may suffer psychological ups and downs.

In general, people I know who have experienced changes from open systems to higher level systems that are more closed have learned to cope and are better, more creative, and more productive people as a result of their encounter with a system that demands self-propulsion. All of the ideas I present above are suitable for testing and I urge educational research teams to address themselves to studies of this complex and difficult problem.

From what I have seen in open systems that operate from kindergarten through grade 12, I infer a pattern such as the one shown in Fig. 4, below.

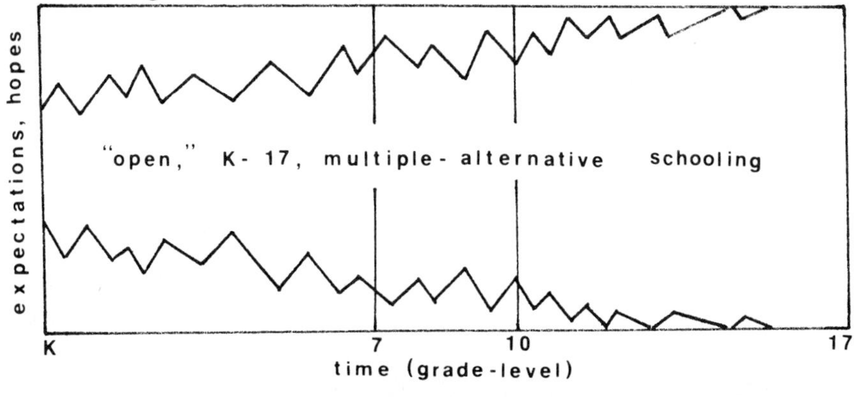

The diagram shows continuous growth of hopes, expectations, feelings about self and creative power and potential. A few schools are operating in this mode and I firmly believe I see the pattern shown in the diagram. Note that the lines are not straight, showing that individuals will always continue to experience highs and lows related to their personal biological cycles, to reward and rejection effects that will always be part of any society, and to other effects. The trend, however, is toward continuous growth.

I have seen my own children go through these abrupt rises in hopes and expectations more than the usual number of times as we have moved about. Moving from one city to another they have been faced with more opportunities for the effect to operate. In a way their motivations has been kept somehow higher than for many children, I feel. At the same time, both they and I are surprised about the uniformity and sameness we find in public schools everywhere.

I remember in myself, in my friends, and in students who have worked with me, this same first-of-the-year spurt, nearly always strongest when an important change of level has been involved. That is one of the reasons I have always especially enjoyed working with freshman students in college during their first months. I feel in them more enthusiasm and anticipation than I often do in sophomores and upperclassmen. This is probably related to what we might now label **The First Year Hypothesis.**

This effect is probably similar to what has been labelled "The Hawthorne effect." The Hawthorne effect is simply that people do better at things (factory production, where the effect was first well documented, in education, and elsewhere) when some new element is introduced. If you increase the level of lighting in a factory for a while, for example, production may increase on a production line. Then it gradually returns to its former level. Then if you decrease illumination back to where it was, productivity may again increase temporarily. Muzak may have worked that way in its early days. Everybody liked the music to start with, productivity and efficiency increased, and then people got tired of the music.

In schools, new curricula are well documented to be more successful in their first year of introduction than at any other time.

The question then becomes, how do you create conditions so there is always something new in the school environment to help keep motivations and expectations high? One anecdote has a young child in an open school asking his facilitator, "Do I have to do what I want to do today?" Sameness seems to be one of the greatest things to overcome.

The best kinds of open schools and ultimately the concept of the free learning resources center may offer the best opportunity for a "perpetual Hawthorne effect." This is ultimately the self-renewing environment of John Gardner, too. In such a place the student who gets "into" science can go do nothing but science for a whole day, week, or month if and when he or she chooses to. The same for math, English, or French. The learner follows his own motivation or responds to stimuli in the environment that he perceives as exciting. Then the environment offers the possibility of continual changes at the learner's option rather than according to someone else's schedule.

AN ODE TO QUALITY AND EXCELLENCE

Parents, teachers, supervisors, principals, superintendents, admissions officers, professors, deans, presidents, trustees, employment officers, bosses, boards of directors! All of you seek "quality." By quality, you usually mean "excellence," especially when you are in charge. You define quality and you expect people who emerge from a lower rung of any hierarchy, real or imagined, to meet your standards of quality before you allow them into a zone you control or influence. You expect quality control in the same way that it is associated with inspection of a piece of furniture or in testing the bounce of a ping-pong ball. Students emerge from their experiences bearing a quality-rating level in their cumulative quality records. Sometimes, when they wonder who they are and how they are doing, they look back over their cumulative ratings. Sometimes they actually **believe** those ratings and begin to think of themselves as "grade B eggs" or as "poor in drawing, good in science, and fair in English."

How do you feel when the next person up the line rates your quality and enters it into the records? Do you really believe the supervisor who says you're a poor plumber, teller, secretary, science teacher, principal, electrician, lecturer, cook, division head, barber? Or do you consider yourself as being involved in a continuous, life-long growth process in which you are always a little bit "better" the next time than you were the last? Do you resent being rated?

Interesting how most teachers resist student evaluations and ratings of **their** work! And yet when the student ratings are favorable they flaunt them. But if the ratings are negative, they rationalize them away—or at least try to, the same way their own students rationalize away poor ratings **they** receive. However you look at it, a quality rating—even though it purports to deal with a person's **product** rather than with him as a person—is frequently internalized.

Jean used to do secretarial work for another department. They asked to have her transferred out because, "the quality of her work was not high enough." Another group took her on and allowed her to create her own role in several important ways. She became an office manager with considerable responsibility. Her work delighted the people she worked with. Note that I said "with" and not "for."

At ES I was required to hand in rating sheets for all of our staff before annual salary increases could be approved. We decided that each person should fill out his or her own rating forms and that we would talk honestly with each other about how we were getting along. This helped to break down the "quality control" feelings, but the idea of recorded, cumulative statements about quality still annoyed all of us.

High quality is not something that you have to do; it is something that you are and become. I like to think of quality and excellence as belonging in the realm of processes. It doesn't matter how badly I just did; what matters is what I **am**, here and now, and what I can become. **Being**, here and now, needs all of my energy if I am to become all that I can. Preoccupation with past products or behavior—with my cumulative record—can only drag me back and reduce the quality of my present experience. Excessive preparation for tomorrow's quality-control-point or rating also reduces the quality of my life—my processes and my products—today. Quality only exists **now**. It also exists as a **potential**.

Quality education occurs only when the origin of learning activities is recognized to be within the learner. As a teacher, facilitator, or parent you are at best an **external** factor. You cannot materially decrease the quality of education and learning, regardless of what you do, if the locus of learning in students is **internal**. This has to do with each student's perception of himself and how much he lives in his own present. You can perhaps improve the quality of education by recognizing the intrinsic nature of real learning and by working to encourage recognition of learners' personal responsibility for their own growth.

I believe in non-academic contacts as primary stage-setters for quality education. Some examples will illustrate my point. Joannie, a girl who was not working directly with me in any academic context, but who is completing her work toward becoming a secondary school teacher, called up the other day. She sounded distressed and said she wanted to talk. When I went to meet her in my room later I found her sitting on the floor in the corner, a poncho-type shawl concealing her almost completely, like a tent. A large hat over her head made Joannie, the person, invisible. She had her arms around her legs and held herself into a tight, almost impregnable ball. She had tried for days to get someone—a teacher—to interact with her on a plane other than academic. Personal distress had led her to cut most classes and the quality of her experience with respect to learning various "subjects" had consequently been terrible. She described a visit to one of her education teachers—a very concerned and well-meaning person. When she arrived, the teacher had spent several minutes fumbling through files looking up her records, without even looking at her, while Joannie sat and wept openly without the teacher's even being aware of her distress. She approached the teacher with a very personal agenda to deal with, but the teacher, without even listening to determine the reason for her visit, gave her a "standard" treatment that ignored the real problem she was dealing with.

Judy, a student in geology, asked one morning if we might meet that afternoon. When we sat down together, we looked at each other for awhile and she finally said, "I really don't have anything in particular to talk about, but, in the 3 years I have been here I have never sat down with a teacher just to talk, and I wanted to see if I could." Her voice trembled and she seemed very nervous, but, having taken the risk to set up a non-academic contact like this, and having been accepted on that basis, she soon relaxed and we dealt with an agenda called "getting to know you." Judy's lack of personal contact had been inhibiting the development of "quality education" for her.

In a college faculty much concerned—at least in their rhetoric—about quality, the student service group has arranged an annual pre-Christmas dinner for Freshman students. At this dinner, faculty members and administrators serve the freshmen. Last year, only 4 out of 150 faculty members volunteered to participate. After some phoning and urging, the number was raised to 10 or 15. Then the administrators called a previously unscheduled faculty meeting to continue discussion of a long-term planning document. In despair the organizers of the dinner cancelled their plans, and the freshmen, as usual, marched again through the cafeteria line. Once again, long-term planning and preoccupation with the future, won out over concern for the real basis for excellence: responsiveness to the present.

I sometimes find myself feeling, "Well, come to the point. I'm a busy person and don't waste my time like this!" but Joannie, Judy several hundred freshman students marching through the cafeteria line again, and dozens of others about whom I might also tell you, keep reminding me that there is probably little quality or excellence in an environment where people restrict their interaction to the superficial level of academic concerns and where preoccupation with the past or future leads to neglect of the present.

Quality and excellence in education are largely states of mind as well as ongoing processes. People who have low opinions of themselves are apt to have experiences of low quality. At a faculty meeting I attended, members of the group talked about "despising themselves" because they thought they were probably getting lower salaries than people in some other institutions. By devoting their time and energy to a problem of this type, they actually **did** lower the quality of the education they are helping to provide. Self-deprecation becomes a self-fulfilling prophesy for teachers, students, administrators, businessmen, preachers, construction workers, anyone. If you think ill of yourself, you are likely to do a bad job and to have experiences of low quality.

The quality of the environment that schools provide for learning has a great deal to do with the quality of education. If the teachers have self-confidence and a high opinion of their own worth, then this attitude will be transmitted to students. If teachers are apprehensive, unsure of themselves as people, ill-at-ease, threatened, or worried, then these attitudes may carry over into their students. I just heard an administrator deploring the relatively little use that is made of excellent language-laboratory facilities in his institution. I was pleased to hear him fault the institution rather than the students, when he said, sadly, "Perhaps we're just not creating a good enough environment for them."

On another occasion, however, the same administrator tried to prevent a group of 15 science students from going off to a national meeting of a professional society. "They would miss too many classes," he said. Many other teachers agreed with him that being in their classes was more important than a several-day trip that would incorporate them right into the heart of the profession they hoped to embrace. The students went anyway and the experience they had was unquestionably a high point in their academic lives. They developed close personal relationships with numerous senior scientists and with students from other institutions. In addition, they learned more science during that week than they could possibly have learned in any full semester of residence in their isolated little school, and they even managed to make up their math, language and philosphy assignments, when they got back, with no apparent losses to anyone.

I want to challenge a certain number of myths that surround the idea of "quality" education: Many people I know consider quality as a definite correlate of quantity. Quantitites involved include number of requirements, number of credit hours, hours spent in class, number of tests and quizzes number of books read, number of lectures, number of pages per term paper, number of projects per term, number of minutes in class, number of experiments, and number of weeks per term. At a recent meeting I heard several science department chairmen veto a forward-looking proposal for a new calendar because they would only have 11 lab weeks instead of 12 lab-weeks. They really **did** equate number of labs and quality of learning! In a college newspaper devoted to blue-sky speculations about possible changes in the direction of creating an ideal, high-quality set of programs, a highly respected faculty member stated, "Three years ago the graduation requirements called for 120 semester hours, normally given as 40 3-hour courses....We now require 32 units and 3 interterms. Does this program provide a better educational experience...as did the former program?" His argument continues on that level. As long as we focus on quantity there is little real chance of improving quality.

In a study reported from Sweden, students in an overcrowded public school were put on a schedule in which they attended school for half of the normal number of hours. Compared with a control group who spent the full number of hours in school, there were no significant differences in the kinds of learning measured by the tests used.

Tests as indicators of quality are also suspect. I find little correlation between quality of a learning experience, subject matter learning (in terms of long-term retention), and the presence or absence of tests or their easiness or difficulty. As a matter of fact, extremely difficult tests can be so injurious to personal self-confidence of some students that they actually inhibit learning. A professor I know recently gave an examination on which he gave 30 F's, a large number of D's and a very small number of C's. Students I talked to were incensed not because of the low grades as much as they were by the misunderstanding they felt. There were excellent students who felt they were doing quality work, but their learning was not congruent with his examination. I experienced a similar situation myself in a physical chemistry course I once took. It was aimed at non-majors and was supposed to be a relatively non-mathematical treatment. The instructor informed us that we must be poor students or we wouldn't be in his course. The good students took the "more difficult" course. We started in his mind as a low-quality, "C" class and he made sure that almost all of us got C or below as grades. (Many people from that class later earned PhD degrees in various sciences and have become high-quality, productive scientists and teachers.) A "difficult" course with many meetings and labs followed by "rigorous" examination in which there is a gaussian curve with a low C average proably represents a learning experience of **low** quality. The quality I wish to improve is the quality of **learning**, not of teaching or of rigor or of difficulty. Something that is "difficult" is usually merely unenjoyable. As such, making it less "difficult" and more enjoyable may be the way to improve quality.

The quality of student papers is often questioned. Many of my teachers used to rip my papers to shreds. The number of red marks indicate the quality of the teacher's critique, they say. Another thing that "quality" editing and the seeking of "high quality papers" through highly critical review can do is severely inhibit people and lead them to fear writing anything. A science faculty member in graduate school once returned a paper to me, covered with red marks. The marks were helpful, but a note informing me, "I'd never pass a thesis written in your current style," almost led me to leave graduate school. Critique must nourish rather than inhibit. Heavy criticism and the requiremnt, "You should write like I do," may lead people not to write or to imitate rather than to develop a unique style. Student papers written in response to requirements have a lesser chance of leading to quality writing than do papers written because of an intrinsic desire to communicate. I've gotten to the point now where I usually say, "Either write it for yourself, or don't write it at all. If you're writing it to please me, I'm not really interested in reading it. If you're writing it because you really want to communicate your ideas and excitement to me and to others then I'd like to read it. Do you want me to comment on it? If so, shall I comment on the ideas, on your style, or on both?" The quality of the writing I now receive has greatly improved, in my opinion.

Another myth is that quality education can only occur in well-equipped schools with high per-student expenditures. High quality education can occur in any setting, regardless of how poorly financed, providing that students are given a chance to base their learning on personally chosen directions rather than having to follow externally specified programs.

A number of indexes of quality exist, and I look for these when I try to judge the quality of a learning situation:

> Is there a feeling of electric excitement in the air?

To what extent do people attend non-required functions? To what extent can and do students and staff re-order their priorities to take advantage of unique opportunities. If a well-known scientist or philosopher visits the town or the school, do the staff and students put aside their routine work to go to the visitor, or does the routine keep staff and students "plugging away." If the latter is true the quality of education is probably low. If a chance for a field trip in earth science or biology comes up, do teachers in English, social studies, etc. gladly and willingly encourage their students to go on the field trip. (The reverse must be true also when a poet visits the school during science time!)

How "hungry" are the students and staff? To what extent do students clamor around a visitor to learn about him or her. To what extent do they come to school eager to talk about last night's science program seen on television?

What quantity of materials are produced? In spite of what I said above, quantity can also indicate quality, when materials produced have **not** been the result of a requirement to produce. When students and staff are relatively free and they **still** produce **because they have something to communicate to others**, this is an index of high quality learning.

How relaxed is the feeling of the school? The absence of aversive, unpleasant controls usually accompanies my idea of a quality learning environment. Uptightness and fear are indices of low quality.

Is there a lack of administrative sanctions and threats at all levels? It takes about 10 or 15 minutes in a teachers' room or one luncheon with a faculty group to sense whether or not administrative harmony exists.

How well are differences accepted and how willing are students and teachers to work together on their own, without requirements to do so?

What access exists to the outside world? Does the school and do the teachers and students accept that people learn and do many learning things better elsewhere than on the school premises? Do teachers help to arrange absence from school and access to the outside world?

Does the atmosphere feel coercive or non-coercive?

How many smiles do I see; how many frowns? How many students and staff encounter me with their eyes, smile and seek to know me?

How much are the school facilities used at times other than normal school hours? Can students use the facilities at almost any time of the day or night?

To what degree are students visitors in faculty homes and vice versa?

Do teachers eat lunch together with the students?

Do teachers share locker-room facilities with the students?

Are there teachers' lounges or any other spaces that are off-limits to students or to faculty?

How much informal versus formal contact do teachers and students have?

What do faculty members and students talk about when they are together? Things that they both consider important or things that either the teacher or the students consider to be trivial?

What do the students talk about when they are away from the teachers?

What do teachers talk about when they are away from the students? If they say bad things about the students, that's an index of low quality environments.

To what extent are certain key library materials used: technical journals, non-fiction, reference sources? To what extent does the library seek inter-library loans from other libraries? (If the library seems adequate, then the quality of learning in the environment is probably low. In a really good learning environment the library will always seem inadequate.

Is everyone totally satisfied? If so, that's probably bad, too, because there is no vision. The question is — how is dissatisfaction expressed? By action leading to improvement and change or just by continuous complaints about why "they" aren't doing something about the situation?

To what extent are prospective students and faculty members trying to get into the institution?

How diverse are the programs of the school. In general I believe that the more diverse the program is, the higher the quality of the school from an educational point of view. Can students learn almost anything at any time they are ready to do so? If so — high quality. If not — low quality.

How can you tell whether an institution has quality education going on in it? Certainly not by looking at cumulative grade point averages, at college board scores, at test results, at graduate record exams, or at the academic credentials of teachers. Most of the criteria mentioned above require an evaluator to have a feeling for the school. Quality is a function of feeling more than anything else.

Quality education is the process of tuning up the body, the intellect, the emotions, the will, and all of the self. It recognizes that we are all striving to reach what Fritz Perls calls the creative mid-point in our lives — the zone of equilibrium where all of our systems are in balance to receive, to work things over, and to communicate. Quality education does not mean stressing the intellect only. Sometimes the gymnasium, the swimming pool, the dance, or the play may just be more important to overall quality than the chemistry lab or the math session. Sometimes hiring a new technician or librarian may do more for quality than hiring a new "teacher."

> If you start out to do
> a masterpiece, how will you ever
> finish it?
>
> —George Balanchine

ENCUMBRANCES

As I work with people, I can allow myself to be encumbered by all sorts of inhibitors to satisfactory relationships.

A person's past record is an encumbrance. Yet usually, people conspire to encumber me with past records. Every time a learner wants to major in our department, the administration sends me all of his transcripts, high school records, etc. The idea is to help me "counsel" the learner.

Dino came over last night to talk about a workshop he is now attending for dormitory head residents. He's heading up the dorm for special interest groups concerned about environmental problems. He hopes to have the place become a real living-learning center, with different people from the sciences and humanities actually meeting groups there in informal settings. In looking over the lists of people who will be residing in the dorms he'll "manage" someone pointed out that three or four names were those of some "real troublemakers." Dino is now encumbered with someone else's prejudgements. He said he wished he didn't know this because now it will be just a little harder for him to approach them as fresh, new people.

I don't want to know who **was** a bad student or a **bad actor.** I don't want to plan in advance how to **handle** someone. This reduces the possibility of my responding spontaneously to others. How about people I knew last year **myself?** Can I erase my previous impressions and feelings and meet each person as a **new** person? Of course I can't. But I can work to unencumber myself. I can focus as much as possible on our interaction of today. I know that I will develop expectations of how people will respond. But I can grow toward, flow toward a me that meets every person, each time **as if** for the first time. If I do this, even with the oldest of friends, I stand a chance of being surprised, of discovering new depths that I might otherwise lose in a web of concealing expectancies.

"You know me better than that!" is something I don't want to say to people or to feel any more!

"I wouldn't have expected that sort of thing from you," is another thing I don't want to say or feel anymore.

I am also encumbered by what I know. If I'm not careful, my interpretation of the world will be limited to modifications of things I have previously observed and synthesized or had synthesized for me in books I read and talks I hear. I loose freshness and growth potential in my attempts to do science, to extend my perception and understanding of my world and my context as I allow my previous knowledge to limit and encumber me. Here, too, I want to look at everything I see **as if** for the first time. Actually I **do** look at everything I see for the first time. The same I is never present in a second observation and the thing I observe is never really exactly the same. If both I and what I am observing do indeed change from moment to moment, then I will be much better off if I can take a fresh, unencumbered look.

Several factors become important to me when I feel boxed-in. I have to take full responsibility for any boxes I perceive. They are really of my making and I can change them to suit me or get completely out of them any time I initiate behavior, attitudes, and feelings necessary to alter a box I become aware of.

First I must be aware that a box is there. Then I must decide whether or not I like the box. I then can take responsibility for either staying in it or getting out of it or modifying it. No one can tell me I **should** get out of it, incidentally. **Anything** is legitimate for me as long as I take responsibility. It's only illegitimate for me if I find myself saying, thinking or feeling, "They make me." I've never been able to find out who "they" really are.

If I don't like the box then I find that the best routes out of it are through trying to allow myself greater **spontaneity** in that particular context. I can try to respond more openly and intuitively to whatever situations arise rather than going by rules. As soon as I feel bound by a rule, I know my response is not likely to be a spontaneous one.

When I become more spontaneous I find myself making more and more fortunate discoveries - seemingly by accident. Serendipity enters my life. I transcend the box.

> I just looked up the word serendipity and found that it was coined by Horace Walpole. The heroes of his tale, **The Three Princes of Serendip** apparently had an aptitude for making useful discoveries during their spontaneous activities.

Synergy is another word I like. According to Buckminster Fuller, it means, "...**behaviors of a whole system unpredicted by the separate behaviors of any of its parts.**"

Integration is a way for me to get out of boxes I find myself enclosed by. If "geology" becomes a box, I just integrate geology with oceanography, geography, meterology, and astronomy, and I get earth science. When that is a box I integrate it with biology, physics, chemistry, and sociology and end up with environmental sciences. As I add art, music, and literature I change it into environmental studies, so that my field for "study" has grown from a limited view of the earth to an all-encompassing one of my total environment. Now I can pursue what I choose to pursue and can feel that it is legitimate. If a box remains, its walls are too far away for me to see. The presence or absence of a box is a function of my awareness and of the length of my view.

If I feel that my current relationships with students are boxed in by a notion of what a teacher-student relationship **should** be, I can integrate here, too. I redefine us all as "learners." This helps things to flow. I also redefine us as "equal people" in terms of power relationships. That can help, further.

Integration becomes a way of linking things up that I had somehow compartmentalized before. It is basically a way of expanding my view. Expansion is growth. I encompass more, I become more. I trust the process.

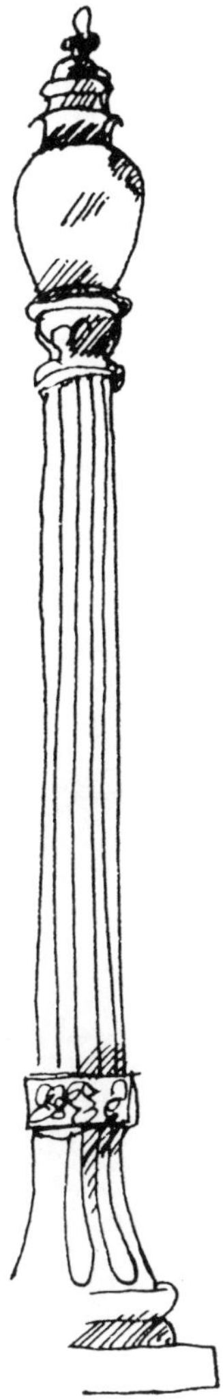

GROWING PAINS

PLANNING, TUMMIES, MY PRODUCTIVITY, YOUR PRODUCTIVITY

Why are you tight, oh tummy of mine?
A week till the conference
Three weeks till the term
Is everything ready?
Is everything there?
Phone up the people
Write them all letters
Order their books
Pads, pencil, and gear
What field trips we'll take!
What labs we will do!
I plan and I plan and I plan,
But still...
Why are you tight, o tummy of mine?

I woke up this morning with a jolt. Only a few days remain before the beginning of our environment studies workshop for teachers. My tummy knotted up. I jotted a list of a dozen people to phone, a dozen more things to buy, stipend checks to be ordered for our participants, salaries for staff members and consultants. Will it work out? Will all the participants show up? Will they have a good experience? Will they like me? What'll happen? **Should** we schedule more structure for them? Will they function? Can we trust the group process yet another time?

A week after the conference ends, our students will be back here at St. Lawrence. What'll I do, then? I want to start having my advisees over for meals, to get them together as people, outside the context of "school." How about all of our majors? Some I've been around for two years and still don't **know**. Regrets well up for last year's seniors, some of whom left without my ever really knowing them. All that richness of people. I want to share a piece of each of them and yet sometimes there seems to be so little of me to go around.

What'll I do with the group that wants to do mineralogy this term? Some of them want me to lay the content on them, they tell me. Yet will they grow — if I just do that? How do I get to the **person** in each of them? How can I be a person to them and not just a walking textbook of mineralogy. I'll take them on field trips. We'll get out together.

I'll handle the content by programming it. But the work involved! WHEN is there time for **them** if I'm always planning and preparing materials. When is there time for the real them, the real people?

So many of the things I plan never really get done and end up being hollow promises. People reproach me for not doing what I said I'd do. If there were only more of me.

But where am I in all of this? Do I lose myself and the things I want to do and need to do to be me? I do when I start trying to take responsibility for other people and their learning and growth.

The phone just rang and I'm told that people from the National Science Foundation will visit our conference. What'll **they** think? Another piece of pressure. If I allow it to be pressure on me. I can make up a dozen — no a hundred — fantasies about what might happen.

But I'm beginning to get comfortable with the notion that what'll happen **will** happen and no amount of expended energy and worry today will change that. I can't predict what'll happen. If I could, all possibility of spontaneity would be dead. In the spontaneity is the life.

I feel a little better for having sat down to write this before running off to deal with all of those lists of things I "have to" do. You know, even if I didn't do one of the things on that list, everything would be all right. But I'll still do that preparation. At least some of it. And writing this down is a kind of preparation, too. I'm a little more in touch with my feelings now than I was a few minutes ago.

My tummy is still tight. And it's OK, too. I don't even want to fight it. I find myself even wanting to savor it. It is becoming almost a high feeling now.

OK, tummy, let's go out and live a little now!

WRESTLING WITH ME ABOUT WHAT I WANT TO DO VERSUS WHAT I "SHOULD" DO

When I started to write this in my journal it was strictly for me. Then as I continued, I decided that I would probably want to share it with a few people I feel close to. I didn't really write it for others to read, however. I wrote it mainly to see what would come out as I wrote. In this way it is really an exploration of me — no changes or editing done.

As I started to write I found myself having a dialogue between two "opposing sides" of me. I've recently been reading some of the things written by Fritz Perls, and I thus unconsciously found myself writing this dialogue as a dialogue. I finally identified the parts of me represented in this as Perls' TOPDOG (the part of me that keeps bugging me with what I really **should** be doing) and his UNDERDOG (the real me—? Whatever that means — the me that wants to live here and now)

After going to Washington yesterday for an editorial board meeting I was thinking about "having to go to Vermont today. I realized that I have been running around like a chicken with it's head cut off — ever since the beginning of the term. I've been doing most things because I feel that I "should." Of course, "should-ness" is related to various long-term goals I've set up for myself. But sometimes I trap myself so much into a pattern of what is **going to be** that I forget that I exist **now** and that **now** is what is really important. Sometimes I lose track of myself.

So I wrestled with the problem of whether to go to Vermont or not. I've already spent $9.00 for pre-registration, $4.00 for a banquet ticket, and $4.00 for the guidebook. The guidebook I have, so it's really only $13.00 that I have "invested." Suppose it were $100.00 or $500.00. Would that need to make a difference? How much am I willing to let $$ control my life? It's a long drive to Vermont, and I'm tired of all this driving around, at least as far as today and tomorrow are concerned.

(Topdog) — But if you don't go, you'll not be there representing the department — and that's against your principles!

(Underdog) — I'm tired of "principles" today. I'm not the only one in the department. Why should I take responsibility for all of us?

— It's your department. You made it the way it is now. You **owe** it to them to keep pushing, being places, putting out.

—But the biggest goal I have is for people to take responsibility for themselves! I'm a people too — and if I go because "they" think I should, then, am I really taking responsibility for me or am I letting "them" control me. How free am I, anyway?

— I guess you're as free as you want to be. Only don't forget what you owe them!

— I don't owe them anything — except to be me as much as I can. The best thing I have to offer them is me, really. If there's not much of me, then I'm not worth much to them either.

— Back to this Vermont thing. You know another reason you **should** go is that several people there are expecting to see you too! How about TB, Barry, Terry, and the others?

— You've really put me on a spot there. That's hitting below the belt. You know that they're the real reason I want to go rather than just going to be on the field trips. I've had these good letters from TB and Terry saying how good it will be to get together. And I've been truly looking forward to seeing these people, touching them, hugging them, and sharing ourselves.

— Then maybe you'd better go! There's still time. It's only 11:20 A. M., and you can still make it to Burlington for the banquet.

— No, today I'm going to do what I **really** want to do: to write, to explore myself, to start on a joint art thing with Lucretia, to be here with Lucretia and the kids, to let my heart beat at a normal rate. Not to throw myself into a pile of 400 miscellaneous people at that meeting, even though there are some very UN-MISCELLANEOUS people there like TB, Barry, and Terry. I **will** miss not seeing them. But we share things of each other across space and time. I think I'll send them a copy of this. I'll not let you control me today, Mr. Topdog!

— OK, so you're not going to Burlington. Since you've got a free day, you'd better drive down to Syracuse and get all those rocks that Dan has suggested you pick up soon. You won't have time next week. When **are** you going to get them if you don't go down today??? You could have stopped to pick up some of them last night when the plane returned you to Syracuse and you had the microbus right there handy. It would have only taken you another hour or two.

— Yeah! I had already had an 18-hour day getting down to D. C., having meetings all day, finishing a manuscript plus a review on the plane up and back.

— Hey! Are you trying to impress me or something? Sounds like you're getting defensive and trying to justify yourself again. Are you sure you don't want to go to Burlington? You really **should**, you know!

—Hey, you're laying it on pretty hard, T.D.! But I must admit that you've caught me at it again.

— Now it's getting a little lighter outside. The sun might even come out. Why don't you be a good boy and go down to Syracuse and get those rocks? — HEY! — There is a patch of sun. Now don't you wish you were going to Burlington? There's still time.

— No, I feel good sitting right here. I like this little den of mine. First time I've really had a den of my own. The leaves are falling outside. There's a pleasant sound of family downstairs. If it gets nicer I think I'll drive over to Madrid (12 miles) and mess around in the old quarry where they got the stone for Sykes Hall. That'll be part of the new thing I want to do with Lucretia. I want to work with her.

— Hey — are you trying to justify yourself again? How sure are you? Maybe you want to do that just to please her?

— Owwww! That's a low blow.

— Now go down and get in the car and either go to Burlington, where you really should be or else to Syracuse and get those rocks. Remember that if you had those rocks you could tell some students that **they** really should look at those rocks and study them, too. Just like you tried to tell some of them that they **should** really go to Vermont, too. Or if you went to Vermont, you could tell them about all of the big shots you know and saw and talked to and how, if they really want to be big deal-geologists they **should** go to these things and make a good impression. You can still control those students more if you want to, too, you know!

— No, I'm getting farther and farther away from wanting to do that, I think. And now that I'm getting to know what **you** are more and more, I'm sure as hell not going to do it because **you** say I should.

— Fooey! I still see the old authoritarian, papa-knows-best coming out in you **plenty**. So don't give me that line!

— Anyway, regardless of what you say, I'm not going to either Burlington or Syracuse just because you or anyone else thinks I **should.**

— Wow! Are you perverse today! What ever became of the old Bill Romey who always did what I told him to do?

— Yep! This weekend is mine, and I'm going to weigh everything in terms of whether I really want to do it or whether my motivation is just to keep **you** happy and smug the way you usually are.

Post scriptum:

T. D. — You really ought to go to the office, then, and work on your correspondence! Remember that business of getting the tape recorders and things set up for the lab next week? And you're responsible for this week's labs, too. And don't forget Colloquy '72. You've got to send out all of that registration information and try to get the "delinquents" to pay up.

U. D. — Nope — I'd rather write this and then go out and visit that quarry or do something completely unrelated to what I "ought" to do — meaning whatever you propose, old dog.

— And there's that manuscript to type up and send to Mary Hawkins, too!

— That's a little different. I know that's an "ought," too. Well, not quite, because it's not due till tomorrow or Monday. But that's different. I like that article. It relates to something that I'm thinking about right now, as a matter of personal pleasure. It has me on a pleasant little ego trip. It's a real "me" thing. So if I do that, it won't be to please **you**. Cricket is playing her flute now. I like that. It's time for lunch, too. A leisurely one at that. And **you** are not invited!

TOM'S ISLAND

We were at upper Saranac Lake for a workshop. Tom soon discovered that the little island directly opposite our conference center provided an ideal camping spot. He could erect his tent as a private place to provide respite and calm. He slept there a couple of nights. Others even joined him there, giving up their beds in camp to sleep beneath the stars or in Tom's "Swiss Chalet," as they called his elegant tent.

Dan got fed up with the workshop program from time to time. He kept threatening to go home. One morning he got up, determined that he **would** go home. But then he realized that he really **could** go home anytime he wanted to. No one was compelling him to stay, and there would be no "penalties" if he did leave. Having realized that he had permission, that he controlled his own going or staying, he **decided** to stay. Knowing he could leave made it possible to take responsibility for staying and for commiting himself to a highly involved participation.

Several nuns did not seem very comfortable in the exceedingly free environment of the workshop. They took every possibile opportunity to go off by themselves on separate field trips of their own. At first, I felt some resentment towards them; I felt they were denying us the inputs they could have provided to the workshop. Also, I wondered how they could take back with them the flavor of a program in which they seemed to be participating so little. Then I realized that the permission for them to go off as they chose to do was a really essential part of the environment we wished to create: a free environment for learning. The quality of their participating was probably improved by the permission they had to leave and return as they chose. As a matter of fact they might not have stayed through the whole workshop at all if they had not **used** their permission in the way they did.

Spo, Karen and Jim attended one of our open-education workshops for science teachers. The second evening, they decided they were not getting enough out of the experience to warrant their staying. At first I felt upset because they were not, I felt, giving the conference or the group a chance. Still, as several of us on the workshop staff talked with them, we realized that an "open" workshop **had** to include permission for anyone to leave, no questions asked. They left. About a half-hour later, Spo returned. For her, the permission to leave had become a functional kind of permission to stay. She contributed actively and vigorously to the rest of the workshop and has gone on to exercise leadership in other areas.

Tom's Island becomes a metaphor representing the need for a refuge, for a place each person creates in any given context as a refuge for himself. When I get to the point where I have had enough of any situation, I like to know there is a place where I can go to be by myself. Sometimes that place is in my fantasy. I can always retreat to my fantasy, to my imagination. I can choose to shut off the outside world in this way. But it is even better if I feel free to go off physically to some different place when I feel the need to do so.

To me it is very important to allow people—to encourage them—to create their own "islands" in any environment we share. I want them to know, explicitly, that they are free to go, physically as well as mentally, to their islands whenever they choose to. An environment without easy access to Tom's Island cannot be very open or free.

CONFLICTING DEMANDS AND WISHES, AWARENESS, POTATOES AND THE FRONT LAWN

This morning I got up all bright and ready to work on this manuscript. It's very nearly finished now. I am mainly filling in holes where there are additional things I want to convey. Actually a book is never really finished, if I can judge from my feelings after **Inquiry Techniques**, and **Risk-Trust-Love.** After I send this in to the printer I'll keep embellishing it in my mind, adding to it, and removing things mentally. A new book is growing already. It may come out. It may not. Putting it down on paper is no final pronouncement. Just a way-station, an attempt to communicate my feelings and ideas of this moment, an attempt to share my process, perhaps to enter into you, and to help you enter into me if we ever meet.

> "Bill, are you going to take those rotten potatoes back to the store?"
>
> "Not now. I'm all set to write. I'll do it this afternoon."
>
> ...Incoherent and coherent fussing.
>
> "Oh, all right! I'll take them back now!" (Then, to myself, "If I'd listened to my own good judgement last night and gone to the supermarket instead of the corner store as you insisted that I do, we probably wouldn't have gotten a bag of rotten ones anyway."
>
> "Whew!" I caught myself, "What kind of a cop-out on responsibility is that? If I went to the corner store instead of the supermarket! That's I that did it, regardless of who said I should."
>
> OK - off to the corner store. Art is very nice about it, so I'm kind of glad I went to the corner store last night after all. Besides, that's past, and dwelling on whether it was good or bad to have done it is just a waste of energy. Besides, I chuckled to myself, that lottery ticket I bought last night along with the potatoes will undoubtedly earn me $50,000 a year for life! That's what the ticket says!
>
> Back at home as I started upstairs to write, Lucretia said, "Are you going to mow the lawn?"

I replied, "This afternoon, — I'm trying to get up and write, you know."

...More fussing, with comments about "Mother and Dad arriving this afternoon."

OK. I really don't care if the lawn looks tidy anyway. I kind of like the weed-flowers and the way the long grass tickles my bare feet. Anyway, I decide I'll go ahead and do it.

As I mow, my mind is going in a million directions. Suddenly, as I push the power mower up over a little hump, the blade catches and the motor grinds to a halt. I realize that I'm not very aware. I've been off in my head thinking about how I wish I was upstairs writing. In my head again. Not experiencing my body, the grass, the machine. I thought about when I first got up. Then, even though eager and ready to go write I felt aware of my body. As I washed my face I was very much aware of the feel of the water, the slipperiness of the soap. No word - thoughts in my mind — just feeling.

Then I thought of a short passage in an article Gunner just gave me about awareness. Here's what John Enright wrote.

> The difference between awareness and unfocused reverie is most clear in the process of eating. Awareness of eating would include the appearance, smell, and taste of the food; the kinesthetic sense of the destruction of the food though chewing and swallowing; and the associated affects of pleasure or disgust....most people while eating are engaged primarily in some sort of reverie. They engage, perhaps, in revenge fantasies about some recent slight, a rerun of the latest Giants' game, or even fantasies about what they are going to eat for dessert in a few minutes....Many people clutter up their lives almost constantly with this internal noise of pointless and only shallowly gratifying fantasy. Since it is not substantially gratifying and does not successfully resolve any unfinished business, its consequences are to make the actual ongoing behavior...less satisfying and to create more unfinished business. For example, consider an obsessive student who interrupts his studying with fantasies of the evening's date. When evening comes, and studying is not completed or well done, he ruins his date worrying about studying.

Word-thoughts get in the way of a lot of my awareness. John Stevens suggests that when you do some normal, ritualistic, everyday activity like dressing or brushing your teeth, you slow yourself to half tempo and try to feel and be aware of your movements, feelings, and bodily sensations. That's the way I had been aware while washing my face this morning.

When I ate my egg, however, I was doing another mind trip about how I'd rather write than deal with moldy potatoes and long grass. All my thoughts did then was to deprive me of pleasure in my egg!

So I tried to become aware of the mowing-the-lawn process and my feelings about it. I got more aware of the lay of the lawn, of the roots and bumps. The machine misbehaved, losing a wheel. OK. I was still operating with low awareness of the machine that had become an extension of my arms, a tool to increase my **power** and productivity, as it were. I was able to replace initial outrage with quiet fixing of the machine. It kept springing out of action due to a lost cotter pin, but somehow a big piece of my awareness included the machine and the shape of the lawn. I felt more comfortable and easy. My energy flowed better. I still wanted to write, and ideas kept coming into my mind, but my body seemed to be there with me, too.

Barry Stevens describes how she is able to extend her awareness to various parts of her body and head and shuttle back and forth from one to the other, capturing a wholeness of self and interaction with things outside of her. She describes her anger at times when she lets her preoccupation with past and future interfere with her awareness of the present. I can't keep out of past and future totally, but when I'm aware that I am dwelling on them and using energy to deal with fantasies rather than to experience the things around me more fully, I can choose to shuttle away from my word-thoughts and picture-fantasies into my feelings and experiences of the moment.

There is often conflict between what I want to do and what I end up doing. Often I have to choose among several alternatives. If, having chosen, I spend energy on, "I wish I had...instead of this." I spin my wheels, do what I **am** doing in a less pleasing and satisfactory way, and feel bad about it besides. If, having **chosen** to mow the lawn, I give myself to that task, I leave myself fresher to write.

As I watch myself and other people in learning environments that involve science and other areas of interest I see these conflicts going on constantly. One of the biggest problems about an open learning environment is that there **are** lots of alternatives. You're always having to choose among them; to make your own decisions. And there are always outside pressures, always a metaphorical lawn to mow and a bag of moldy potatoes to deal with.

When we were having regular Wednesday afternoon field trips last term, Martha kept deciding she wanted to go on **them** instead of to her gym class. She acted, ran over to inform the physical education people, and went with us. She also gave herself completely to the activity and her energy flowed and learning followed strongly. Becky came on one trip, knowing that she "had to" be back for a supper date for which the departure was scheduled at 4:00 P.M. She spent the last hour fretting about being back on time. No learning. Low awareness. We got back on time, but the others had left without her. I felt terrible, having "made her miss." But if I try to take responsibility for Becky's decisions, I'm letting myself in for more energy waste of my own and for less effective and satisfactory functioning.

At Syracuse, when we were having some outstanding guest lectures, very few of our graduate students and majors were showing up. As one of the committee responsible for setting up the special events I got furious and felt more and more frustrated. For one thing, what would the guests **think of us?** (The old "image" hang-up.) I wrote a memo expressing my feelings and expectations that they should participate in these experiences rather than deciding in favor of tomorrow's structural geology assignment or test. I'm glad I expressed my anger, because that's what I was really feeling, and I cleared the air by announcing it. — It was a risk for me to express it and to take responsibility for my own feelings. I'm less satisfied that I ended with a threat about how my performance on their examining committees might be influenced by my evaluation of their degree of participation in outside functions like these. That becomes an attempt to enforce and to take responsibility for them. That's an extrinsic way of approaching learning rather than hoping for an intrinsic one.

This recalls my own behavior when I felt "forced" to go to lectures that had no attraction for me. I often spent the whole time of the lecture fuming about how I hated it for "them" to make me come when I wanted to be doing something else. Mentally I wasn't present at these lectures anyway, and I wasn't profiting by the experience available to me there nor by the one I could have had if I had done something else. The sum total of my real experience was an hour of anger, blaming someone else for my own decision to come, energy waste, and enervation.

Just like fretting about mowing the lawn rather than giving myself to it once I had committed myself to it.

Just like taking the rotten potatoes back.

I can't take responsibility for the way someone else feels when he chooses to keep himself in a conflict-regurgitation-and-mastication situation. I know that I can chew on an I'd-rather-be-doing-something-else situation like a cud. I know that lots of other people do this, too. Perhaps I can be more sensitive to other people when I observe this conflict in them.

I frequently sense conflicts of this type at home. Lucretia wants to work on her art and is frustrated because of the conflict she feels with housework, cooking, children. William felt it yesterday because he wanted to go out in our new canoe, but no one could be enticed into transporting it to the river and going along with him. Bill Elberty wanted to go to Indian Lake to meet with the "Interface" group and talk about off-campus programs, but conflict from the home front led him to do repair work there.

The freer the matrix we are in, the more alternatives we have, the more such real personal conflicts are possible. The greater the need becomes for deeper awareness of my conflicts if I want to grow and develop my potential and my production. Even when I do something to please someone else, **I** decide to do it. Taking responsibility for the choice frees me to conserve energy I would otherwise expend in angry ruminations and frees me to profit from the experiences I am actually involved in. I know that I can learn and grow through any experience. I also know that when I really choose **not** to participate in an experience, even when I am virtually compelled to be there, I can often leave physically without really getting hurt, as long as I am open and honest and take full responsibility for leaving. I also know that I can take "mental leave." I can retreat into fantasy, and this, too, can be an acceptable and enjoyable experience for me as long as I enter into it fully.

I live in a society. I am affected by other people. I affect them. If there is to be any sense of community, there is also tradeoff. I can choose not to cooperate; I can cooperate but fuss while doing it; I can cooperate and communicate honestly. If I accept responsibility for any of these paths I take, community has a better chance of working.

I also need to be out of community sometimes. Clear away from other people. In Scandinavia, there are some plans by which housewives get separate paid vacations away from their families. Not a bad idea! When Maggie went off by herself on a western jaunt - without any friends, family, or other people, she felt an important rebirth of self, a freedom from others.

In our open learning environment, how do I build time for myself and how do I encourage others to do the same for themselves. How do we choose to be away from all others? Bill Coulson describes a time when he had accepted "supervisory responsibilities" for two dozen doctoral condidates. This was while working for a university on a part-time basis. As students kept coming to him he realized that the flood of community was keeping him away from other important things he wanted to do, too. So, when students came to him and asked for appointments he always said, "Monday at 3:00 P.M." He said this to all of them, so Monday afternoon became a group community meeting in which everyone expressed his feelings, concerns and research problems. Instead of advice from Coulson only, most problems, personal and academic, affective and cognitive, got the benefit of community ideas. They finally had to establish an agenda to make sure everyone's concern was gotten around to.

This is one of the biggest single problems we face in an open science department. When I started work at St. Lawrence I began to feel the pressure of "my door is always open" tremendously. I wasn't getting even simple administrative papers in as required and this was causing avoidable unpleasantness with the college administration. I was also president of the National Association of Geology Teachers at the time, associate editor of a journal, involved in consulting work and writing, and trying to get back into a personal research program. All of these "professional" conflicts had their interface against the family and all of the people I wanted to work with at the college. When I would get too uptight I would close my door and hang signs up, "Please, let me have some time for me, now." A sarcastic note from "Doom" once said to me, "How open is this place when your door is closed every time I walk by?" The "every time" was only about three mornings a week, but I felt stung pretty deeply. Jack Carter at Colorado College tells me that he tells learners, "Mornings are yours, afternoons are mine." Maybe it works for him. It hasn't really worked for me yet, but I'm working on it. I find myself increasingly able to resist answering the telephone now when I choose not to. It's interesting to watch other people's reactions to me when I just let the telephone ring. Many people are shocked. Some can't stand it, so compulsive is their feeling that the telephone has priority over anything we might be doing, and answer it for me even though I ask them to "leave it." This acceptance of control by the telephone is so strong that I've even suggested to some people that they use the telephone in my room to telephone to the offices next door to talk to Russ or Jim when those two seem occupied. Sure enough, Russ and Jim then abandon what they are doing and respond to the telephone. I control my own attitude toward interruptions and I must decide for myself and take responsibility for how I deal with them. I no longer want to say "Excuse me while I answer the phone. (I **have** to you know!)" I now want to say, "I **choose** to answer this phone now and to interrupt our conversation or I choose **not** to answer it." Why accept anyone's right to interrupt me from clear across campus or clear across the world. I can allow the telephone to control me if I choose to do so. I can compulsively open my mail each morning and allow my mail to dictate what I should do. Or I can open my mail and deal with it or not to deal with it. When I carry a briefcase full home every night or try to do what I **want** to do or what I've agreed to do as part of administrative or other professional functions, then I get the "How about us?" routine from my family.

> PULL, PULL, PULL, PULL!
> How can I ever be me instead of what all of them want me to be.
> How can I ever do what I want to do instead of always thinking of **their** expectation of me.

These are all **real** conflicts. I experience them. You experience them. Every learner I work with has a whole set of his own pressures.

If we can develop any sense of community, and if we can communicate our tensions and feelings of pressure honestly, if I can be aware of what I'm feeling and choose to allocate energy fully to my experience of the moment, if I can find my balance point in what is going on **now** (teetering precariously back and forth between thoughts of the past and the future), then I may be able to feel comfort, resolution, and responsibility as I act rather than dwelling in the zone of conflict.

NOTES

NAMES: How to handle names has been a problem in a book like this. Giving details about people's identities would have cluttered up the text, and yet some readers might want to know just a little more about some of the principal "characters." My compromise is this short note. Lucretia is my wife and has kindly let me use a number of her sketches for the book. Cricket (18), Gretchen (17), and William (13) are our three children. "Bill" is Bill Elberty, friend, colleague, and constant source of support and encouragement. Gunner, Hugh Gunnison, and Fritz, Fritz Renick, are humanistic psychologists who provide further support. Jonathon is Jonathon Swinchatt, who has had an important effect on me during the process of growth of consciousness. John Thompson and Bob Samples have left their tracks through the book, too. Some of the other people in the text appear under their real names. Others bear names other than their own, in the interest of their privacy. I want to acknowledge the profound effects that these people and the many whose names I have not included in the text have had upon me during the preparation of the book.

Acronyms for a number of organizations have been used. Among these are ES (Environmental Studies for Urban Youth), ESTPP (Earth Science Teacher Preparation Project), ESCP (The Earth Science Curriculum Project), ESEP (Earth Science Educational Programs), AGI (American Geological Institute), and NSF (National Science Foundation).

Some additional acknowlegedments; Special thanks to Jeanne Van Auken for superb help with the manuscript, to Bill Elberty, J.B. Buddington, Chuck Wall, and many others who read substantial parts of the manuscript and provided helpful comments, to Aileen Vincent-Barwood for use of some of the facilities of the St. Lawrence **Plaindealer,** to Arie Westdijk and his fine compositors of the Northern New York Publishing Company, to Arnie Poltenson of Salina Press, and, perhaps most of all, to several hundred students, mostly from St. Lawrence University, who continue to affect my thinking, feeling, and consciousness.

REFERENCE NOTES: (Full publishers' data will be given only for the first reference to a given publication.)

p. 3 Verses from A.A. Milne, "Waiting at the Window" in **Now We Are Six,** Methuen and Co., London, 1927.

p. 8 Theodore Roszak, **Where the Wasteland Ends,** Anchor Books, Garden City, N.Y., 1973.

p. 9 Jerome Bruner, **Essays for the Left Hand,** Belknap Press, Cambridge, Mass., 1963. Robert Ornstein, **The Psychology of Consciousness,** Viking, N.Y., 1973.

p. 10 Aldous Huxley, **The Doors of Perception,** Harper and Row, N.Y., 1954.

p. 11 John Lilly, **The Center of Cyclone: An Autobiogography of Inner Space,** Julian, N.Y., 1972.

p. 12 Denis Goulet, **The Cruel Choice,** Atheneum, N.Y., 1973. Charles Reich, **The Greening of America,** Random House, N.Y. 1973. Jane Roberts, **Seth Speaks,** Bantam Books, 1974, pp. 31, 36.

p. 17 A. Maslow, **Motivation and Personality,** Harper and Row, N.Y., 1954. A. Maslow, **Toward a Psychology of Being,** Van Nostrand, N.Y., 1962. G. Goble (on Maslow), **The Third Force,** Pocket Books, N.Y., 1971.

p. 23 A.S. Neill, **Summerhill: A Radical Approach to Child Rearing,** Hart, N.Y., 1960. Carl Rogers, **On Becoming a Person,** Houghton-Mifflin, Boston, 1961. Carl Rogers, **Freedom to Learn,** Charles Merrill, Columbus, O., 1969. A. Maslow, **The Psychology of Science,** Harper and Row, N.Y., 1966. Federick Perls, **Gestalt Therapy Verbatim,** Real People Press, Lafayette, Cal., 1969. Barry Stevens, **Don't Push the River:** (It Flows by Itself), Real People Press, Lafayette, Calif. 1970. George I. Brown, **Human Teaching for Human Learning: An Introduction to Confluent Education,** Viking, N.Y., 1971. Eric Berne, **Games People Play,** Grove Press, N.Y., 1964.

p. 25 Carl Rogers, "The Interpersonal Relationship: The Core of Guidance," **Harvard Educational Review**, v. 32, no. 4, 1962.

p. 30 quote from Carl Rogers and Barry Stevens,**Person to Person**, Pocket Books, N.Y., 1971, p. 177.

p. 32 G.B. Shaw, **Pygmalion**, 1913.

p. 38 William R. Coulson, **A Sense of Community**, Charles Merrill, Columbus, O. 1973.

p. 40 Ronald Clark, **Einstein, The Life and Times**, World, N.Y., 1971.

p. 46 The Coleman Report: James S. Coleman et al., **Youth: Transition to Adulthood: Report on Youth of the President's Science Advisory Committee**, U. of Chicago Press, 1974.

p. 47 The Jencks Report: Christopher Jencks: **Inequality: A Reassessment of the Effect of Family and Schooling in America**. Harper and Row, N.Y., 1973.

p. 50 Eric Berne, **Games People Play**.

p. 51 Alvin Toffler, **Future Shock**, Random House, N.Y., 1970. Carl Rogers, **Person to Person**, p. 186.

p. 53 George Leonard. **Education and Ecstasy**, Delacorte, 1968.

p. 55 Maslow's hierarchy: See Goble, **The Third Force**. B.F. Skinner, **Beyond Freedom and Dignity**, Knopf, 1971.

p. 57 Richard Bach, **Jonathan Livingston Seagull**, Macmillan, N.Y. 1970. Jane Roberts, **Seth Speaks**. Andre Gide, **Les Caves du Vatican**, Gallimard, Paris, 1950.

p. 62 John Gardner, **Self-Renewal: The Individual and the Innovative Society**, Harper and Row, N.Y., 1964.

p. 63 about John L. Coleman, see **Time**, June 25, 1973, p. 74. Also: John L. Coleman, **Blue-Collar Journal: A College President's Sabbatical**, Lippincott, 1974. Alvin Toffler, **Future Shock**.

p. 70 Carl Rogers, **Carl Rogers on Encounter Groups**, Harper and Row, N.Y., 1973.

p. 71 Barry Stevens, **Person to Person**, p. 109. Martin Duberman, **Black Mountain: An Exploration in Community**, E.P. Dutton, N.Y., 1972, Anchor Books Edition, p. 503. William Bryce-Douglas in William R. Couslon's **A Sense of Community**.

p. 74 Excerpts from **Norwegian Folk Tales**, translated by P.S. Iversen and C. Norman, Dreyers Forlag, Oslo.

p. 77 Maslow, **Psychology of Science**. Rogers, **Freedom to Learn**. John O. Stevens, **Awareness, Exploring, Experimenting, Experiencing**, Real People Press, Lafayette, Calif. 1971. Michael Polanyi, **The Tacit Dimension**, Doubleday, Garden City, N.Y., 1967.

p. 84 Bill Keane, **The Family Circus**, Jan. 12, 1975, Sunday funnies. J.D. Salinger, **Catcher in the Rye**, Penguin Books. Kinglsey Amos, **Lucky Jim**, Viking, N.Y., 1958.

p. 87 John Lissner, "The Duke and I" (article appearing in one of the Airline magazines, Fall, 1974, reference lost.)

p. 91 Franz Kriwanek, **Keramos**, Kendall-Hunt, Dubuque, Iowa, 1970.

p. 94 Lawrence Kubie, **Neurotic Distortion of the Creative Process**, Farrar, Strauss, and Giroux, N.Y., 1961.

p. 95 Clark, **Einstein**, p. 106.

p. 97 Frank Barron, **Creative Person and Creative Process**, Holt, Rinehart, and Winston, N.Y., 1969.

p. 98 James Austin, "The Roots of Serendipity", **Sat. Review-World**, Nov. 2, 1974, pp. 60-64.

p. 100 William F. Fry, "Mind Over Mattress, " **Flightime**, Sept. 1974, pp. 20-22.

p. 102 "gestalt"-Frederick Perls, **In and Out The Garbage Pail**, Bantam, N.Y., 1972, pp. 62-64.

p. 105 Maslow, **Psychology of Science**.

p. 110 W.J.J. Gordon, **Synectics**, Harper and Row, N.Y. 1961. G.M. Prince, **The Practice of Creativity**, Harper and Row, N.Y., 1970.

p. 112 **The Notebooks of Leonardo da Vinci,** Dover, N.Y., 1970.

p. 113 C. Wahrhaftig, "Stepped Topography of the Southern Sierra Nevada, Calif." **Geol. Soc. America Bull.,** v. 76, 1965, pp. 1165-1190. D.W. Oldenburg and J.N. Brune, "Ridge Transform Fault-Spreading Pattern in Freezing Wax," **Science,** v. 178, p. 304, 1972.

p. 114 J.D. Watson, **The Double Helix: Being a Personal Account of the Discovery of the Structure of DNA,** Atheneum, N.Y., 1968. W.D. Keller, "The Green Spots in the Red Beds," **American Journal of Science,** 1929.

p. 115 David Hawkins, "Messing About in Science," **Science and Children,** v. 2, no.-5, 1965.

p. 117 "stroking"-see Eric Berne, **Games People Play.** J. Dyer and F. Dyer, "The Corporate Creativity Factor," **Passages,** v. 5, No. 1, p. 17, 18. The source is in **Julius Caeser,** I, ii, 138: "The fault, dear Brutus, is not in our stars-But in ourselves, that we are underlings."

p. 118 Margaret Mead, "Creativity in Cross-Cultural Perspective," in **Creativity and its Cultivation,** H. Anderson (ed.) Harper and Row, N.Y., 1959. Jerome Bruner, "Conditions of Creativity," in **Contemporary Approaches to Creative Thinking,** H.E. Gruber, G. Terrell, and M. Wertheimer (eds.), Atherton Press, N.Y., 1962.

p. 120 J. Piaget as quoted by F. Jennings in "Jean Piaget, Notes on Learning," **Saturday Review,** May 20, 1967, pp. 81-83. J. Bruner, **Toward a Theory of Instruction,** Harvard U. Press, Cambridge, Mass., 1966. R. Bacon, as quoted by R. Ornstein in **The Psychology of Consciousness.**

p. 124 questioning of witnesses under hypnosis: see **Newsweek,** Aug. 5, 1974, p. 57.

p. 125 Polanyi, **The Tacit Dimension.** W.T. Gallwey, **The Inner Game of Tennis,** Random House, N.Y., 1974.

p. 126 Janos Starker: **Newsweek,** Jan. 29, 1973, p. 75.

p. 128 J.A. Passmore, **Science,** v. 181, 1972, p. 327. J. Bronowski, quoted by D.G. Barry in Science, v. 152, pp. 1011-1012. P. Brandwein, from a speech at a regional meeting of the National Science Teachers Assn, Grand Rapids, Mich. P.W. Bridgman, **The Way Things Are,** Harvard. U. Press, Cambridge, Mass. 1959.

p. 129 T.S. Kuhn, **The Structure of Scientific Revolutions,** U. of Chicago Press., 1970.

p. 131 T. Roszak, **The Making of a Counterculture,** Doubleday, Garden City, N.Y. 1969. T. Roszak, **Where the Wasteland Ends.**

p. 135 A. Einstein, address to the National Academy of Science, Washington, D.C., April 26, 1921, as quoted in the **N.Y. Times,** April 27, 1921. Kuhn, **The Structure of Scientific Revolutions,** p. 65. Morris Holland, **Newsweek,** May 21, 1973, p. 105.

p. 138 Geomorphology: G.H Dury, "Some Current Trends in Geomorphology," **Earth Science Reviews,** v. 8, 1972, pp. 45, 46.

p. 140 **Vasari's Lives of the Artists,** ed. by Betty Burroughs, Simon and Schuster, N.Y., 1964, p. 187.

p. 141 Max Born, as quoted by Clark in **Einstein,** p. 339. T. Roszak, **Where the Wasteland Ends,** p. 215. Werner Heisenberg, **Physics and Philosophy,** Harper and Row, N.Y., 1958, p. 58.

p. 142 Norman Hackerman, "Ignorance as the Driving Force," **Science,** v. 183, 1974, p. 907. C.T. Tart, "States of Consciousness and State Specific Sciences," **Science,** v. 176, p. 1203. Bruner and Postman, "On the Perception of Incongruity: a Paradigm," in **Journal of Personality,** v. 18, 1949, pp. 206-222.

p. 143 Simon and Chase, "Skill in Chess," **American Scientist,** v. 61, 1973, pp. 394-403. Jonathan Swinchatt, "Miscellaneous Observations from a Wandering Mind," **Journal of College Science Teaching,** v. 3, 1974, pp. 197-199.

p. 145 Lewis Carroll, **Through the Looking Glass,** Macmillan edition, N.Y., 1963, pp. 34, 35. Roszak, **Where the Wasteland Ends,** p. 375.

p. 148 Cicero, quoted by Michel de Montaigne, **Essays** (as excerpted in J. Noll and S. Kelly in **Foundations of Education in America: an Anthology of Major Thoughts and Significant Actions**, Harper and Row, N.Y., 1970, p. 73. W. Boyd, "The Emile of Jean Jacques Rousseau," Bureau of Publications, Teacher's College, Columbia U. 1962. Polanyi, **The Tacit Dimension.**

p. 150 Rogers and Stevens, **Person to Person,** p. 10.

p. 154 William Wiley, quoted by Peter Selz in "Six Artists in Search of a Definition of San Francisco, " **Art News,** Summer, 1973, p. 36.

p. 158 Robert Hughes on Leonardo: **Time,** Oct. 14, 1974, p. 93.

p. 159 A. Einstein as quoted by C. Seelig in **Albert Einstein: A Documentary Biography**, London, 1956, p. 209. K. Krauskopf, "A Tale of 10 Plutons," **Geol. Soc. America Bull.**, v. 97, 1968,1 pp. 1-8,(presidential address for 1967.) F.J. Turner, "Uniqueness Versus Conformity to Pattern," American Mineralogist, v. 55, 1970, p. 339.

p. 161 Maslow, **The Psychology of Science.** Kuhn, **The Structure of Scientific Revolutions.**

p. 162 Maslow, **The Psychology of Science,** p. 14.

p. 163 Rogers and Stevens, **Person to Person,** p. 79.

p. 165 Carnegie Inst. of Washington, Geophysical Laboratory, Annual Yearbook, 1972, p. 623. B. Griffith and N.Mullins, **Science,** v. 177, 1972, pp. 959-966.

p. 166 L.N. Tolstoy, **War and Peace,** conversation between Platon Karatayev and Pierre Bezukhov.

p. 167 Einstein, from Clark, **Einstein.**

p. 171 Barry Stevens, **Don't Push the River,** p. 140. Lewis Carroll, **Alice's Adventures in Wonderland.**

p. 173 Barry Stevens, **Person to Person,** p. 257. Pappas: **Newsweek,** June 25, 1973.

p. 180 A. Einstein, inscription at the portal of the Canadian National Museum of Science and Technology, Ottawa.

p. 181 Eight-year study: D. Chamberlin, E. Chamberlin, N. Drought, and W. Scott, **Adventures in American Education: Did They Succeed in College?** Harper, N.Y., 1942.

p. 182 Kuhn, **The Structure of Scientific Revolutions.** Reich, **The Greening of America.** Bruner, **Toward a Theory of Instruction.**

p. 183 W. Romey and J. Merrill, "A Comparison of the Performance of Ninth-Grade and College Students in an Earth Science Laboratory Activity," **The Science Teacher,** v. 31, no. 9, 1964, pp. 49-52.

p. 184 Most details from Clark, **Einstein.**

p. 189 Einstein: from autobiographical notes quoted in P.A. Schilpp, ed., **Albert Einstein: Philosopher-Scientist**, Evanston, Ill. 1949.

p. 191 O.J. Harvey, Dept. of Psychology, Univ. of Colorado, Boulder, Colo. Einstein: R. Clark, **Einstein,** pp. 36, 37.

p. 194 **The Notebooks of Leonardo da Vinci.**

p. 195 SAPA: **Science-A Process Approach,** a curriculum prepared by the American Association for the Advancement of Science and now distributed by the Xerox Corporation (for elementary schools).

p. 203 Ivar Giaever, "Electron Tunneling and Superconductivity," in **Science,** v. 183, March 29, 1974, p. 1258, (lecture delivered when Giaever received the Nobel Prize in Physics, 1973).

p. 207 Frederick Perls, **Gestalt Therapy Verbatim.**

p. 209 Eric Berne, **Games People Play.** Muriel James and Dorothy Jongeward, **Born to Win,** Addison-Wesley, Reading, Mass., 1971.

p. 212 Susan Sontag, quoted by Lynn Hershman in Peter Selz's article, "Six Artists in Search of a Definition of San Francisco," **Art News,** Summer, 1973, p. 36.

p. 213 Carl Rogers, **Carl Rogers on Encounter Groups.**

p. 214 Perls, **Gestalt Theraphy Verbatim.**

p. 215 D.L. Rosenhan, "On Being Sane in Insane Places," **Science**, v. 179, Jan., 1973, pp. 250-258.

p. 218 Reich, **The Greening of America.** Roszak, **The Making of a Counterculture.**

p. 219 T. Armstrong, "Coordinating Science Teaching Methods with Levels of Student Awareness," **Journal of College Science Teaching**, v. 3, 1974, pp. 187-188.

p. 223 M. Duberman, **Black Mountain, p. 5.**

p. 225 R. Townsend, **Up the Organization**, Knopf, N.Y., 1970. D. McLean, "Volvo Brings Team Idea to Land of the Assembly Line," **Boston Sunday Globe**, June 30, 1974, p. A3. Saab magazine adds, e.g. **Time**, June 11, 1973.

p. 228 Barry Stevens, **Don't Push the River.**

p. 232 Thomas Edison: a similar anecdote exists about Einstein, with respect to a paper on the unified field theory. See Clark's **Einstein**, p. 535.

p. 233 D. Allen as quoted in W. Romey and J. Thompson, "Colloquy '72-A Meeting Report," **Journal of Geol. Education**, May, 1973, pp. 130-133.

p. 237 Jencks, **Inequality, A Reassessment of the Effect of Family and Schooling in America.**

p. 239 J. Salinger, **Catcher in the Rye**, Penquin ed., p. 14.

p. 243 J. Gardner, **Self Renewal.**

p. 256 Buckminster Fuller, **Intuition**, Doubleday, Garden City, N.Y., 1970, p. 27.

p. 261 F. Perls, **Gestalt Therapy Verbatim.**

p. 268 John Enright, "Awareness, Consciousness, Insight, and the Mentally Healthy Person," in **Gestalt Therapy Now**, ed. by Fagan and Shepherd. J. Stevens, **Awareness.**

p. 269 B. Stevens, **Don't Push the River.**